CONTEMPORARY'S

GED

PREPARATION FOR THE HIGH SCHOOL EQUIVALENCY EXAMINATION

TEST 2:

THE SOCIAL STUDIES TEST

GARY WALLER

DE LORES WEAVER
Consultant
Coordinator
Centers for Adult Learning
Community College of Philadelphia

CAREN VAN SLYKE
Editorial Director

Contemporary Books, Inc.
chicago

Library of Congress Cataloging in Publication Data

Waller, Gary.
    Contemporary's GED.

    1. Social sciences—Examinations, questions, etc.
2. General educational development tests—Study guides.
3. High school equivalency examination—Study guides.
I. Contemporary Books, inc.   II. Title.   III. Title: GED.
H87.W35   1985   300'.76   84-28515
ISBN 0-8092-5587-1

Published by Contemporary Books, Inc.
180 North Michigan Avenue, Chicago, Illinois 60601
Manufactured in the United States of America
International Standard Book Number: 0-8092-5587-1

Published simultaneously in Canada by
Beaverbooks, Ltd.
195 Allstate Parkway
Valleywood Business Park
Markham, Ontario L3P 4T8
Canada

_____

Editorial
Ellen Carley Frechette
Art Strobeck, Jr.
Christine M. Benton
Elizabeth Rubin

Editorial Assistant
Karin Evans

Production Editor
Deborah Rank Popely

Art and Illustrations
Princess Louise El
Ophelia M. Chambliss-Jones

Typography
Terrence Alan Stone

ACKNOWLEDGMENTS

Cartoon on page 12 by Dana Summers, from *Best Editorial Cartoons of the Year*, 1983 edition, edited by Charles Brooks. Reprinted by permission of Dana Summers.

Chart on page 13 reprinted from *A Geography of Mankind*, by Jan O. Broek and John W. Webb, copyright © 1978 by McGraw-Hill Book Company. Used by permission.

Graph on page 14 copyright © 1983 by the New York Times Company. Reprinted by permission.

Graph on page 15 from *Editorial Research Reports*, April 8, 1983. Published by the Congressional Quarterly, Inc. Used by permission.

Graph on page 51 from the book *Economics Explained*, by Robert Heilbroner & Lester Thurow, © 1982 by Robert L. Heilbroner and Lester C. Thurow. Published by Prentice-Hall, Inc., Englewood Cliffs, NJ 07632. Reprinted by permission.

Graph on page 56 from *Urban Geography*, by Ray Northam. Copyright © 1979 by John Wiley & Sons, Inc. Published by John Wiley & Sons, Inc. Reprinted by permission of the publisher.

Graphic on page 58 reprinted by permission of the *Chicago Tribune*.

Map on page 62 reprinted with permission from *Urban Geography*, by James H. Johnson, copyright © 1967, Pergamon Press, Ltd.

Map on page 63 reprinted from *A Geography of Mankind*, by Jan O. Broek and John W. Webb, copyright © 1978 by McGraw-Hill Book Company. Used by permission.

Cartoon on page 65 by Tony Auth, from *The Philadelphia Inquirer*. Reprinted by permission of Tony Auth.

Cartoon on page 66 from *Best Editorial Cartoons of the Year*, 1983 edition, edited by Charles Brooks, copyright © 1983 by Charles Brooks, used by permission of the publisher, Pelican Publishing Company, Inc.

Letter on pages 82–83 from the private collection of Art Strobeck, Jr. Reprinted by permission.

Letter on pages 89–90 from *In Their Own Words—A History of the American Negro*, edited by Milton Meltzer. Copyright © 1964 by Milton Meltzer. Published by Harper & Row Publishers, Inc. Reprinted by permission of the publisher.

Excerpt on page 104 from *The Story of Alice Paul and the National Woman's Party*, by Inez Hayes Irwin. Copyright 1964, 1977, by the National Woman's Party. Published by Denlinger's Publishers, Ltd. Reprinted by permission of the National Woman's Party.

Graphs on page 109 from the *Hammond Atlas of U.S. History*. Copyright permission: Hammond Incorporated, Maplewood, NJ.

Excerpt on page 113 from *Hard Times: An Oral History of the Great Depression*, by Studs Terkel. Copyright © 1970 by Studs Terkel. Published by Pantheon Books, a division of Random House, Inc. Reprinted by permission of Random House, Inc.

Cartoon on page 118 reprinted by permission of Tim Skelly.

Chart on page 141 from "The Political Parties: Reform and Decline," by Austin Ranney, in *The New American Political System*, ed. Anthony King. Copyright © American Enterprise Institute for Policy Research; used by permission.

Excerpt on pages 141–142 from "Voter Turnout," in *Social Policy*, Winter 1983, vol. 13 no. 3. Used by permission of Social Policy Co., Inc.

Cartoon on page 185 from *Psychology and Life*, 9th edition, by Philip G. Zimbardo and Floyd L. Ruch. Copyright © 1975, 1971, 1967, by Scott, Foresman, and Co. Reprinted by permission.

Graph on page 185 from Albert Bandura, *Aggression: A Social Learning Analysis*, Copyright © 1973, p. 145. Reprinted by permission of Prentice-Hall, Inc., Englewood Cliffs, NJ.

Graph on page 195 courtesy of the United States Department of Justice, Bureau of Justice Statistics.

Graph on page 196 from *Child Psychology*, by Mavis Hetherington and Ross D. Park. Copyright © 1979 by McGraw-Hill Book Company. Reprinted by permission of the publisher.

Excerpt on pages 201–202 from "Body Ritual Among the Nacirema," by Horace Miner, in *American Anthropologist* 58(3), 1956. Not for further reproduction.

Graphs on pages 214 and 228 from the book *Economics Explained*, by Robert Heilbroner & Lester Thurow, © 1982 by Robert L. Heilbroner and Lester C. Thurow. Published by Prentice-Hall, Inc., Englewood Cliffs, NJ 07632. Reprinted by permission.

Graph on page 277 from *The Nation*, August 21–28, 1982. Reprinted by permission.

Graph on page 279 from the book *Economics Explained*, by Robert Heilbroner & Lester Thurow, © 1982 by Robert L. Heilbroner and Lester C. Thurow. Published by Prentice-Hall, Inc., Englewood Cliffs, NJ 07632. Reprinted by permission.

Chart on page 284 from *Post-Conservative America: People, Politics, and Ideology in a Time of Crisis*, by Kevin P. Phillips. Copyright © 1982 by Kevin P. Phillips. Published by Random House, Inc. Based on surveys by Louis Harris and Associates reported in *Public Opinion*, October/November 1979:30. Reprinted by permission of Random House and the American Enterprise Institute for Public Policy Research.

Cartoon on page 286 by Richard Crowson, from *Best Editorial Cartoons of the Year*, 1983 edition, edited by Charles Brooks. Reprinted by permission of Richard Crowson.

Table of Contents

POLITICAL SCIENCE————————————————————130

BEHAVIORAL SCIENCE————————————————174

ECONOMICS————————————————————————209

Introducing The Social Studies Test

Perhaps it has been a long time since you took an important test. Maybe you are not sure about what is required to pass the social studies test, or you are nervous about the test-taking situation.

This book has been designed to help you succeed on the GED social studies test. It will provide you with instruction in the skills you need to pass the test, plenty of GED-type practice exercises, and test-taking hints. If you work carefully through this book, you should do well on the social studies test.

USING THIS BOOK

Contemporary's GED series is a program that you or a teacher can use to determine your individual strengths and weaknesses.

1. Start your work with the pre-test at the beginning of the book. This will help you to preview what the social studies test includes, but more importantly, it will help you to diagnose which areas you need to concentrate on. Use the skills chart at the end of the pre-test to see what areas need special work.

It would be best for you to work your way carefully through the entire book. However, if your time is limited, and you need more work on another test, you can use the pre-test and skills chart to decide what areas to focus on for the social studies test.

2. The first two chapters of this book are devoted to specific reading and interpretation skills. To pass the test, you need to understand social studies passages and answer questions based on them. Also, 25 percent of the test questions require you to interpret graphs, charts, maps, and cartoons.

The following sections concern the five content areas the test is based on: history, political science, behavioral science, economics, and geography. Each section has two key features: (1) background essays to familiarize you with social studies terms and concepts and (2) exercises to give you practice answering questions about passages and pictorial materials.

3. One of the key features of this book is the explanations of answers. If you make a mistake, you can learn from it by reading the explanation that follows the answer and then going back to the question and analyzing your error. The answer key for the content areas also indicates which comprehension skill the question was testing.

4. Finally, the post-test is a simulated GED test. It represents GED-type format and difficulty of questions. It will give you a chance to determine if you are ready for the test and, if not, what areas of the book you still need to review.

THE SOCIAL STUDIES TEST

There are sixty multiple-choice questions on this test. Forty of them test your ability to interpret social studies passages, charts, graphs, cartoons, and maps. About twenty-five of the forty questions are based on passages, while the remaining fifteen are based on pictorial materials.

Twenty of the test questions are single isolated questions that require an understanding of basic social studies concepts. For the most part, these questions are based on general principles and the testing of isolated facts and dates is avoided.

These types of questions are intermixed through the test. The Canadian version of the test differs from the U.S. editions. Canadian history replaces U.S. history and the test contains 20 percent geography questions and 15 percent economics questions (see chart, *The GED Test*).

THE GED TEST

Q: What does GED stand for?

A: GED stands for the Tests of General Educational Development. The credential received for passing the test is widely recognized by colleges, training schools, and employers as equivalent to a high school diploma. The GED is a national examination developed by the GED Testing Service of the American Council on Education.

    The GED tests consist of five examinations in the areas of writing skills, social studies, science, reading skills, and mathematics. While the GED measures skills and knowledge normally acquired in four years of high school, much that you have learned informally or through other types of training can help you pass the test.

    The GED test is available in English, French, and Spanish, and on audiocassette, in braille, and in large-print editions.

Q: What should I know to pass the test?

A. The chart below outlines the main content areas, the breakdown of questions, and the time generally allowed per test.

THE GED TEST			
Content	**Minutes**	**Number of Questions**	**Percentage of Test**
Test 1 Writing Skills	75	80	
Spelling		10	12.5%
Capitalization & Punctuation		10	12.5%
Grammar & Usage		24	30%
Diction & Style		12	15%
Sentence Structure		12	15%
Logic & Organization		12	15%
Test 2 Social Studies	90	60	
U.S. History		15	25%
Economics		12	20%
Geography		9	15%
Political Science		12	20%
Behavioral Science		12	20%
Test 3 Science	90	60	
Biology		30	50%
Earth Science		12	20%
Chemistry		9	15%
Physics		9	15%
Test 4 Reading Skills	60	40	
Practical Reading		6	15%
General Reading		12	30%
Prose Literature		12	30%
Poetry		5	12.5%
Drama		5	12.5%
Test 5 Mathematics	90	50	
Arithmetic		28	55%
Geometry		10	20%
Algebra		12	25%

On all five tests, you are expected to demonstrate the ability to read and understand what you are reading. You are also tested on many skills you have acquired from life experiences, reading, television, radio, newspapers, contracts, consumer products, and advertising. By and large, you are not expected to recall facts. However, parts of the social studies and science tests require you to remember some information from your past reading and learning.

In addition to the above information, keep these facts in mind:

1. Three of the five tests—reading, science, and social studies— require mainly that you answer questions based on reading or interpreting pictorial materials in these content areas. Developing strong reading and analysis skills is the key to succeeding on these tests.

2. The writing skills test does not require you to write, but rather to detect errors of grammar and usage, punctuation, capitalization, and spelling. Also, you must be able to recognize correct sentence and paragraph construction.

3. The math test consists mainly of word problems to be solved. Therefore, you must be able to combine your ability to perform computations with reading comprehension skills.

Someone once said that an education is what remains after you've forgotten everything else. In many ways, this is what the GED measures.

Q: Can I take the test?

A: Each year, more than 800,000 people take the GED test. In the United States, Canada, and many territories, people who have not graduated from high school and who meet specific eligibility requirements (age, residency, etc.) may take the test. Since eligibility requirements vary, it would be useful to contact your local GED testing center or the director of adult education in your state, province, or territory for specific information.

Q: What is a passing score on the GED?

A: Again, this varies from area to area. To find out what you need to pass the test, contact your local GED testing center. However, you must keep two scores in mind. One score represents the *minimum score* you must get on each test. For example, if your state requires minimum scores of 35, you must get at least 35 points on every test. Additionally, you must meet the requirements of a *minimum average score* on all five tests. For example, if your state requires a minimum average score of 45, you must get a total of 225 points to pass. The two scores together, the minimum score and the minimum average score, determine whether you pass or fail the GED.

To understand this better, look at the scores of three people who took the test in a state that requires a minimum score of 35 and a minimum average score of 45 (225 total). Heino and Bob did not pass, but Maria did. See if you can tell why.

	Heino	Bob	Maria
Test 1	45	38	43
Test 2	47	43	48
Test 3	33	42	47
Test 4	50	40	52
Test 5	50	39	49
	225	202	239

Heino made the total of 225 points but fell below the minimum score on Test 3. Bob passed each test but failed to get the 225 points needed; just passing each test was not enough. Maria passed all the tests and exceeded the minimum average score.

Generally, to receive a GED credential, you must correctly answer half or a little more than half of the questions on each test.

Q: What happens if I don't pass the test?

A: You are allowed to retake some or all of the tests. Again, the number of times that you may retake the tests and the time you must wait before retaking them depend on your state, province, or territory. Some states require you to take a review class or to study on your own for a certain amount of time before retesting.

Q: How can I best prepare for the test?

A: Many libraries, community colleges, adult education centers, churches, and other institutions offer GED preparation classes. Some television stations broadcast classes to prepare people for the test. If you cannot find a GED preparation class locally, contact the director of adult education in your state, province, or territory.

Q: I need to study for the other tests. Are there other materials available?

A. Contemporary Books publishes a wide range of materials to help you prepare for the tests. These books are designed for home study or class use. Contemporary's GED preparation books are available through schools and bookstores and directly from the publisher.

Now let's focus on some useful test-taking tips. As you read this section, you should feel more confident about your ability to succeed on *The Social Studies Test*.

TEST-TAKING TIPS

1. Get prepared physically. Eat a well-balanced meal and get plenty of rest the night before the test so that you will have energy and will be able to think clearly. Last-minute cramming will probably not help as much as a relaxed and rested mind.

2. Arrive early. Be at the testing center at least fifteen to twenty minutes before the starting time. Have time to find the room and to get situated. Keep in mind that many testing centers refuse to admit latecomers.

3. Think positively. Tell yourself you will do well. If you have studied and prepared for the test, you should succeed.

4. Relax during the test. Take a half-minute several times during the test to stretch and breathe deeply, especially if you are feeling anxious or confused.

5. Read the test directions carefully. Be sure you understand how to answer the questions. If you have any questions about the test or about filling in the answer form, ask before the test begins.

6. Know the time limit for each test. *The Social Studies Test* has a time limit of ninety minutes.

Some testing centers allow extra time, while others do not. You may be able to find out the policy of your testing center before you take the test, but always work according to the official time limit. If you have extra time, go back and check your answers.

For this sixty-item test, you should allow a maximum of one and a half minutes per question. However, this is not a hard and fast rule. Use it only as a guide to keep yourself within the time limit.

7. Have a strategy for answering questions. You should read through the reading passages or look over the pictorial materials once and then answer the questions that follow. Read each question two or three times to make sure you understand it. It is best to refer back to the passage or illustration in order to confirm your answer choice. Don't try to depend on your memory of what you have just read or seen. Some people like to guide their reading by skimming the questions before reading a passage. Use whichever way works best for you.

8. Don't spend a lot of time on difficult questions. If you're not sure of the answers, go on to the next questions. Answer easier questions first and then go back to the harder questions. If you skip a question, be sure that you have skipped the same number on your answer sheet. Although this is a good strategy for making the most of your time, it can be very easy to get confused and throw off your whole answer key.

Lightly mark the numbers of the questions you did not answer in the margin of your answer sheet so that you know what to go back to. Be sure to erase these marks completely after you answer the questions. In this way, there won't be any confusion when your test is graded.

9. Answer every question on the test. If you're not sure of an answer, take an educated guess. When you leave a question unanswered you will <u>always</u> lose points, but you can possibly gain points if you make a correct guess.

If you must guess, try to eliminate one or more answers that you are sure are not correct. Then, choose from the remaining answers. Remember, you greatly increase your chances if you can eliminate one or two answers before guessing. Of course, guessing should be used only when all else has failed.

10. Clearly fill in the circle for each answer choice. If you erase something, erase it completely. Be sure that you give only one answer per question; otherwise no answer will count.

Use the exercises, reviews, and especially the post-test in this book to better understand your test-taking habits and weaknesses. Use them to practice different strategies such as skimming questions first or skipping hard questions until the end. Knowing your own personal test-taking style is important to success on the GED.

SOCIAL STUDIES PRE-TEST

Directions

Before beginning to work with this book, take this pre-test. The purpose of this test is to help you determine which skills you need to develop in order to pass *The Social Studies Test*.

The Social Studies Pre-Test consists of 30 multiple-choice questions. Some of the questions are based on maps, charts, graphs, cartoons, and reading passages. Others are discrete, or self-contained, questions, which are not accompanied by any passage or illustration.

Answer each question as carefully as possible, choosing the best of five answer choices and marking it on the grid below. If a question is difficult, do not waste time on it. Work ahead and come back to it later when you can think it through carefully.

When you have completed this test, check your work with the answers and explanations at the end of the section.

Use the Evaluation Chart on page 20 to see in which areas you need the most work. However, we strongly advise you to work through this entire book for the best possible preparation for *The Social Studies Test*.

Answer Grid

1 ① ② ③ ④ ⑤	11 ① ② ③ ④ ⑤	21 ① ② ③ ④ ⑤
2 ① ② ③ ④ ⑤	12 ① ② ③ ④ ⑤	22 ① ② ③ ④ ⑤
3 ① ② ③ ④ ⑤	13 ① ② ③ ④ ⑤	23 ① ② ③ ④ ⑤
4 ① ② ③ ④ ⑤	14 ① ② ③ ④ ⑤	24 ① ② ③ ④ ⑤
5 ① ② ③ ④ ⑤	15 ① ② ③ ④ ⑤	25 ① ② ③ ④ ⑤
6 ① ② ③ ④ ⑤	16 ① ② ③ ④ ⑤	26 ① ② ③ ④ ⑤
7 ① ② ③ ④ ⑤	17 ① ② ③ ④ ⑤	27 ① ② ③ ④ ⑤
8 ① ② ③ ④ ⑤	18 ① ② ③ ④ ⑤	28 ① ② ③ ④ ⑤
9 ① ② ③ ④ ⑤	19 ① ② ③ ④ ⑤	29 ① ② ③ ④ ⑤
10 ① ② ③ ④ ⑤	20 ① ② ③ ④ ⑤	30 ① ② ③ ④ ⑤

1. In 1968, Congress passed the Truth in Lending Act. This act requires that lenders tell people buying on credit the annual percentage rates (APR) for interest and the total interest charges over the life of the loan. This act is an example of
   (1) consumer protection legislation
   (2) Congress following a policy of economic protectionism
   (3) Congress legislating profit controls
   (4) the Federal Reserve trying to control credit
   (5) a government policy of laissez-faire toward lenders

2. A high school student explains that she has been using drugs heavily because her parents put too much pressure on her. This explanation is characteristic of
   (1) a psychosis
   (2) an innate characteristic
   (3) a learning disability
   (4) a defense mechanism
   (5) an intelligence problem

Questions 3–4 refer to the following passage.

The Fall Line, which demarcates the edge of the eastern coastal plain, had a great influence on early settlement patterns in the eastern United States. Barge traffic from the coast had to stop at the Fall Line because of steep waterfalls and rapids in the rivers caused by sharp decreases in altitude. This forced traders to break down their larger bulk shipments suitable for river transportation into smaller units that could be carried over land. Towns grew up at these points to handle such changes.

In addition, the water power provided by the falls and rapids along the Fall Line was harnessed for industrial uses. As a result, textile plants, shoe manufacturers, lumber mills, and other industry grew, creating the nucleus for further growth of towns and cities.

3. The Fall Line was important to early towns in the eastern United States because it
   (1) provided water for drinking
   (2) protected towns from flooding
   (3) helped river navigation
   (4) provided water power for industry
   (5) prohibited all land travel

4. Based on this passage, you can conclude that
   (1) climate determines city location
   (2) geographic factors that aid economic activity can influence a town's location
   (3) geographic factors do not affect city location
   (4) westward expansion was blocked by the Fall Line
   (5) the Fall Line was responsible for new methods of transportation

GO ON TO THE NEXT PAGE.

Questions 5–6 refer to the following passage.

The Articles of Confederation were passed by the Continental Congress in 1781 as the constitutional framework for the new nation. The articles gave much power and independence to the states and relatively little influence to the central federal government. Subsequent developments proved that the federal government was too weak to deal with the needs of the new nation in securing frontiers, creating a military defense, protecting trade, and handling domestic unrest during the troubled times of the 1780s.

Most of the leaders of the revolution decided that decentralization of power had gone too far. They were worried about the ineffective federal government, and they called a Constitutional Convention to develop a constitutional framework with a stronger central government. They hoped to keep the United States from dissolving into separate states. The convention was called in 1787, and a new constitution was written that established a strong central government.

5. The Articles of Confederation were replaced because
   (1) they gave too much authority to the president
   (2) they gave too much authority to the central government
   (3) the states were dissatisfied with them
   (4) they created an all-powerful national Congress
   (5) they created a weak and ineffective federal government

6. You could infer from this passage that the leaders of the revolution supported a more centralized system because
   (1) they feared the nation would not survive without the change
   (2) they wanted more political power for themselves
   (3) they wanted to establish the president as a power like the king
   (4) they wanted the U.S. to become a world power
   (5) they wanted to protect their own wealth and investments

7. The American political system is often described as a pluralist system. This is a system that gets its strength from the large number of interest groups that take part in politics. These groups must share power and make continual compromises to get things done.
   Which of the following is characteristic of decision making in such a system?
   (1) Political decisions are always made very rapidly.
   (2) One group always tends to dominate in the process.
   (3) No single group wins all the time.
   (4) There is very little political conflict and argument.
   (5) Political parties play a very small role.

Question 8 refers to the following chart.

NATIONAL BUDGET FIGURES	
Highways, roads, and railroads	10%
Education and welfare	20%
Industrial development	15%
Land reform and agricultural research	15%
Public health	10%
Military and police	30%

8. Social scientists say that one important way to determine the real priorities of a society is to examine how it spends its money. Based on this idea, you could say that a government with the above national budget placed highest priority on
   (1) external and internal security
   (2) economic development controlled by private business
   (3) agricultural improvements
   (4) education and welfare
   (5) economic development controlled by the government

GO ON TO THE NEXT PAGE.

Questions 9–10 refer to the following passage.

Today, almost all U.S. citizens over the age of eighteen have the legal right to vote, but this was not always the case. The U.S. Constitution originally let the states determine qualifications for voting, and the right to vote was usually restricted to white male property owners.

Property qualifications were gradually eliminated, and by 1830 most white males over the age of twenty-one could vote. Blacks gained the legal right to vote from the 15th Amendment, ratified in 1870. Women gained the right to vote after several decades of struggle with the passage of the 19th Amendment in 1919.

Unfortunately, although these Americans now had the legal right to vote, some states used a variety of devices to deny this right to blacks. Poll taxes, literacy tests, and sometimes open terror were used to keep them from casting ballots.

The poll tax on voting in federal elections was finally erased by the 24th Amendment in 1962, and the civil rights movement of the 1960s led to the Voting Rights Act of 1965, which guaranteed the right to vote to all citizens, regardless of race or sex.

9. What provision did the original U.S. Constitution make for voter qualifications?
   (1) It gave all white adult males the right to vote.
   (2) It gave all citizens the right to vote.
   (3) It left it up to the Supreme Court to decide.
   (4) It left it to the states to set qualifications.
   (5) It gave all property owners the right to vote.

10. The main idea of this passage is that
    (1) equality in voting rights has always been a well-established principle of American democracy
    (2) voting rights have been extended without any social struggle
    (3) the right to vote in the United States was not won by all citizens at the same time, but over time, and with much social conflict
    (4) the Voting Rights Act was the most important legislation of the 1960s
    (5) without the 15th Amendment, women and blacks would still not have the legal right to vote

11. Which of the following would be included on a geographic, or physical, map?
    (1) Cultural features of different regions
    (2) Racial distribution
    (3) Mountain ranges
    (4) Major industries
    (5) Population density

Questions 12–13 refer to the following passage.

Many social science researchers have linked the changing nature of the American family in recent years to the growth of the women's liberation movement. The rights and freedoms won by women have increased their participation in the work force. This in turn has changed child-rearing patterns, as more and more children attend day care centers while their mothers work. The increase in the number of working women has also changed the division of labor between husbands and wives in the home. Many experts argue that increased job opportunities for women have increased the rate of divorce because women feel more economically secure on their own. Furthermore, this increase in job opportunities for women has caused a decrease in the population growth rate because more women are delaying childbirth or not having children at all.

12. The main idea of this passage is that
    (1) women's liberation has destroyed the American family
    (2) the women's liberation movement has brought about many changes in the American family
    (3) men now take most of the responsibility for child rearing
    (4) women's liberation has had little effect on anyone except children
    (5) the nature of the American family has changed due to the high rate of divorce

13. What principle of social change can you conclude based on this passage?
    (1) Change is bad for the family unit.
    (2) Change in one aspect of society is unlikely to affect other aspects of that society.
    (3) Too much freedom will ruin a society.
    (4) Change in one aspect of society usually brings about changes in other aspects.
    (5) Social change has little effect on people's daily lives.

GO ON TO THE NEXT PAGE.

Questions 14–15 refer to the following passage.

In recent years, the most important factor affecting home purchases has been the rate of interest on mortgages. Some economists say that each rise of 1 percent in mortgage interest rates makes homes unaffordable to more than one million families. The effects of this were clearly seen in 1983. Declining mortgage rates in early 1983 increased home sales very rapidly. The rates bottomed in May at around 12½ percent. By August they had climbed to almost 14 percent. Economists said that this took 2.4 million families out of the home market and slowed home sales by 35 percent.

14. Based on the details in this passage, you can conclude that a continuing rise in mortgage interest rates would
    (1) increase home sales
    (2) not affect home sales
    (3) not affect the price of homes
    (4) cause more homes to be built
    (5) decrease home sales

15. Which of the following steps might the government take to aid the housing industry?
    (1) Try to bring rising mortgage interest rates under control
    (2) Refrain from controlling rising interest rates
    (3) Tighten the money supply
    (4) Put a lid on the cost of new homes
    (5) Fix the mortgage interest rate at a flat 15 percent

Question 16 refers to the following cartoon.

DANA SUMMERS
Courtesy The Sentinel

16. The main idea of this cartoon is that
    (1) it is useless to vote in any election
    (2) people complain about government but often fail to vote
    (3) the unemployed should not have the right to vote
    (4) unemployment benefits and the ability to vote are two important rights given to Americans
    (5) the government should do more to help the unemployed

GO ON TO THE NEXT PAGE.

17. What has been the influence of large-scale militant social movements on American political history?
 (1) They have been mainly negative because they focus too much on problems.
 (2) They have caused the existing political parties to adopt many of their demands.
 (3) They have led to the emergence of lasting political parties during the twentieth century.
 (4) They have had little influence on American political parties because the parties do not pay attention to popular demands.
 (5) They have usually been tools of foreign countries.

18. Social Darwinism was a doctrine that was followed by many influential Americans during the late nineteenth and early twentieth centuries. It stressed that society was based on the survival of the fittest and the government was wrongfully tampering with nature when it aided the disadvantaged. Which of the following would best describe a Social Darwinist's reaction to a government food stamp program?
 (1) He would want to expand the program.
 (2) He would want to maintain the present level of spending on the program.
 (3) He would want state governments to run the program.
 (4) He would make sure that the unemployed received the aid.
 (5) He would want to cut out the program.

Questions 19–20 refer to the following chart.

FORECAST OF POPULATION INCREASE, 1975–2000
(In Millions)

	Population		Increases, 1975–2000	
	1975	2000	Absolute	Percent
Anglo-America	242	295	53	22
Europe	474	540	66	14
Soviet Union	254	314	60	24
Oceania	21	33	12	57
Subtotal	991	1,182	191	19
Latin America	328	610	282	86
Asia	2,407	3,800	1,393	58
Africa	420	830	410	98
Subtotal	3,155	5,240	2,085	66
World Total	4,146	6,422	2,276	55

19. According to the chart, which area of the world will have the largest absolute increase in population between 1975 and 2000?
 (1) Anglo-America
 (2) Soviet Union
 (3) Latin America
 (4) Asia
 (5) Africa

20. By what percent is the population of the world projected to increase between 1975 and 2000?
 (1) 19
 (2) 2,276
 (3) 55
 (4) 191
 (5) 22

GO ON TO THE NEXT PAGE.

Questions 21–22 refer to the following graph.

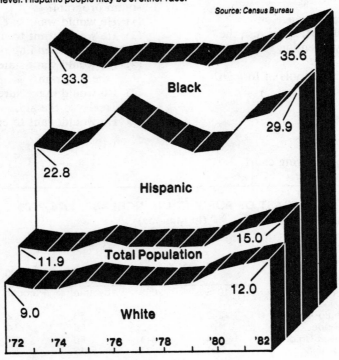

Poverty Rates in the U.S., 1972-82

For each category, percentage of the population living below the poverty level. Hispanic people may be of either race.

Source: Census Bureau

33.3

35.6

Black

29.9

22.8

Hispanic

15.0

11.9   **Total Population**

12.0

9.0   **White**

'72   '74   '76   '78   '80   '82

21. Which of the following conclusions is best supported by the data on this graph?
    Between 1972 and 1982, the percentage of people living below the poverty level
    (1) increased among blacks and Hispanics but decreased in the total population
    (2) decreased among whites and Hispanics and increased among blacks
    (3) increased for all categories
    (4) decreased for all categories
    (5) decreased among blacks and whites and increased among Hispanics

22. Which of the following represents the category and year of the highest percentage of people living below the poverty level?
    (1) Blacks in 1973
    (2) Total Population in 1982
    (3) Hispanics in 1976
    (4) Blacks in 1982
    (5) Hispanics in 1982

GO ON TO THE NEXT PAGE.

23. During the 1970s and 1980s, there were several federal court decisions concerning the respective powers of the president and the Congress. In the Watergate affair, the courts ruled that the president could not claim executive privilege as a reason to keep certain materials away from Congress. In 1983, the Supreme Court halted the use of the so-called "legislative veto," which had been used by Congress to control and limit many actions of the executive branch.

  The series of events described in this passage demonstrates that the separation of powers provided for under the Constitution is actually
   (1) very dictatorial
   (2) too rigid
   (3) not guiding the government efficiently
   (4) flexible and open to interpretation and change
   (5) the weakest part of the Constitution

Question 24 refers to the following graph.

WHO PAYS FOR HEALTH CARE?

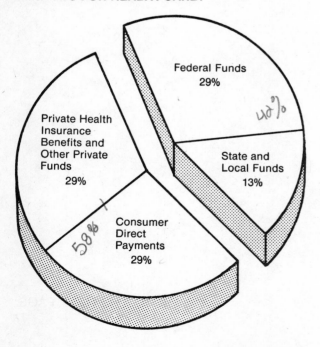

24. Which of the following statements is true according to the data on the graph?
   (1) Private health insurance and other private funds pay most of the cost of health care.
   (2) State and local funds should pay more for health care.
   (3) The high cost of health care is hardest on the consumer.
   (4) Consumer payments, private health insurance benefits, and state and local funds pay equal portions of the total cost of health care.
   (5) Private health insurance benefits, federal funds, and consumer direct payments cover close to 90 percent of the total cost of health care.

GO ON TO THE NEXT PAGE.

Questions 25–26 refer to the following passage.

". . . the peculiarity of American institutions is the fact that they have been compelled to adapt themselves to the changes of an expanding people—to the changes involved in crossing a continent, in winning a wilderness, and in developing each area of progress out of the primitive economic and political conditions of the frontier. . . ."

Frederick Jackson Turner

25. The main idea of this passage is that
    (1) the rise of cities was a major influence in economic and political development
    (2) American character has been dominated by its origins in Europe
    (3) settlement of the frontier has been the dominant force in the development of the American character
    (4) industrialization has been the dominant force in American institutions
    (5) the primitive economic conditions of the frontier have created American institutions that are resistant to change

26. To the writer of this passage, what event would signal an end to American originality and innovation?
    (1) The end of exploring new frontiers
    (2) The development of the wilderness into a place of economic and political power
    (3) The rise of large cities in the east
    (4) The end of our close ties to European culture
    (5) The crossing of the continent

27. In the last twenty years of the nineteenth century, many American small farmers were driven off the land or reduced to the position of tenants by changing economic conditions. They formed protest organizations and demanded various government reforms they thought would save the small farmers and their way of life, but their efforts were unsuccessful. The small farmers continued to decline in number as agriculture became more mechanized, and larger farms took over the small ones.
    In the terms of a social scientist, the American small farmer of the late nineteenth century was a member of a
    (1) rising social class
    (2) political elite
    (3) powerful majority
    (4) declining social class
    (5) revolutionary social class

28. In 1954, the unanimous Supreme Court decision in the *Brown* v. *the Board of Education* case was a major historical event. This decision
    (1) upheld the "separate but equal" policy of the late 1800s
    (2) denounced all violent protests over segregated schools
    (3) struck down legal racial segregation in public schools
    (4) was the only impetus for the 1964 Civil Rights Act
    (5) created segregated public schools in the U.S.

GO ON TO THE NEXT PAGE.

Questions 29–30 refer to the following map.

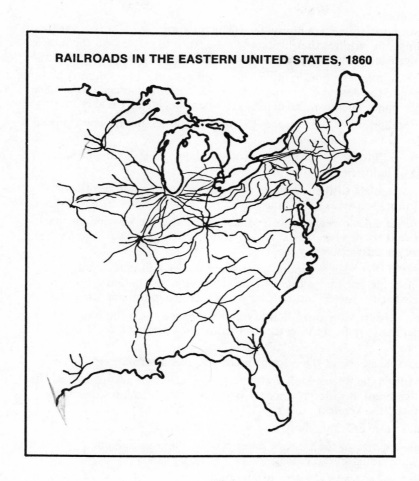

RAILROADS IN THE EASTERN UNITED STATES, 1860

29. This map depicts
  (1) tributaries of the Mississippi River
  (2) 1860 state boundaries
  (3) the first telegraph lines in the eastern
     United States
  (4) U.S. railroads in the East as of 1860
  (5) major highways in the United States in
     1860

30. You can infer from this map that
  (1) the Northeast was more developed
     commercially and industrially than the
     Southeast
  (2) river travel was more extensive in the
     Northeast
  (3) communication among northeastern cities
     was well developed by 1860
  (4) few highways had been built in the
     Southeast
  (5) Texas was not yet a state in 1860

END OF EXAMINATION

ANSWERS AND EXPLANATIONS

1. (1) People who buy things are consumers. The question tells you that the Truth in Lending Act requires that lenders tell the truth to buyers, so the people who are protected by this legislation are consumers.

2. (4) Rather than taking responsibility for her own actions, the student is blaming someone else for her problems. People use defense mechanisms to protect their self-image. These can be dangerous when they distort reality.

3. (4) The last paragraph of the passage is about the harnessing of water power along the Fall Line for industry.

4. (2) The passage illustrates that towns sprouted along the Fall Line because of the need of industry for power.

5. (5) The passage refers to the central government as having "little influence," and as being "too weak" and "ineffective."

6. (1) The third sentence gives a list of problems faced by the new nation that suggests that its survival was at stake. There is no evidence in the passage for the other answers.

7. (3) You are told that "These groups must share power and make continual compromises to get things done." This sentence suggests that all groups get some of what they want but that no particular group dominates.

8. (1) The most money is spent on military and police, so (1) is the best answer. The other answers relate to categories with lower percentages of national spending.

9. (4) The second sentence of the passage gives you this information.

10. (3) The details of the passage tell you how several different groups gained the right to vote, all at different times. They also describe the obstacles that blacks faced in exercising this right.

11. (3) "Mountain ranges" is the only physical feature listed.

12. (2) The first sentence of the passage gives you the main idea. None of the other answers are stated in the passage.

13. (4) The passage illustrates changes brought about in several areas of people's lives as a result of the changes in women's employment patterns.

14. (5) The passage tells you that, when mortgage interest rates rise, fewer families can afford to buy homes and sales fall.

15. (1) The housing industry would be aided by lower interest rates, since more families would be able to afford to buy homes.

16. (2) The cartoonist is showing people complaining but not voting to show that people's apathy is the cause of ineffective government.

17. (2) The most popular demands of militant social movements have been adopted into the programs of major political parties. These demands have been absorbed into the existing two-party structure without forcing basic political realignment.

18. (5) A Social Darwinist would think that giving out food stamps would artificially assist those who are not capable of taking care of themselves.

19. (4) Looking down the column headed "Increases; Absolute," you will find that the highest number in the column is for Asia.

20. (3) The bottom row of the chart gives you the world totals in all the categories. The forecasted total percentage increase is 55.

21. (3) Each category on the graph has a starting figure for 1972 and an ending figure for 1982. If you compare these figures, you will see that the ending number is higher than the starting number for all categories.

22. (4)   The 1982 figure for blacks is the highest point on the graph (35.6%).

23. (4)   The paragraph describes recent reinterpretations of the constitutional balance of power. The other answers are not supported by the information given.

24. (5)   If you test each of the answers against the data on the graph, you will see that (5) is the best answer.

25. (3)   This answer best restates the main idea of the passage, which asserts that American institutions have had to serve an expanding and pioneering nation.

26. (1)   The writer's tone is one of enthusiasm for the achievements of the American people in settling and developing a wilderness. You can infer that he believes that the challenge of the frontier brought forth originality and innovation.

27. (4)   The situation described in the passage is one of a declining social class. American farmers, as part of the class of small-scale producers, were forced to change their way of life due to massive economic and technological changes.

28. (3)   This ruling made illegal the practice of deliberate racial segregation.

29. (4)   You can see from the title of the map that (4) is the correct answer.

30. (1)   The map shows a greater concentration of railroads in the Northeast than in the Southeast. Railroads made the movement of goods and raw materials in the Northeast easy and enabled this region to develop much faster economically than the Southeast.

PRE-TEST EVALUATION CHART

The evaluation chart below will give you an idea of what you need to work on to pass the GED social studies test.

The rows across tell you the social studies content areas, and the columns down indicate the reading skills being tested. The heading *Prior Knowledge* refers to questions that require you to recall facts you may have previously learned or read.

The numbers in darker type indicate questions based on graphic or pictorial materials. If you miss more than 3 of these, you should pay especially close attention to the chapter that starts on page 45.

	Prior Knowledge	Main Idea	Finding Details	Inferences and Conclusions	Application of Ideas	Evaluation of Logic
History	17	10, 25, 29	9	*30*	18	26
Political Science	28	5, *16*		6	23	7
Behavioral Science	2	12	*22*	13, *21*		27
Economics	1		*24*	*8*, 14		15
Geography	11	3	*19, 20*	4		

Social Studies Reading Skills

The Social Studies Test requires well-developed reading skills. This section will help you to evaluate and develop those skills.

The starting point for improving your reading skills is to understand that social studies writers have a purpose in mind; they want to present an idea or convince you of a point of view. Writers communicate their basic point, or main idea, and then use details to support and defend it. They may further illustrate an idea by demonstrating how it relates to other examples. Sometimes, they may attempt to sway you emotionally by using a certain style or tone.

IDENTIFYING THE MAIN IDEA

The **main idea** is the basic topic of a passage; it sums up what the writer is trying to tell you. The other ideas and details in a paragraph or passage are used to support and develop the main idea. Understanding the main idea of a paragraph or passage will help you to answer many types of questions on the GED social studies test.

Most often, the main idea of a paragraph is found in the first sentence, although it may appear elsewhere, such as in the last sentence. In a longer passage, the main idea can usually be found in an introductory or concluding paragraph. To identify the main idea, use the following method.

(1) Read the entire paragraph or passage.

(2) Determine what the paragraph or passage is about.

(3) Finally, check the first and last sentences of a paragraph or the first and last paragraphs of a passage. You will often find the main idea stated in one of these places.

Now, look at a sample passage.

E
X
A
M
P
L
E

Because of the lack of popular support, the military command was very reluctant to get involved in direct action in Central America. High-level Pentagon sources reported that the military leaders were well aware of the public's memories of the Vietnam War, a war that had cost the United States more than 200,000 casualties and more than $100 billion.

The military leaders said they did not want to become involved in another unpopular war. They felt that the experience in Vietnam had demoralized the military and had cost it valuable public support for its modernization plans.

Because of these reservations, the military leadership urged the administration to take a cautious approach to direct military involvement.

What is the main idea in this passage?
(1) Military leaders did not want the United States to suffer heavy casualties in Central America.
(2) Military leaders were worried about the cost of military action.
(3) Military leaders wanted to initiate direct military intervention in Central America.
(4) Because of the lack of public support, military leaders were reluctant to get involved militarily in Central America.
(5) Military leaders thought there was sufficient public support to justify military intervention in Central America.

The answer is (4). The passage states, "Because of the lack of popular support, the military command was very reluctant to get involved in direct action in Central America." The rest of the passage supports this central idea. Look back at the passage and note the references to an "unpopular war," and the loss of "valuable public support."

The following exercise offers more practice in understanding the main idea.

EXERCISE 1

Directions: Read the following passage and answer the questions. Fill in the circle that corresponds to the correct answer.

A team of sociological researchers has just released a five-year study of youth problems in the United States. The study has caused a stir because it uncovered a disturbing new trend—the rise of teenage suicide.

5   Suicide is now the third highest cause of death among youths fifteen to nineteen years old, ranking it just behind accidents and homicide. Youth suicide increased nearly 250 percent between 1950 and 1980. In 1979 alone, 5,000 young people committed suicide and an estimated 400,000 attempted suicide. While public
10   and official attention has been focused on teenage drug abuse and pregnancy, teenage suicide has been increasing at an alarming rate.

1. What is the main idea of this passage?
    (1) The increase in teenage suicide is a disturbing new trend.
    (2) Drug abuse is the main problem our youth are facing.
    (3) Pregnancy is a growing problem among teenagers.
    (4) Sociologists study all youth problems.
    (5) Youth problems are on the decline.

2. The most logical follow-up story would be one that answers the question:
    (1) Why are our teenagers on drugs?
    (2) Why are our teens getting pregnant?
    (3) Why do sociologists study teenagers?
    (4) Why are teenagers suddenly giving up drugs?
    (5) Why are teenagers committing suicide?

For answers and explanations, see page 42.

FINDING DETAILS

The author supports his main idea with details. These **supporting details** clarify or expand on the main idea. On *The Social Studies Test*, you will have to locate facts or details in a reading passage. To do this, you will often have to reread the passage to see how the facts are presented.

Scanning is an important skill that will help you to save time when finding details. **Scanning** is the practice of rapidly looking over a passage and locating a specific detail. For example, suppose you have read an interesting article on the history of immigration to the United States. Later, you realize that you have forgotten which countries the immigrants came from, so you look at the article again, this time scanning only for this information. Your eyes focus on the word *immigrant* and on references to nationality.

Look at the following passage on immigration. Try to scan for only the details that you wish to know now: the national origins of immigrants. Underline this information as you find it.

> E
> X
> A
> M
> P
> L
> E
>
> Throughout the years, people have immigrated to the United States for a variety of reasons. The earliest immigrants came to North America from northern Europe in the 1600s, some in search of political and religious freedom and some to escape imprisonment for debts and criminal activity. At the same time, there was also a group who were forcibly "immigrated": African people who were enslaved to work on large plantations. Later, in the 1800s, many Chinese and Irish people moved to the United States for economic and political reasons. In the early twentieth century, many more came from Italy, Greece, and other European countries. The most recent immigrants to this country, from Mexico, Central America, and Southeast Asia, have come seeking better jobs and political freedom.

If you did the above exercise efficiently, your scan of the reading passage should have looked something like this: . . . immigrants . . . from northern Europe . . . forcibly "immigrated": African people . . . Chinese and Irish people . . . many more came from Italy, Greece, and other European countries. . . . immigrants . . . from Mexico, Central America, and Southeast Asia. . . .

To prepare for the GED test, you should practice scanning for detail in reading passages. First, read the passage carefully and get the sense of what is being said by identifying the main idea. Then read the questions that will direct you back to the passage to scan for key details. Look back for the key words, numbers, or dates that are needed to answer each question.

EXERCISE 2

Directions: Read the following passage and answer the questions. Fill in the circle that corresponds to the correct answer.

The southern slave owners won many victories in the decades preceding the Civil War. In 1820, the Missouri Compromise opened new areas of the country to slavery. More areas were

cleared for the potential growth of slavery with the passage of the
5   Kansas-Nebraska Act in 1854. The greatest victory for the
supporters of slavery came in 1857 with the Dred Scott decision.
The decision opened virtually all of the territories to slavery.

3. Which event first opened new areas to slavery?
    (1)   The beginning of the Civil War
    (2)   The passage of the Kansas-Nebraska Act
    (3)   The Missouri Compromise
    (4)   The Dred Scott decision
    (5)   The Decision of 1854

4. The 1857 Dred Scott decision
    (1)   was welcomed by the slave owners because it
         limited the expansion of slavery
    (2)   was not as important as the Missouri Compromise
    (3)   was a signal to prepare for war
    (4)   preceded the Kansas-Nebraska Act
    (5)   was a great victory for the slave owners

For answers and explanations, see page 42.

ORGANIZATION OF IDEAS

Writers use different methods to organize their ideas in a passage. On the
GED social studies test, be aware of the three common methods of
organizing supporting details in passages.

       (1)   Comparison and Contrast
       (2)   Cause and Effect
       (3)   Sequence of Events

Comparison and Contrast

Comparison and contrast is a method used to show the similarities and
differences between two or more things. A writer uses **comparison** when he
wants to examine similarities and **contrast** when he wants to look at
differences. For example, a writer might compare rates for similar crimes
in two different societies, or he might contrast different lifestyles in the
same societies.

Now look at a passage that uses comparison and contrast.

EXERCISE 3

Directions: Read the following passage and answer the questions. Fill in the circle that corresponds to the correct answer.

American cities are returning to a pattern similar to that of European cities during the Middle Ages. At that time, the rich and their servants lived in the inner city, while the working classes and poor lived on the city's outer edge. For much of this century,
5 the inner areas of American cities were inhabited by poor people and the suburbs were inhabited by the rich. However, in recent years, the central cities have become wealthier in places like Chicago, New York, and San Francisco.

Many of the wealthy have moved back into the cities as part of
10 the process referred to as "gentrification." Inner cities have been rehabilitated and, once again, the poor have been pushed to the outer edge of the city or to the older suburbs.

5. How are American cities of recent years becoming like the cities of the Middle Ages?
   (1) The cities are generally very poor.
   (2) The rich have their servants with them.
   (3) The suburbs are inhabited by the wealthy and the inner cities by the poor.
   (4) Rich people live in luxurious houses and apartments.
   (5) More rich people are living in the central areas, while the poor are pushed to the outer edge.

5 ① ② ③ ④ ⑤

6. How did the growth of American cities earlier in this century differ from today's patterns of urban development?
   (1) The rich used to live in the suburbs, and the poor lived in the inner city.
   (2) Poor people lived in the suburbs, and rich people lived in the center.
   (3) The servants used to live with rich people.
   (4) The rich used to live in houses, not apartments.
   (5) The cities used to be wealthier.

For answers and explanations, see page 42.

Cause and Effect

The use of **cause and effect** is a very common way of organizing a social studies passage. In this type of presentation, a writer shows how one event causes another to happen. For example, the development of high technology has allowed machines to do much of the work previously done by people. As a result, workers in many industries are now unemployed. In this situation, the *cause* is the development of high technology, and the *effect* (or result) is an increase in unemployment.

Now look at a passage that uses cause and effect.

EXERCISE 4

Directions: Read the following passage and answer the questions. Fill in the circle that corresponds to the correct answer.

The rapid growth of Third World populations has been greatly influenced by public health measures. The extension of public health to many poor countries, largely through the efforts of the United Nations, has had a big impact on controlling malaria,
5   yellow fever, and many other diseases. One result of this has been the reduction of infant mortality. In some countries, the infant mortality rate has dropped from 200 deaths per 1,000 births to 50 per 1,000 births. This rapid decline in infant mortality has been the main source of increased population growth. Even further
10 growth is expected because more young women will reach childbearing age.

7. According to the passage, what has been a major cause of the reduction in infant mortality?
   (1) More young women can reach childbearing age.
   (2) Public health measures have controlled diseases.
   (3) Increased population growth
   (4) Better food and housing conditions
   (5) Malaria, yellow fever, and other diseases

7 ① ② ③ ④ ⑤

8. According to the passage, what effect will increased survival of infants have on future population growth?
   (1) Reduce it by increasing the demand for effective family planning
   (2) Increase it because more girls will reach childbearing age
   (3) Decrease the number of child-bearing women
   (4) Reduce population growth because it causes food shortages
   (5) Reduce the need for public health measures

8 ① ② ③ ④ ⑤

For answers and explanations, see page 42.

Sequence of Events

Many writers use a **sequence of events** or a series of steps or operations. This is a very common way of arranging information in social studies writing, especially in history passages. When passages contain a sequence, you have to follow and keep in mind the series of events that is described in the passage. You will often find key words used such as *first, second, third, finally, before, after, next,* and *then.*

The passage below is about a sequence of events.

EXERCISE 5

Directions: Read the following passage and answer the questions. Fill in the circle that corresponds to the correct answer.

In October 1962, an American U-2 plane found evidence of the existence of Soviet nuclear missile bases in Cuba. President Kennedy rejected calls for direct military retaliation against the bases and instead instigated a naval blockade of Cuba. He also
5   threatened to invade Cuba and retaliate against the Soviet Union if any attack was launched from the bases. When confronted with photographic evidence of the bases, the Soviets agreed to negotiate. First, they offered to remove the bases if the U.S. removed its own missiles from Turkey. The U.S. refused, however, and in
10 the end, the Soviet Union agreed to withdraw the missiles and dismantle the bases. After the bases were dismantled, the United States ended its blockade of Cuba.

9. When did the United States blockade Cuba?   9 ① ② ③ ❹ ⑤
    (1) When the Soviets asked the United States to
        remove its missiles from Turkey
    (2) When the Soviet Union first set up missile bases
    (3) When the negotiations between the United States
        and the Soviet Union broke down
    (4) When the United States found evidence that the
        Soviets had established nuclear missile bases in
        Cuba
    (5) When Cuba launched an attack from the nuclear
        missile bases

10. When did the United States end the blockade?
  (1) After the missile bases were dismantled
  (2) When the USSR agreed to negotiate
  (3) When the USSR agreed to dismantle the bases
  (4) When the USSR removed the missiles from the bases
  (5) When the USSR threatened to attack the United States

10 ① ② ③ ④ ⑤

For answers and explanations, see page 42.

INFERENCE SKILLS

Making Inferences

In the previous section of this chapter, you learned how to identify the main idea and locate supporting details. This type of reading skill, called **literal understanding**, simply requires that you go back to the passage and understand information that is stated directly. On *The Social Studies Test*, you will need **inferential understanding** as well as literal understanding. **Making inferences** requires a reader to go beyond the directly stated information in a passage. A reader goes beneath the surface meaning of words and finds a meaning that is only suggested. An inference is actually a form of "educated guess" based upon the various facts. Before making an inference, a reader must be very sure of what the passage is stating directly.

Below is a short paragraph followed by a question that requires an inference.

> **EXAMPLE**
>
> There is some evidence that people who take sleeping pills over long periods of time become irritable or depressed. One possible explanation is that sleeping pills inhibit normal dreaming. Thus, many doctors do not recommend the consistent use of sleeping pills.

What inference about dreaming can be made based on the passage?
(1) Dreaming makes people depressed and irritable.
(2) Too much dreaming is abnormal.
(3) Not everyone needs to dream.
(4) Sleeping pills do not affect dreaming.
(5) Dreaming may be necessary for good mental health.

The answer is (5). While the paragraph does not state explicitly that dreaming is necessary for mental health, it shows a connection between the inhibition of normal dreaming and irritability or depression. From this connection, we can infer that normal dreaming promotes mental well-being.

Now practice your inference skills with the following passage.

EXERCISE 6

Directions: Read the following passage and answer the questions. Fill in the circle that corresponds to the correct answer.

Until recently, the Catholic church was very closely tied to the Spanish government. This meant that both divorce and abortion were illegal. However, by the 1960s, not everyone in Spain was happy with such laws, perhaps because religion had become less
5   important in people's daily lives. Nonetheless, it was hard to break the link between church and state that had endured for so many hundreds of years. These ties began to fray after the death of Generalissimo Franco in 1975 and have almost completely broken off under the new Socialist government because of policy differ-
10   ences over issues important to the church.

11. What can we infer about religion in Spain?
    (1) Catholicism is the religion of a small minority in Spain.
    (2) Catholicism is the traditional religion of Spain.
    (3) Catholicism has guided the Socialist government.
    (4) Only the rich and powerful are Catholic.
    (5) People in Spain have no special religious affiliation.

11 ① ② ③ ④ ⑤

12. What can we infer about the policies of the new Socialist government?
    (1) The government supports legal divorce and abortion.
    (2) The government continues to reject divorce and abortion.
    (3) The government abides by the church's stand on divorce and abortion.
    (4) The government supports legal abortion, but not divorce.
    (5) The government supports legal divorce, but not abortion.

12 ① ② ③ ④ ⑤

For answers and explanations, see page 42.

Unstated Main Idea

One special type of inference skill is understanding an implied or **unstated main idea**. In a previous section, you learned how to locate a main idea when it is stated directly. How would you identify a main idea when it is not stated directly?

An unstated or implied main idea is only suggested. To understand it, you must read the passage, study the details, and ask yourself what is being said. On the basis of the details, you determine the main point that the writer is trying to make. Ask yourself, "What is the passage all about?" and then change what you believe to be the unstated main idea into a clear statement.

Now you can practice finding an unstated main idea.

EXAMPLE St. Louis, Missouri, and Chicago, Illinois, competed for regional domination throughout the nineteenth century. They both had access to the productive western farming areas. St. Louis had an early lead on Chicago because of the former's history as the jumping-off point for westward expansion up the Missouri River Valley. Chicago gained the lead on St. Louis during the Civil War. The Mississippi River was closed to trade during the war while Chicago's railroads and access to the Great Lakes were not halted. As a result, Chicago flourished as a grain-trading and meat-packing center.

What is the unstated main idea of this passage?
(1) The Civil War caused Chicago and St. Louis to grow rapidly.
(2) During the Civil War, St. Louis dominated the Midwest because of its better location.
(3) Chicago became more of a regional power than St. Louis because of its superior access to trade routes during the Civil War.
(4) The Civil War was the major cause of the decline of both St. Louis and Chicago.
(5) Chicago pushed ahead of St. Louis because it was a more modern city.

The correct answer is (3). The unstated main idea of this passage is that access to trade and transportation routes is what made Chicago grow. St. Louis lost ground because its transportation routes were shut off during the Civil War. If Chicago had not had access to the railroads and Great Lakes trade routes, the war would have had little impact on its growth.

EXERCISE 7

Directions: Read the following passage and answer the questions. Fill in the circle that corresponds to the correct answer.

Realignment of political party coalitions occurs when one or both of the traditional parties lose their usual base of support. Recent polls indicate that increasing numbers of people identify themselves as independents. Twenty percent of voters said they were
5   strong Democrats in 1960; however, only 15 percent identified themselves that way in 1976. The number of people identifying themselves as strong Republicans decreased from 14 percent to 9 percent during the same period.

These figures could also be stated in a different way. The total
10   number of people identifying strongly with either of the two major political parties decreased from 34 percent of all the voters in 1960 to 24 percent in 1976. This change has given an unpredictable quality to recent elections and caused observers to question the future of the two parties.

13. Which of the following best summarizes the main idea
    of this passage?
    (1) More and more people are leaving the Republican
         party to become Democrats.
    (2) The Republicans and Democrats are losing hard-
         core support, and this points to the possibility of
         party realignment.
    (3) Republicans are having a hard time holding on to
         their base of support.
    (4) The Democrats can no longer assume the support
         of union members.
    (5) The two-party system is not likely to change.

13 ① ② ③ ④ ⑤

For answers and explanations, see page 43.

Drawing Conclusions

The ability to draw conclusions is an important inference skill. You **draw a conclusion** when you predict the outcome of events or determine the implication of facts given in a passage. For an example of drawing conclusions, look at the passage below.

EXAMPLE

When the federal government has to borrow large amounts of money to finance its spending, the supply of available money for loans becomes tightened and interest rates for borrowing tend to rise. Thus, when companies need to borrow money, they must pay more in interest. This extra cost is usually passed along to consumers.

If the government had to borrow a lot of money to finance a
big increase in defense spending, what could be a possible
effect on consumer prices?
(1) They would fall.
(●) They would rise.
(3) They would fall and then rise.
(4) They would rise and then fall.
(5) They would stay the same as they were before.

The answer is (2). The facts in this passage indicate that large-scale
government borrowing leads to higher interest rates. Companies must
spend more money when they borrow, so they usually raise their prices to
compensate.

Now practice drawing conclusions with the passage below.

EXERCISE 8

Directions: Read the following passage and answer the questions. Fill in
the circle that corresponds to the correct answer.

Having a credit card can be a wonderful convenience because you
never have to worry about having ready cash when you want to
buy something. Rather than paying right away for the full price of
an item, you can pay for it in small monthly installments.
5   Remember, though, you always have to pay the cost or a portion
of the cost at the end of the month. If you can't afford to pay the
entire bill, you'll be charged interest on the remaining amount.
You will continue to pay interest until you finally pay off all that
you charged. If you don't pay your balance in full by the due date
10 on the first statement, you'll end up spending much more than if
you had made your purchase in cash.

14. Which piece of advice is based on this passage?   14 ① ② ● ④ ⑤
    (1) Use credit cards because they are cheaper.
    (2) Never use a credit card because you pay more.
    (●) Make sure that your credit card payments don't
        exceed your ability to pay monthly installments.
    (4) Always use cash because it is easier.
    (5) Use credit cards so that you can establish yourself
        as a good credit risk.

15. According to the passage, a disadvantage of buying with credit cards is that

    (1)   you'll never have cash on hand

    (2)   it's hard to remember to carry the cards around

    (3)   you may underestimate how much you ultimately pay for an item

    (4)   interest rates are rising

    (5)   it's difficult to establish credit

15 ① ② ● ④ ⑤

For answers and explanations, see page 43.

Application of Ideas

Another common inference skill is application of ideas. When you **apply an idea**, you are using information from one situation as a means of interpreting or understanding information in another. For example, if an airplane continues to fly on a straight course for a sufficient length of time, you can determine that it will eventually return to the approximate point where it started. How do you figure this out? Use the idea that the earth is round and apply this idea to the flight of the airplane. Now practice applying ideas by reading and answering a question about the following passage.

> **EXAMPLE**
>
> President Monroe announced the Monroe Doctrine in a speech to the United States Congress in 1823. In that speech, he declared that the U.S. would not allow European powers to intervene in the affairs of the Western Hemisphere. This speech came at the time that Spain had lost control of its colonies in Latin America, and many Americans feared that other European powers might attempt to take over these colonies. The President stated that, if any European power interfered with an independent state in this hemisphere, the U.S. would see it as "the manifestation of an unfriendly disposition toward the United States."

The United States would feel that the Monroe Doctrine had been violated if a European power were to send military forces to intervene in the politics of

    (1)   Libya

    (2)   Saudi Arabia

    (3)   Brazil

    (4)   Thailand

    (5)   China

The answer is (3). The question requires that you understand the basic principle of the Monroe Doctrine (the U.S. will not tolerate European interference in the Western Hemisphere). You must then apply this principle to a situation involving European military intervention in a nation in the Western Hemisphere, Brazil.

EXERCISE 9

Directions: Read the following passage and answer the questions. Fill in the circle that corresponds to the correct answer.

At the heart of economic growth is the growth in labor productivity. One way to measure productivity is by the output of each worker per hour of labor. The more that can be produced per hour, the more productive the economy. The more productive the
5   economy, the faster the economy can grow.

There are several ways to improve productivity. The most important method has been the introduction of modern technology. In the past, the introduction of technology to agriculture produced the greatest surge in farm productivity in European and
10   American history. Today, the introduction of modern technology, such as computers, is leading to increased manufacturing productivity. Other means of increasing productivity include more efficient organization of management, improvement in worker morale, and speed-up of the work process.

16. The Japanese now have a large lead on the U.S. in the successful use of modern technology, such as robotics, to increase industrial productivity. Based on the ideas in the above passage, what effect will this have on the growth of Japan's economy?
    (1) It will be slower than in the U.S. because of lower productivity.
    (2) It will decline because robots cannot buy anything.
    (3) It will be about the same as the U.S.
    (4) It will grow faster than the U.S. economy.
    (5) It will be slower because of the cost of maintaining robots.

16 ① ② ③ ④ ⑤

17. A company wishing to increase productivity should focus its efforts on which of the following?
    (1) Better marketing
    (2) Better supervision of workers
    (3) Introducing new technology
    (4) Reducing its prices
    (5) Reducing the costs of raw materials

17 ① ② ③ ④ ⑤

For answers and explanations, see page 43.

EVALUATION OF LOGIC

After reading a passage, you might ask yourself, "Does the writer make sense? Are his ideas logical?" To answer these questions, you must use evaluation of logic, another inferential reading skill. Think of **evaluation of logic** as your judgment of the way a writer presents and uses his ideas. When evaluating logic, you may have to draw upon any or all of the various reading skills you have previously learned.

Probably the most important aspect of evaluating a writer's logic is judging his logical consistency. *Logical consistency* simply means the writer's use of sound reasoning in developing an idea. Some of the things that you should be aware of are listed below.

(1)   A writer's facts should support his conclusions.

The writer should use only facts or details that are relevant to her conclusion. For example, an author who concludes that teenage suicide is becoming a serious problem should support her argument with facts about teenage suicide.

(2)   A writer should correctly apply his ideas.

You should carefully examine how a writer takes an idea or a principle that applies to one situation and applies it to an entirely different situation. For example, a political scientist writing recommendations for U.S. foreign policy in Latin America should not base his argument on American experience in Southeast Asia unless he can show a meaningful connection.

On the GED, you may have to evaluate whether a statement or an assertion is supported by certain facts. The example below illustrates this.

EXAMPLE
Critics of government assistance programs for the poor often charge that such aid is not effective. However, recent research indicates otherwise. Nationwide studies show that some of the War on Poverty's programs of assistance to the needy significantly helped narrow the gap between the school performance of black and white children. Most black children who participated in the Headstart preschool education program, all-day kindergarten, breakfast and lunch programs, or family counseling programs showed improved school performance in later grades.

Which of the following statements could be supported by this passage?
(1)   Increased spending on education does not improve performance.
(2)   Early help in education has no relation to later performance.

(3) Needy children, black and white, can do just as well without enrichment programs.
(4) Early help in education can affect later performance.
(5) Nutrition programs are the most successful social programs in improving school performance of black children.

The details in the passage support the conclusion stated in answer (4). The passage states that most black children who participated in the antipoverty programs showed improved school performance. You should notice that the details in the passage do not support any of the other answer choices.

The following passage provides more practice with evaluation of logic.

EXERCISE 10

Directions: Read the following passage and answer the questions. Fill in the circle that corresponds to the correct answer.

No one knows for sure why the crime rate is soaring. Crime is a problem that affects everyone in the United States. A great deal of thought and research has been devoted to finding out the reasons for the rise in crime.

5   One theory is that there are too many rewards for the criminal in our society and too few incentives to do honest work. Hence, many intelligent and able young people pursue a career of crime because they consider it the quickest way to get what they want. If, in fact, it is the fastest and easiest manner of making a living,
10   we must make crime less desirable and work more attractive.

Another viewpoint is that most crime is a result of economic and social conditions. These conditions affect men and women who have no opportunity to advance their economic status. They are without hope in a society that promises an equal chance for
15   everyone.

18. Which of the following conclusions could be supported by the details in this passage?   18 ① ② ③ ④ ⑤
    (1) Crime does not pay.
    (2) The rise in the crime rate is not caused by a single factor.
    (3) The elimination of poverty would mean an end to crime.
    (4) Crime is rising because society is too easy on lawbreakers.
    (5) Lax parole standards turn many criminals loose on society.

19. According to the passage, different views of the causes
     of crime reflect different perceptions of
     (1) work
     (2) societal influences
     (3) law enforcement
     (4) the criminal justice system
     (5) poverty

19 ① ② ③ ④ ⑤

For answers and explanations, see page 43.

TONE

Tone is an element a writer uses to influence the reader's reaction to a situation. **Tone** refers to an emotion, such as delight or outrage, that is communicated in a piece of writing. It often reflects the writer's own bias or opinion on the subject. However, not all writing reveals the writer's feelings. In many cases, a piece is written in a straightforward and objective manner.

The skill of recognizing tone requires the reader to analyze the way a selection is written and the feeling that underlies it. When determining tone, it is important to pay careful attention to the writer's choice of words. For example, look at the two paragraphs below.

EXAMPLE

1. Starvation is rampant, and hunger haunts the humble hovels of the needy. Will nothing be done? How can people continue to support an administration that so callously ignores the urgent needs of the poor and underprivileged?

2. Until recently, concern about hunger focused on Third World nations. Lately, however, hunger has become an issue in the United States. Many accuse the current administration of contributing to the problem by cutting back programs that aid the poor. The administration has denied these charges, saying that it has consistently provided assistance to the needy.

The first paragraph is an attempt to create an emotional response in the reader. The writer's bias on the subject of government responsibility for the problem of hunger is clear. Notice the words that are used. Starvation is "rampant"; the administration "callously ignores" the "urgent needs" of the poor, and "hunger haunts the humble hovels" (not homes) of the poor.

(*Hovel* means a "small, wretched dwelling.") The writer, of course, hopes the reader will become angry, maybe even indignant over the plight of the poor.

In contrast, the second paragraph has adopted an objective tone. It is difficult to determine the writer's own feelings on the subject of government responsibility for hunger because he has simply reported, without comment, on the opinions of two different sides. His word choices ("hunger," "the poor," "the needy," and "the problem") are straightforward and not emotionally charged.

Now carefully observe how the writer chooses her words in the following passage.

EXERCISE 11

Directions: Read the following passage and answer the questions. Fill in the circle that corresponds to the correct answer.

> As we stood at the entrance to the Senate chambers, we could see the two protagonists approaching from opposite directions. The senator from North Carolina was striding briskly, with an air of confidence, toward the Senate floor. He was chatting amiably
> 5   with reporters about strategy for the upcoming debate in the Senate. Meanwhile, the senator from New York darted into sight and scurried down the hallway from the other direction. He paused very briefly to huddle nervously with his aides about possible parliamentary maneuvers in the debate.

20. How does the writer of this passage feel about the two senators?   20 ① ② ③ ④ ⑤
    (1) She does not admire either man.
    (2) She admires the senator from North Carolina and dislikes the senator from New York.
    (3) She has no feelings about either man.
    (4) She dislikes the senator from North Carolina and admires the senator from New York.
    (5) She respects both senators.

21. Which word conveys a positive image?   21 ① ② ③ ④ ⑤
    (1) *darted*
    (2) *scurried*
    (3) *amiably*
    (4) *nervously*
    (5) *maneuvered*

For answers and explanations, see page 43.

WORD MEANINGS: CONTEXT AND CLUES

While reading this book or taking the GED test, you may encounter words or phrases that are unfamiliar. Always assume that you can get the general meaning of a passage even if you don't know a particular word or words.

> **E X A M P L E**
>
> It was recently learned that rebel city council members held a *conclave* last month. At the secret meeting, they discussed ways to embarrass the mayor.

If you did not know the meaning of *conclave*, you could guess from the words following it that a conclave is a secret meeting. Here you have used a word's **context**—the words surrounding the unknown word—for clues to its meaning.

Sometimes, you can determine the meaning of an unfamiliar word from its opposite meaning. For example, look at the sentence below.

> **E X A M P L E**
>
> Unlike the United States, with its official policy of racial integration, South Africa practices *apartheid.*

If you did not understand the meaning of the word *apartheid*, you could guess that it means "the official policy of racial segregation" (the opposite of a policy of integration). The word *unlike* is the clue to look for an opposite meaning.

Finally, the meaning of a word may not be stated directly, and you will have to infer from it the supporting details. This skill is similar to inferring the meaning of an unstated main idea. For example, see if you can determine the meaning of *Gross National Product* from the details in the passage below.

> **E X A M P L E**
>
> The U.S. Gross National Product (GNP) began growing rapidly during the economic recovery of 1983–84. This was determined by adding together the total sales values of goods and services bought by both consumers and businesses. The results showed that the GNP was actually growing at an annual rate of 6–8 percent.

From this passage, you could infer that the GNP is the
(1) total value of consumer goods
(2) total value of consumer and business goods and services ⁃
(3) total value of consumer and business services
(4) total value of business goods and services
(5) total value of consumer goods and services

The answer is (2). Without directly stating the meaning of *Gross National Product*, the passage breaks it down into its component parts: the goods and services bought by consumers and those bought by business. These are added together, and the total value is the GNP. You were able to determine the meaning of GNP by carefully reading the passage.

Below is some more practice in determining word meaning from context.

EXERCISE 12

Directions: Read the following passage and answer the questions. Fill in the circle that corresponds to the correct answer.

Many supporters of school prayer would like to see the institution of a standard prayer to be recited by all schoolchildren. They insist that such a prayer would be acceptable to all because it would be *nondenominational*. That is, it would refer to God in a
5   nonspecific way only, making no *explicit* mention of Jesus Christ, the Holy Trinity, Mohammed, or any other religious figures or beliefs of particular religious groups.

22. You could infer from the passage that
nondenominational means
(1) standardized
(2) not dominant
(3) acceptable to none
(4) not associated with a particular religious group
(5) associated with a particular religious group

22 ① ② ③ ④ ⑤

23. You could infer that *explicit* means
(1) nonspecific
(2) specific
(3) acceptable
(4) religious
(5) educational

23 ① ② ③ ④ ⑤

For answers and explanations, see page 44.

ANSWERS AND EXPLANATIONS

EXERCISE 1

1. (1) The main idea is in the first paragraph: the study "uncovered a disturbing new trend—the rise of teenage suicide." The rest of the passage provides details about this trend.

2. (5) The topic in answer (5) is most closely related to the main idea of the passage, the increase in teenage suicide.

EXERCISE 2

3. (3) In lines 2–3, the passage states, "In 1820, the Missouri Compromise opened new areas of the country to slavery."

4. (5) The writer says, "The greatest victory for the supporters of slavery came in 1857 with the Dred Scott decision."

EXERCISE 3

5. (5) This question asks you to compare the cities of the Middle Ages with today's American cities. Lines 2–4 tell you that, in the Middle Ages, the rich lived in the center of the city and poorer people lived around the outer edge. This is becoming increasingly characteristic of American cities today.

6. (1) To answer this question, you must contrast American cities of today with those of the past. The third sentence of the passage says, "For much of this century, the inner areas of American cities were inhabited by poor people and the suburbs were inhabited by the rich."

EXERCISE 4

7. (2) The third sentence says, "One result of this has been the reduction of infant mortality." "This" refers to the cause, the control of disease through public health measures, which is described in the previous sentence.

8. (2) Based on the last two sentences of the passage, you can see that the decline in infant mortality is expected to result in more girls' reaching childbearing age.

EXERCISE 5

9. (4) See lines 1–4. The first event in the sequence, the discovery of missile bases, is followed by Kennedy's instigation of a naval blockade.

10. (1) The last sentence of the passage states, "After the bases were dismantled, the United States ended its blockade of Cuba."

EXERCISE 6

11. (2) You can guess that Catholicism is the traditional religion of Spain because the passage tells you that the Catholic church and the state were closely tied together for hundreds of years.

12. **(1)** You can infer that the Socialist government supports legal divorce and abortion because the passage tells you that divorce and abortion used to be illegal when the church and the government were more closely tied and that there are now policy differences between the church and the Socialist government.

EXERCISE 7

13. **(2)** Answer (2) best states the main idea because it summarizes the statistics given in the passage about political party affiliations of voters and the implications of the current trend toward independent voting.

EXERCISE 8

14. **(3)** An implication of the passage is that when you buy something that you plan to pay off a month at a time, you should be sure that you'll be able to pay the amount of the monthly installment.

15. **(3)** You can conclude from the last sentence that charging an item may increase its final cost because you will also be paying interest.

EXERCISE 9

16. **(4)** Lines 6–8 state, "The most important method [of improving productivity] has been the introduction of modern technology." You can apply this idea to the information that Japan leads the United States in the area of modern technology and conclude that the Japanese economy will grow faster because of its higher level of productivity.

17. **(3)** In the second paragraph, the passage tells you that "the introduction of modern technology, such as computers, is leading to increased manufacturing productivity."

EXERCISE 10

18. **(2)** The passage tells you that much effort has been directed toward discovering the "reasons for the rise in crime." Then the writer goes on to tell you about two theories concerning the reasons.

19. **(2)** Choice (2) is the only answer that is stated broadly enough to include both of the theories presented in the passage.

EXERCISE 11

20. **(2)** Look at the way the writer depicts each of the senators. Imagine the way each one looks based on the description in the passage. The senator from North Carolina is brisk, confident, and amiable. The senator from New York darts and scurries and is nervous.

21. **(3)** *Amiably* means friendly and relaxed. The other answers describe a sneaky person.

22. (4)   The word *nondenominational* in the passage refers to prayer. The last sentence tells you that a nondenominational prayer is not specific to any particular religious beliefs. You can then infer the meaning of *nondenominational*.

23. (2)   In the last sentence, you can tell that a nonspecific reference to God means that no explicit references to particular religious figures are used. If *nonspecific* means "not explicit," then *explicit* has to mean "specific."

Graphs, Charts, Maps, and Cartoons

For *The Social Studies Test*, you will need to be familiar with the various ways that social studies material can be displayed in pictorial form. This section will acquaint you with tables, graphs, maps, and political cartoons.

In order to work with such materials, it is very important that you pay attention to all of the information that is given in both pictures and words. This means that you must look at how the material is labeled and the types of figures and numbers used. You may be asked to find a particular number or fact, or you might have to make an interpretation that requires making an inference or drawing a conclusion.

1. TABLES

A table is a list of statistics displayed in columns and rows to make it easier for you to make comparisons. A table will have a title at the top. The separate columns and rows within the table will also be labeled so that you will know what information they contain.

Look at the table below.

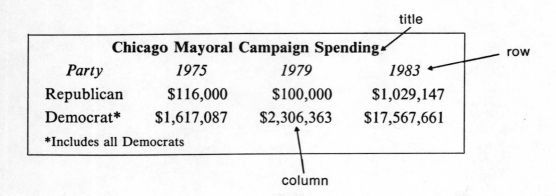

Chicago Mayoral Campaign Spending			
Party	*1975*	*1979*	*1983*
Republican	$116,000	$100,000	$1,029,147
Democrat*	$1,617,087	$2,306,363	$17,567,661

*Includes all Democrats

The title on the table tells you that this is information about mayoral campaign spending in Chicago. The column headings tell you that this information is broken down for the years 1975, 1979, and 1983. The row headings name the political parties. Notice the asterisk (*) used as a reference mark following the label "Democrat." This alerts you that additional information is given at the bottom of the table.

This table is a simple one, but it can be used to make comparisons of the spending of the two parties over a period of time or to compare the spending of the Democratic and Republican mayoral candidates at particular points.

To learn more about reading tables, study the three questions below and the answers and explanations that follow.

In 1983, all of the Democratic candidates spent approximately how much more than the Republican?
(1) $100 thousand
(2) $1 million
(3) $2 million
(4) $16½ million
(5) $18 million

According to the data in this table, the campaign expenditures of Republican mayoral candidates
(1)   declined steadily from 1975 to 1983
(2)   were about the same from 1975 to 1983
(3)   rose steadily from 1975 to 1983
(4)   rose from 1975 to 1979 and then declined
(5)   declined from 1975 to 1979 and then rose

The information in this table could support which of the following conclusions?

(1) In the two elections prior to 1983, the Republicans did not have a serious candidate for mayor.
(2) The 1979 campaign was tainted by corruption scandals.
(3) The Chicago Democratic machine was dissolved in 1975.
(4) In 1975, there were more registered Republicans than Democrats in Chicago.
(5) There are more wealthy Republicans than Democrats in Chicago.

The answer to the first question is (4), $16½ million. Look at the column labeled "1983." The difference between $17½ million (Democrats) and $1 million (Republicans) is closest to the choice $16½ million.

For the second question, the best answer is choice (5). It describes the changes in the Republicans' expenditures over the years shown. The total declined in 1979 and then rose dramatically in 1983.

For the third question, (1) is the best conclusion based on the data. There is no direct statement of this, but the figures for the Republicans would seem to bear this out. Prior to 1983, the Republicans spent far less than would be necessary to contend seriously in a big city mayoral election.

EXERCISE 1

Directions: Answer the questions that follow based on the table below. Fill in the circle that corresponds to the correct answer.

CONSUMPTION OF MAJOR FOOD COMMODITIES PER PERSON PER YEAR (in pounds)		
	1980	1981	1982
Meat	147.6	144.5	139.4
Fish	12.8	13.0	16.4
Poultry Products	34.6	33.6	35.8
Fats & Oils	56.5	57.3	56.8
Fresh Fruit	85.7	87.3	87.4
Fresh Vegetables	99.5	95.2	150.9

1. The food category in which consumption rose by about 50 percent from 1980 to 1982 was
   (1) meat
   (2) fish
   (3) poultry products
   (4) fresh fruit
   (5) fresh vegetables

   1 ① ② ③ ④ ⑤

2. The material in this table supports which of the following conclusions?
   (1) Most people are becoming vegetarians.
   (2) Health-conscious Americans are consuming less meat and more fruit and vegetables.
   (3) Americans consume too much sugar and salt.
   (4) The price of fresh vegetables has risen by 50 percent.
   (5) Between 12 and 16 percent of all Americans eat fish regularly.

   2 ① ② ③ ④ ⑤

For answers and explanations, see page 67.

GRAPHS

Graphs are used to simplify the presentation of information. Long passages of facts and figures can be confusing and difficult to understand. Social studies books and publications, such as magazines and newspapers, use graphs to present material pictorially. Graphs make figures easier to understand and interpret.

Whenever you are reading a graph, make sure to look first at all of the important features: its title, its organization, and a key that indicates the meanings of figures, bars, or lines. If a graph doesn't have a title, the labels on the axes should give you an idea of the topic. Always read figures carefully and be sure to base any interpretation on the material given.

In this section, you will work with four important types of graphs: pictographs, circle graphs, bar graphs, and line graphs.

Pictographs

Pictographs are the simplest type of graphs to interpret. They use a series of symbols to show an amount or quantity. Look at the graph below and answer the following questions. These will give you a good idea of what to look for in a pictograph.

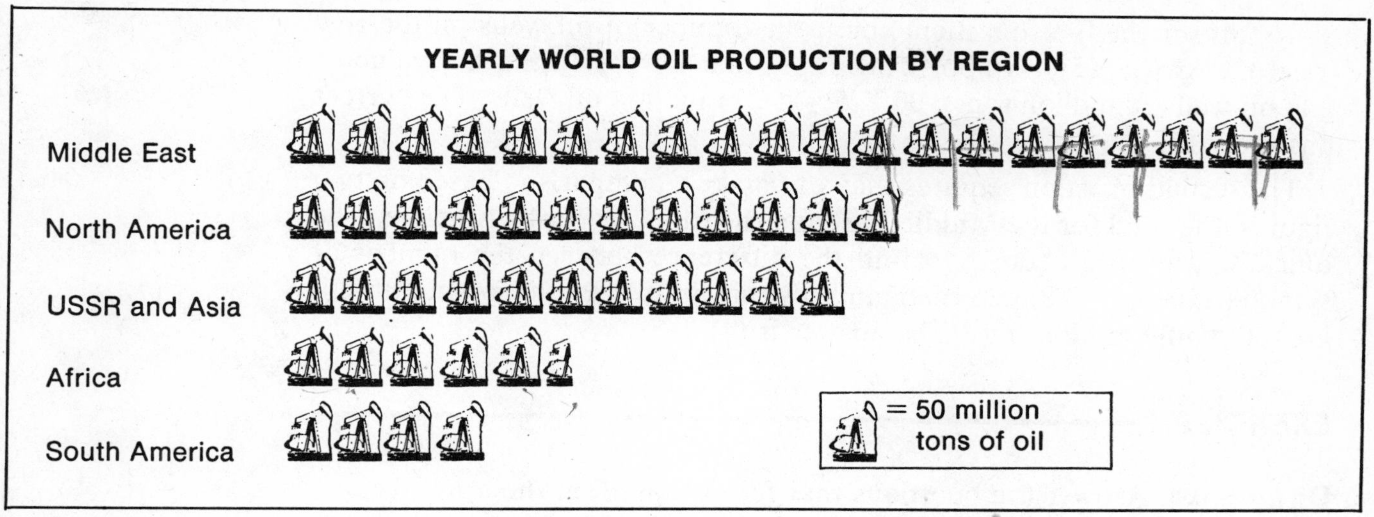

YEARLY WORLD OIL PRODUCTION BY REGION

Middle East

North America

USSR and Asia

Africa

South America

= 50 million tons of oil

To understand the main idea of any graph, ask yourself some questions like these:

- What is the topic (title) of this graph?
  (yearly world oil production)

- What does each oil well represent?
  (50 million tons of oil)

- The graph compares oil production in different _____.
  (regions)

The basics were pretty simple. To read the graph, you will need to do some simple arithmetic and make comparisons. To find the quantities on a pictograph, multiply the value that you are given for a symbol by the number of times it appears on a line. Also notice that partial symbols are used. Most of the time, ½ of a symbol is used, but it is not uncommon to see ¼, ¾, ⅓, or ⅔ of a symbol.

Now answer the questions below based on the graph above.

How much oil was produced by the nations of Africa?
(1) 5 million tons
(2) 25 million tons
(3) 27½ million tons
(4) 250 million tons
(5) 275 million tons

How much more oil was produced in the Middle East than in North America?
(1) 8 million tons
(2) 50 million tons
(3) 80 million tons
(4) 400 million tons
(5) 600 million tons

To answer the first question, count the number of oil wells on the row labeled "Africa" (5½ symbols). Multiply that number times the value of one oil well (50 million tons). 50 × 5½ = 275 million oil wells. The correct answer is (5).

The second question requires that you make a comparison based on two figures: the total for the Middle East and the total for North America. The quickest way to do this is to find the difference between the number of symbols (20 − 12 = 8) and then multiply this times the value of an oil well. 8 × 50 = 400 million tons. The answer is (4).

EXERCISE 2

Directions: Answer the questions that follow based on the graph below. Fill in the circle that corresponds to the correct answer.

3. In 1980, there were approximately how many Air Force officers and enlisted personnel?
   (1) 9,500
   (2) 95,000
   (3) 550,000
   (4) 800,000
   (5) 950,000

3 ① ② ● ④ ⑤

4. Based on the material in the graph, you could say that   4 ① ② ● ④ ⑤
   (1) the number of Air Force personnel dropped steadily from 1955 to 1983
   (2) more people joined the Air Force in 1983 than in 1955
   (3) between 1955 and 1983 the number of Air Force personnel was at its high point in 1955 and its low point in 1980
   (4) more people joined the Air Force in 1955 than in any following year
   (5) the number of people joining the Air Force is expected to decline

For answers and explanations, see page 67.

Circle Graphs

Circle graphs are sometimes called *pie graphs* because of their shape. They are used to show how a total amount of something is divided into parts. The parts of the circle, called *segments*, must add up to a whole or 100 percent. These graphs are often used to show how a total amount, such as a population, is made up of certain groups. Another common use for circle graphs is to show how a budget is divided into separate categories.

Use the graph below to practice reading a circle graph.

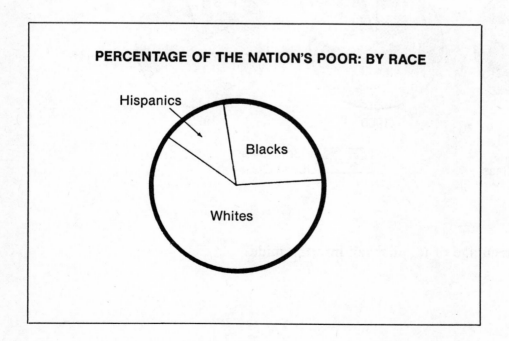

PERCENTAGE OF THE NATION'S POOR: BY RACE

Hispanics

Blacks

Whites

The highest percentage of the nation's poor comes from
which racial group?
(1)   White
(2)   Black
(3)   Hispanic

   To determine this, you simply read the values on the segments of the
circle. The segment labeled "Whites" (1) has the largest percentage of the
nation's poor—63 percent.

   The three circle graphs below give you an opportunity to make comparisons of different amounts. You must be able to read each graph individu-
ally and also compare changes over time. Additionally, you must use the
key below the graphs to know what the different shadings stand for.

   These graphs take the total number of families for each of the years listed
and divide the total (100 percent) into percentages based on income levels.
By looking at the graphs, you can evaluate the breakdown for each
particular year and see how the percentage of families that fall into each
income layer has changed over the years.

PERCENTAGES OF FAMILIES IN DIFFERENT INCOME LAYERS

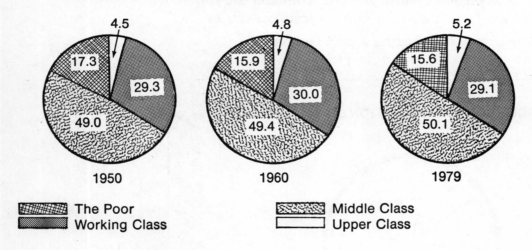

In 1960, what percentage of families fell into the middle
class?
(1)   4.8
(2)   15.9
(3)   49.0
(4)   49.4
(5)   50.1

Between 1950 and 1979, the percentage of families considered poor
(1)   rose steadily
(2)   rose but then declined
(3)   was greater than the middle class
(4)   was smaller than the upper class
(5)   declined

The correct answer to the first question is (4) 49.4 percent. To answer this, you only had to locate the graph for 1960 and the segment that the key indicated as representing the middle class.

To answer the second question, you had to look at all three graphs and draw a conclusion. First you had to determine which shading represented the poor. Then you had to see that the percentages declined steadily from 1950 (17.3 percent) to 1960 (15.9 percent) to 1979 (15.6 percent). The correct answer, therefore, is (5).

EXERCISE 3

Directions: Based on the graphs below, answer the questions that follow. Fill in the circle that corresponds to the correct answer.

PERCENTAGE OF TOTAL IMMIGRATION BY REGION OF LAST RESIDENCE

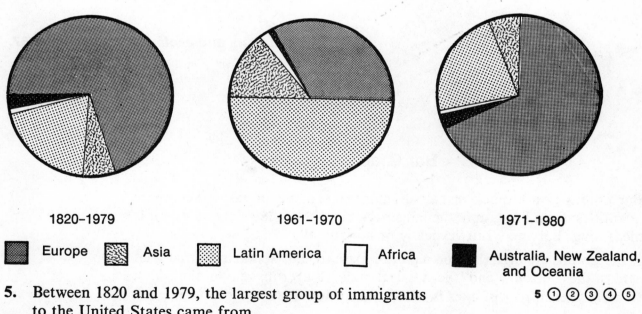

| 1820–1979 | 1961–1970 | 1971–1980 |

■ Europe   ▓ Asia   ▒ Latin America   ☐ Africa   ■ Australia, New Zealand, and Oceania

5.   Between 1820 and 1979, the largest group of immigrants   **5** ① ② ③ ④ ⑤
     to the United States came from
     (1)   Europe
     (2)   Asia
     (3)   Latin America
     (4)   Africa
     (5)   None of the above.

6. From the 1960s through the 1970s, the biggest change
   in immigration was

   6 ① ② ③ ④ ⑤

   (1)   an increase in the percentage of immigrants from
         Europe accompanied by a sharp decrease in the
         percentage of immigrants from Latin America
   (2)   a decrease in the percentage of immigrants from
         Europe accompanied by a sharp increase in the
         percentage of immigrants from Latin America
   (3)   a sharp decrease in the percentage of immigrants
         from Australia, New Zealand, and Oceania
   (4)   a sharp increase in the percentage of immigrants
         from Asia and Latin America
   (5)   a sharp decrease in the percentage of immigrants
         from Africa

7. The region whose percentage of immigration in the
   1970s was double its rate for the 1960s was

   7 ① ② ③ ④ ⑤

   (1)   Europe
   (2)   Asia
   (3)   Africa
   (4)   Latin America
   (5)   Australia, New Zealand, and Oceania

For answers and explanations, see page 67.

Bar Graphs

Bar graphs give a quick visual summary that makes it easy to compare
quantities. On a bar graph, the longer the bar, the greater the quantity it is
measuring. Bars may run vertically or horizontally.

Bar graphs are organized on a pair of axes: the horizontal axis (that goes
across the bottom) and the vertical axis (that runs along the side).
Generally, each pair of axes is labeled and has values assigned to it.

To read a bar graph, you have to be able to tell the value that the top of
the bar indicates. You do this by reading across from the top of the bar to
the axis at the side of it. If the line across from the top of a bar does not
precisely meet a certain value, you must estimate your answer. Fortunately,
the GED gives you five choices, so you will be able to pick the best of the
possible answers.

Use the graph below to practice reading bar graphs.

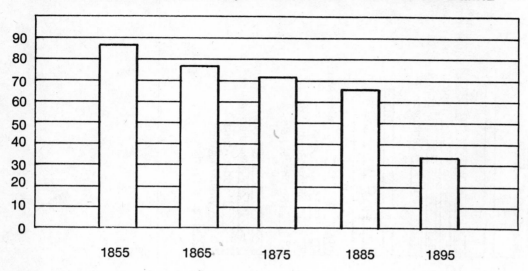

DOLLAR VALUE (IN MILLIONS) OF ORE TAKEN FROM FRIGATE MINE

What was the approximate worth of ore taken from the
Frigate Mine in 1865?
(1) $80 thousand
(2) $70 thousand
(3) $78 million
(4) $80 million
(5) $88 million

The ten-year period that showed the greatest decline in the
value of the ore taken from the mine was between
(1) 1855 and 1865
(2) 1865 and 1875
(3) 1875 and 1885
(4) 1885 and 1895
(5) 1895 and 1905

To answer the first question, simply find the bar labeled "1865." Read
across from the top of the bar to the points on the vertical axis. The top of
the bar falls between "70" and "80," more than halfway up. Choice (3), $78
million, is the best answer.

The second question requires that you make a comparison. The greatest
decline comes from 1885 to 1895, choice (4).

Some bar graphs are more complicated, with several groups of values to
compare and contrast. Based on the graph below, you could compare levels
of urbanization within regions (such as Europe) or between different
regions of the world.

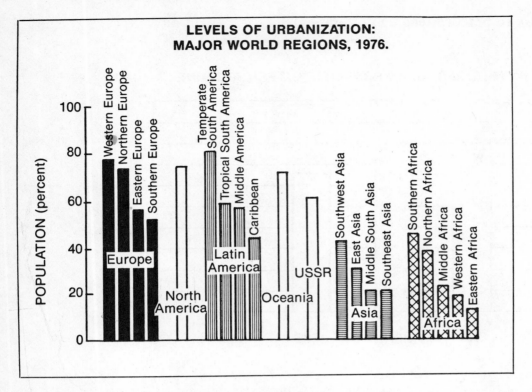

Within the continent of Africa, which area has closest to
50 percent urbanization?
(1)   Southern Africa
(2)   Northern Africa
(3)   Middle Africa
(4)   Western Africa
(5)   Eastern Africa

Of all the regions shown, which has the highest overall level
of urbanization?
(1)   Europe
(2)   North America
(3)   Latin America
(4)   Oceania
(5)   U.S.S.R.

To answer the first question, locate the set of bars labeled "Africa."
Within that group, choice (1), Southern Africa, is the highest—at about 50
percent urbanization. To be sure that this is the best answer, go across from
the top of the bar labeled "Southern Africa" to a point between "40" and
"60" on the side axis labeled "Urban Population (percent)."

The second question requires you to make a comparison of the sets of
bars labeled with the names of the major world regions. Europe, North
America, and Latin America are possible choices. However, two of the
areas in both Europe and Latin America have urbanization levels lower
than 60 percent. North America is represented by a single bar close to 80

percent. Therefore, it is possible to infer that choice (2), North America, is the best answer.

EXERCISE 4

Directions: Answer the questions that follow based on the graphs below. Fill in the circle that corresponds to the correct answer.

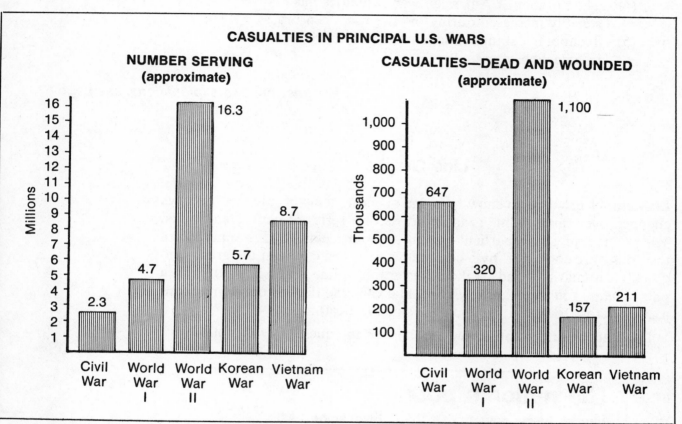

CASUALTIES IN PRINCIPAL U.S. WARS

NUMBER SERVING (approximate)

CASUALTIES—DEAD AND WOUNDED (approximate)

8. According to the graphs, the greatest number of casualties occurred in which war?
   (1) Civil War
   (2) World War I
   (3) World War II
   (4) Korean War
   (5) Vietnam War

8 ① ② ③ ④ ⑤

9. The war in which approximately one in four soldiers became casualties was
   (1) the Civil War
   (2) World War I
   (3) World War II
   (4) the Korean War
   (5) the Vietnam War

9 ① ② ③ ④ ⑤

10 ① ② ③ ④ ⑤

10. The data on this graph would support which of the
following conclusions?
  (1) Modern weapon systems have accounted for a
       great increase in war casualties.
  (2) The greatest number of American casualties took
       place in the Civil War and World War II.
  (3) Modern medical techniques are failing to save lives
       on the battlefield.
  (4) The number of American war casualties has
       steadily increased during the twentieth century.
  (5) Technological innovations in warfare have resulted
       in a decline of casualties.

For answers and explanations, see page 67.

Line Graphs

Line graphs are used to show how one or more items of information have
changed over time. A line graph consists of a series of connected points.
The points represent a particular value at a particular point in time. When
the points are connected by a continuous line, you can scan the graph and
quickly summarize trends. Like a bar graph, a line graph is plotted on a
pair of axes. You can read down to find a value on the bottom (horizontal)
axis or across to find a value on the side (vertical) axis.

Look at the line graph below and answer the questions that follow.

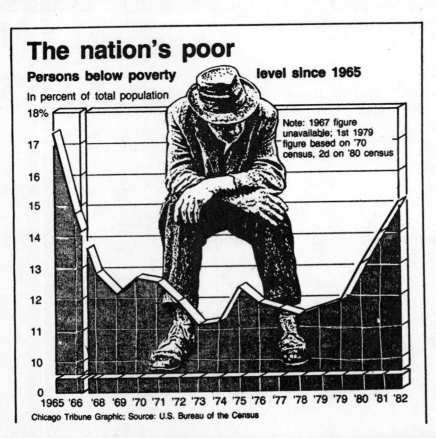

The nation's poor

Persons below poverty   level since 1965

In percent of total population

Note: 1967 figure
unavailable; 1st 1979
figure based on '70
census, 2d on '80 census

1965 '66 '68 '69 '70 '71 '72 '73 '74 '75 '76 '77 '78 '79 '79 '80 '81 '82

Chicago Tribune Graphic; Source: U.S. Bureau of the Census

According to the graph, the percentage of the U.S. population living in poverty in 1973 was a little more than
(1) 11%
(2) 12%
(3) 13%
(4) 15%
(5) 17%

Which of the following statements best summarizes the graph?
(1) From 1965 to 1982, the percentage of people living in poverty remained the same.
(2) From 1965 to 1982, the number of people on unemployment compensation fell and then rose.
(3) From 1965 to 1982, the percentage of the U.S. population living in poverty fell and then rose.
(4) The percentage of the nation living in poverty will never be more than 18%.
(5) In 1973, 11% of the people in the U.S. were unemployed.

To answer the first question, find the line that is labeled "1973." Then follow it up to where the line graph cuts across a line labeled "11" on the vertical axis. Choice (1) comes closest to this.

The second question requires you to analyze the overall trend shown by the graph. Only response (3) is correct. Notice that choice (2) refers to unemployment compensation—not poverty, which is the focus of the graph.

Another type of GED question is one that requires you to match the information on a table with a graph that best represents the data in the table. The following is an example.

PER CAPITA INCOME TRENDS IN COUNTRY Y									
(in dollars)									
1970	1971	1972	1973	1974	1975	1976	1977	1978	1979
1,000	1,100	1,500	1,750	1,250	1,700	2,200	2,500	3,000	2,500

Which of the following line graphs most accurately sums up the data in this table?

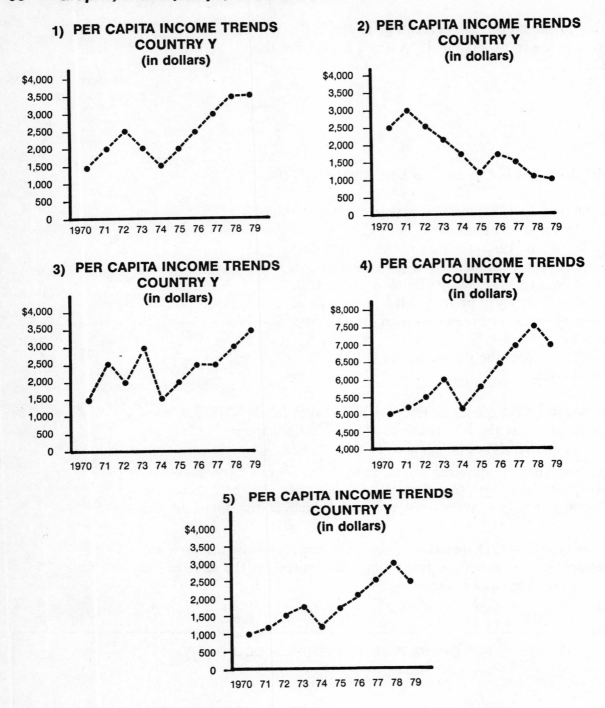

1) PER CAPITA INCOME TRENDS COUNTRY Y (in dollars)

2) PER CAPITA INCOME TRENDS COUNTRY Y (in dollars)

3) PER CAPITA INCOME TRENDS COUNTRY Y (in dollars)

4) PER CAPITA INCOME TRENDS COUNTRY Y (in dollars)

5) PER CAPITA INCOME TRENDS COUNTRY Y (in dollars)

The most accurate graph is (5). Graph (2) has the same data, but it has been graphed backward. Graph (4) follows the correct pattern, but the numbers on the axes have been changed; they are not accurate.

EXERCISE 5

Directions: Answer the questions that follow based on the graphs below. Fill in the circle that corresponds to the correct answer.

POLITICAL DIVISION IN THE U.S. CONGRESS
1969–1985

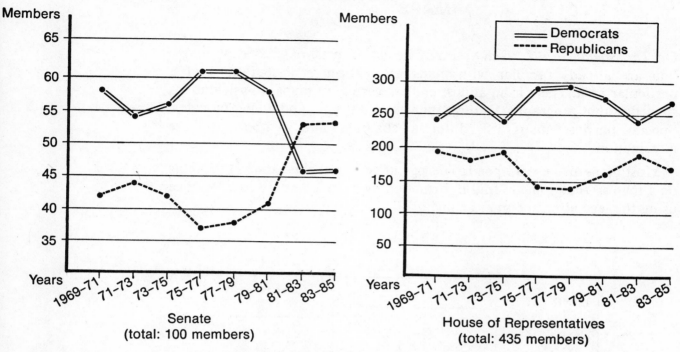

Senate
(total: 100 members)

House of Representatives
(total: 435 members)

11. The data on the graphs above indicate that   11 ① ② ③ ④ ⑤
  - (1) the Democrats controlled both houses of Congress until 1981
  - (2) the Republicans have controlled the House of Representatives since the early 1970s
  - (3) the Republicans lost control of the Senate in 1981
  - (4) at no time did the Republicans or Democrats control both houses of Congress
  - (5) Republican membership in the House of Representatives has declined steadily since 1969

12. Which of the following could be inferred from the   12 ① ② ③ ④ ⑤
graphs?
  - (1) A Republican president has no chance for Congressional support.
  - (2) The 91st Congress (1969–71) was the high point of Democratic power in Congress.
  - (3) The overwhelming victory of Ronald Reagan in 1980 swept the Republicans to power in the Senate.
  - (4) Congress became more involved in foreign affairs in the 1970s and 1980s than in preceding decades.
  - (5) Increased voter registration has helped the Republicans more than the Democrats.

For answers and explanations, see page 67.

MAPS

On *The Social Studies Test*, you may be asked questions based on maps. You are already familiar with maps as pictorial representations of a particular area. There is an almost endless variety of maps. Physical maps show different geographic features such as land masses and bodies of water. Special purpose maps use different shadings and symbols to give information.

Most maps also use a legend. The legend defines the meaning of symbols on a map so that you can find information or make comparisons. Practice using the legend on the map below.

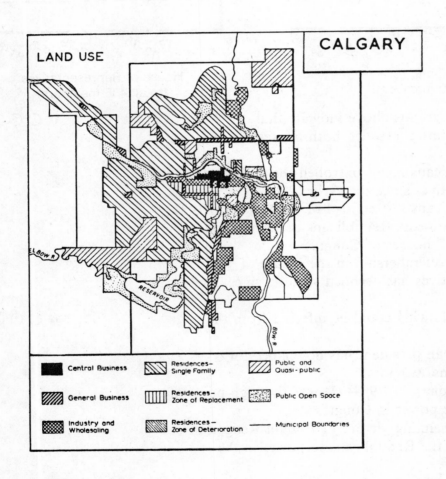

This map shows Calgary's
(1) racial makeup
(2) reservoir system
(3) various land uses
(4) elevation
(5) voting districts

According to the map, public open spaces are
(1) surrounded by the central business district
(2) near the reservoir and outlying areas
(3) beyond the city limits of Calgary
(4) adjacent to the Elbow River
(5) found in only one area of the city

The answer to the first question is (3). Both of the titles—"Calgary" and "Land Use"—indicate that.

The answer to the second question is (2). Look at the legend to find the markings for "Public Open Space." On the map, you find these dots near the reservoir and the outlying areas.

EXERCISE 6

Directions: Based on the map below, answer the questions that follow. Fill in the circle that corresponds to the correct answer.

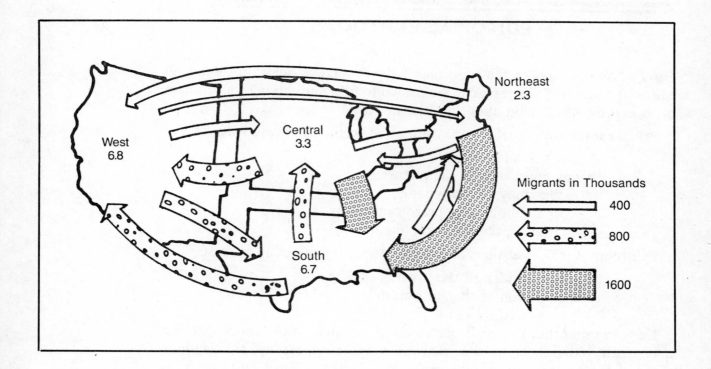

13. According to the map, the area that is attracting the most people is the   13 ① ② ③ ④ ⑤
    (1) West
    (2) Central
    (3) South
    (4) Middle West
    (5) Northeast

14. Based on the map, which of the following is a logical conclusion?   14 ① ② ③ ④ ⑤
    (1) The industrial areas of the Northeast and Central regions attracted the most people.
    (2) More people immigrated to the Northeast than left it.
    (3) More people left the South than moved there.
    (4) The "Sun Belt" areas of the South and West attracted the most people.
    (5) Most of the people who left the West went to the Northeast.

For answers and explanations, see page 68.

EDITORIAL CARTOONS

On *The Social Studies Test*, you may have to answer questions about an editorial cartoon. Such cartoons are drawn to bring attention to a problem or to express an opinion about politics or social issues.

When examining a cartoon, pay attention to the following features.

- any title or caption
- any characters in the picture:
    they may be real people;
    or symbolic of a person or group
- any labels, conversation, etc.

Before answering questions about a cartoon, try to get an idea of

- the main idea of the cartoon
- the opinion of the cartoonist

Keep in mind that humor is one of the main tools of the cartoonist. He may draw individuals in a humorous manner or set up a ridiculous situation. Cartoonists also make great use of irony—depicting things in a way opposite from the way they really are.

Since cartoons reflect an opinion, the cartoonist is free to let his biases show. For example, two cartoonists with strongly different feelings about a candidate might show her in two very different ways. One might show her as strong and caring; the other might show her as weak and indifferent.

The example below gives you a chance to practice interpreting a cartoon.

United Nations

The artist who drew this believes that
(1)   the U.S. is appreciated in the United Nations
(2)   other nations have "ganged up" on the U.S. in the U.N.
(3)   the U.S. is the most powerful nation in the U.N.
(4)   the Third World's power in the U.N. should be
       expanded
(5)   U.N. peacekeeping forces serve a useful function

The cartoonist would most likely be in favor of
(1)   increased U.S. participation in the U.N.
(2)   United States withdrawal from the U.N.
(3)   a one-world government
(4)   increasing United States funding of United Nations
       activities
(5)   increasing the U.N.'s power in international relations

Before answering the questions, be sure that you understand what the cartoonist is depicting and how he feels about it. The cartoon is called "United Nations." This is a play on words: the United Nations is the name of an organization, and the nations are shown as being united against one. The tied up man is Uncle Sam, symbolizing the U.S. The answer to the first question is (2).

To answer the second question, you have to infer the cartoonist's opinion. Since the cartoonist believes that the U.S. is being treated unfairly in the U.N., the best answer choice is (2).

EXERCISE 7

Directions: Answer the questions that follow based on the cartoon below.
Fill in the circle that corresponds to the correct answer.

JERRY BARNETT
Courtesy Indianapolis News

15. The main idea of this cartoon is that   15 ① ② ③ ④ ⑤
   (1) most people are not cashing their Social Security
        checks
   (2) bankers have a hard time deciding on good credit
        risks
   (3) the national debt is higher than ever
   (4) people should not pay their income tax
   (5) the nation's Social Security system is going broke

16. You can infer that the cartoonist   16 ① ② ③ ④ ⑤
   (1) does not keep his money in banks
   (2) used to be a banker
   (3) has little faith in the Social Security system
   (4) opposes more taxation
   (5) feels that the nation's economy is strong

For answers and explanations, see page 68.

ANSWERS AND EXPLANATIONS

EXERCISE 1

1. (5) Most of the food categories that rose did so by only a small amount. The rise in consumption of fresh vegetables from almost 100 pounds to a little more than 150 pounds is an increase of approximately 50 percent.

2. (2) While some of the other choices may or may not be true, this is the only answer supported by data from the table. This is the choice that shows a decline in the consumption of meat accompanied by a rise in the consumption of fruit and vegetables.

EXERCISE 2

3. (3) Multiply the number of symbols next to 1980 (5½) by the value of a symbol (100,000) to get a total of 550,000.

4. (3) This choice is the only one supported by the graph. The high point was in 1955 (950,000 people) and the low point was in 1980 (550,000 people).

EXERCISE 3

5. (1) Look at the first graph, titled "1820–1979." The greatest percentage of immigrants came from Europe.

6. (1) Although other changes took place during this period, the sharpest change was the increase in the percentage of European immigrants and the decrease in the percentage of Latin American immigrants.

7. (1) This question requires that you compare the two graphs titled "1961–1970" and "1971–1980." Only Europe appears to have doubled.

EXERCISE 4

8. (3) On the graph called "Casualties—Dead and Wounded," the highest bar is the one labeled "World War II."

9. (1) To answer this, compare the information on both graphs. The war in which there was an approximate ratio of one casualty to every four soldiers was the Civil War. A little more than ½ million out of about 2 million soldiers became casualties of the war.

10. (2) This is the only choice supported by data on the graph. The bars on the graph "Casualties—Dead and Wounded" are the highest for the Civil War and World War II.

EXERCISE 5

11. (1) Both graphs show a Democratic majority until the 97th Congress (1981–83). At that time, a majority of Republicans were elected to the Senate.

12. (3) Only choices (2) and (3) have a factual basis. However, choice (2) is incorrect because there were several years following that had larger Democratic majorities. Choice (3) is an inference based on the dramatic shift that took place in the Senate in 1980.

13. (3)   The most and largest arrows are headed into the South.

14. (4)   This conclusion is based on the number and size of the arrows going into the South and West.

15. (5)   Judging from the picture of "Social Security" sitting at the loan officer's desk and the worried look on the other customers' faces, you can assume that the cartoonist believes that Social Security is going broke.

16. (3)   The best of the choices is that the cartoonist has little faith in the Social Security system.

U.S. History

_____

1. EXPLORATION AND DEVELOPMENT
OF THE NEW WORLD   1492–1783

indentured servant—laborer who bound himself (or was involuntarily bound) to a period of service in the American colonies as payment of a debt

mercantilism—popular seventeenth-century economic practice in which the colonies supplied the mother country with raw materials and became a market for manufactured goods

consent of the governed—a political concept established at the time of the American Revolution—that a government achieves its legitimacy through the approval of the people it governs

Exploration and Colonization

The European exploration and settlement of the Americas, North and South, was motivated by the European powers' struggle for new sources of wealth. Spain got a head start when Columbus sailed west across the Atlantic in 1492. Although he was trying to find a new route to India and the East, he actually discovered the Western Hemisphere, which the Europeans called the New World. Spain followed this discovery with the conquest of many of the Caribbean islands, Mexico, and most of Central and South America. The other European powers were influenced to develop colonies in the West when they saw the large amount of gold and silver that Spain had plundered and sent home.

England and France led the settlement of North America, although the Dutch and Spanish also settled in some areas. England established colonies along the Atlantic coast. Some of the more important English colonies were founded in the early 1600s at Jamestown, Virginia; Plymouth, Massachusetts; and Massachusetts Bay.

Meanwhile, France established settlements in what is now Canada as well as along the Ohio and Mississippi River valleys, all the way south to New Orleans on the Gulf Coast.

The English colonies along the Atlantic coast grew slowly. They were usually organized by well-to-do Englishmen in search of even greater fortunes, but they were populated mainly by those seeking to escape poverty or prison in Europe. Between 50 and 75 percent of the colonials came as **indentured servants** bound to spend a certain number of years serving a master, usually in payment for their passage to the New World. Others, like the Puritans, came to establish religious communities. Black slaves, forcibly imported from Africa for cheap labor, also became a significant part of the colonial population.

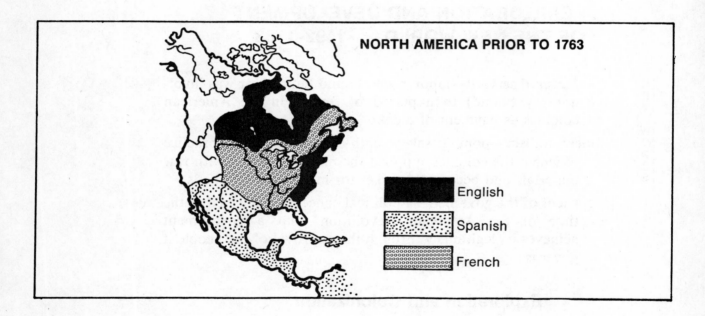

NORTH AMERICA PRIOR TO 1763

English

Spanish

French

Development of the American Colonies

The English colonies developed an expanding trade in lumber, tobacco, rice, indigo, beef, and other agricultural products. Enormous profits were also made from the growing slave trade. Native industries began to develop in the fields of shipbuilding, textiles, shoes, and iron making. Large and busy towns, like New York and Boston, grew up around the seaports.

England controlled trade with the colonies and followed the policy of **mercantilism**. Under this policy, the colonies supplied raw materials to the mother country and, in return, received manufactured goods. Independent economic development was restricted in the colonies because English economic interests did not want competition. England passed specific laws in an attempt to severely retard the growth of colonial industry and to force the colonies to be dependent on the motherland for their manufactured goods.

American colonial government was somewhat more democratic than the government in England. Each American colony had a governor (some were appointed by the king) and an elected representative body to pass laws on taxes and other matters. The towns usually had some form of elected body. These representative bodies eventually became the centers of opposition to the English colonial policies.

As the colonies grew, they looked to the West. Their westward expansion was blocked by an alliance of the French and native Indians. The long simmering rivalry between France and England came to a head during the French and Indian War (1756–1763), ending with the defeat of France. France lost all of her North American territories and could no longer block the way to the West.

Directions: Based upon what you have just read, fill in the circle that corresponds to the correct answer.

1. The European countries' main motivation for colonizing America was to   1 ① ② ③ ④ ⑤
   (1) provide religious freedom
   (2) provide a productive use for slaves
   (3) find new sources of wealth and power
   (4) bring political freedom to the native people
   (5) find outlets for excess European wealth

2. Consider a present-day nation in Asia, Africa, or Latin America that is used as a cheap source of raw materials by an industrialized country. If the underdeveloped country were also heavily dependent on manufactured goods from the developed country, the situation would be described as   2 ① ② ③ ④ ⑤
   (1) taxation without representation
   (2) an example of modern mercantilism
   (3) independent economic growth
   (4) aid for economic development
   (5) the international division of labor

3. When compared to English government at that time, colonial American political institutions were   3 ① ② ③ ④ ⑤
   (1) dictatorial
   (2) less democratic
   (3) more effective
   (4) more democratic
   (5) less effective

For answers and explanations, see page 125.

Road to Revolution and Independence

Following the end of the French and Indian War in 1763, England wanted to make the colonies bear the financial burden of the conflict. Laws were passed to increase taxation and to take more money from the colonies. These included the Sugar Act, the Stamp Act, and the Tea Act. The English also tightened political control over the colonial government and courts.

The colonials resisted these measures with protests that ranged from signing petitions to the forceful dumping of tea into Boston Harbor. The Sons of Liberty and the Committees of Correspondence were formed to organize protests. The colonial protesters cried out: "Taxation without representation is tyranny!" The colonies had no political representation in England, where the tax laws were passed.

The English responded to the Boston Tea Party with more repressive measures known as the Intolerable Acts. These acts closed Boston Harbor to commerce until the destroyed tea was paid for and forced colonial citizens to pay to house English soldiers. They also restricted the powers of the colonial courts and elected legislatures. Citizens in Massachusetts were now forced to seek permission from their appointed governor before they could hold town meetings.

The First Continental Congress was called by the colonists in 1774. It brought together the representatives of all the colonies—except Georgia—to consider ways to resist the increasing English restrictions on the colonies' economic and political freedom. The Congress organized a boycott of English imports and set up local militias. The English king George the Third, responded by sending additional troops.

In April 1775, British troops were sent to arrest colonial leaders and destroy the colonists' military stores. Massachusetts militiamen, warned of the British advance by Paul Revere and Dr. Samuel Prescott, fought pitched battles with the British soldiers at Lexington and Concord, Massachusetts. These battles marked the beginning of the American Revolution.

The Second Continental Congress met later in 1775, voted to equip an army, and named George Washington as commander in chief. The Declaration of Independence was adopted by the Congress in July 1776. Five years of hard fighting followed. The war finally ended in 1781 with the surrender of British forces at Yorktown, Virginia, and independence was won. A treaty formally ending the fighting was signed in 1783.

The colonists, who originally had appealed only for their rights as Englishmen under English law, were forced into revolution. In carrying out their revolution, the Founding Fathers went beyond the English traditions and created even more rights for citizens. The revolution firmly established the principle that government must be based on the **consent of the governed.**

The American Revolution marked the first time that a European power had lost a colony to an independence movement. The American movement for independence directly influenced many other independence movements, especially the successful slave revolution against the French in Haiti (1795–1803) and later independence struggles against Spanish rule throughout Latin America in the early nineteenth century.

Directions: Based upon what you have just read, fill in the circle that corresponds to the correct answer.

4. The American Revolution had an impact that was   4 ① ② ③ ④ ⑤
   (1) limited to the English colonies
   (2) unimportant outside North America
   (3) important only in American history
   (4) important to the Latin American independence struggles in the 1800s
   (5) not important to other anticolonial struggles

5. The colonists' response to the British laws in the 1760s to 1770s would lead you to conclude that   5 ① ② ③ ④ ⑤
   (1) the British were fair and sought to protect the rights of the colonists
   (2) the colonists were unreasonable
   (3) repressive laws can often lead to greater resistance
   (4) the colonists should have obeyed the laws
   (5) if the British had passed more laws, they could have stopped the revolution

6. Which of the following best characterizes the initial reaction of the colonists toward the problems with England?   6 ① ② ③ ④ ⑤
   (1) They used arms against the British as soon as they felt economically exploited.
   (2) They made military alliances with the Spanish against England.
   (3) They offered no organized resistance to the British until the First Continental Congress.
   (4) They adopted the Bill of Rights and made it their rallying point.
   (5) They started their protests by proclaiming their rights as Englishmen.

For answers and explanations, see page 125.

HISTORY EXERCISE 1 —————————————————————————

Directions: Read this passage based on the historical period covered in the preceding essay. Fill in the circle that corresponds to the correct answer.

The Triangular Trade

The ships of the African slave trade have been referred to as shuttles weaving together the fate of the colonies in the Americas, the African slaves, and slave merchants of Europe. The Portuguese started this trade, and the English later perfected it. Fifteen
5 million Africans were violently torn away from their homes and forced into slavery in the New World.

Slavery proved to be very profitable for the traders, as each voyage produced between 100 and 1,000 percent profit. The trade also provided the cheap labor that was necessary to run planta-
10 tions in Brazil, the West Indies, and North America. Slavery created the foundation of modern world trade. Significant portions of the profits accumulated from this trade in human misery were later used to finance the large-scale industrial and economic growth that took place in England during the early nineteenth
15 century.

Many of the slave trading ships had American captains and sailed from Boston, Massachusetts, or Charleston, South Carolina. The economic impact of these voyages was very important to the American colonies. More than 700 American ships were
20 involved, and more than 100 New England rum distilleries supplied the drink for trading.

Many Yankee slavers followed the triangular trade route, taking rum to Africa to trade for slaves, then going on to the murderous "middle passage" across the Atlantic to the West
25 Indies. There the slaves were sold for money or traded for molasses. The molasses was taken back to New England and distilled into rum for another trip to Africa. Other American ships took slaves directly to southern ports such as Charleston, South Carolina, where slaves were sold on the auction block.

30 Slaves could not be legally imported into the United States after 1808. However, the highly profitable trade was not effectively halted until slavery was outlawed in the West Indies in 1838. It took the American Civil War to put an end to slavery in the United States.

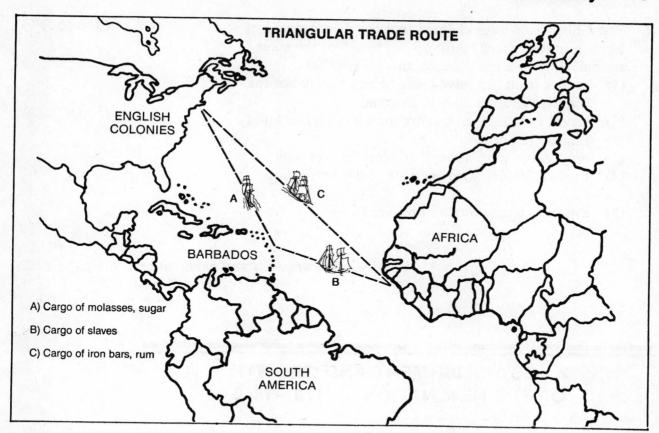

TRIANGULAR TRADE ROUTE

ENGLISH
COLONIES

A

C

AFRICA

BARBADOS

B

A) Cargo of molasses, sugar

B) Cargo of slaves

C) Cargo of iron bars, rum

SOUTH
AMERICA

7. Which of the following can we infer about the economic importance of the Atlantic slave trade?

  7 ① ② ③ ④ ⑤

  (1) It was of limited importance in American history.
  (2) It was actually a drain on American economic resources.
  (3) It accounted for a significant part of the colonial American economy.
  (4) It was limited to southern ports.
  (5) It quickly ended when the slave trade was made illegal.

8. Considering the profitability of slave trading, you might expect the Yankee ship owners to

  8 ① ② ③ ④ ⑤

  (1) oppose the slave trade
  (2) be indifferent to slavery since it had no economic importance to them
  (3) stop trading in slaves as soon as it was made illegal
  (4) be willing to support the slave-holding states on the constitutionality of slavery
  (5) be strong supporters of the antislavery movement.

9. Some historians have claimed that the development of
English industry was "built on the back" of the slave
system. Based on the passage, this means that

(1) profits from the slave trade helped to finance the
Industrial Revolution in England
(2) slaves were used as construction workers to build
English factories
(3) only slaves were allowed to work in factories
(4) English factory workers were really only wage
slaves
(5) English factory owners preferred to have slave
labor

For answers and explanations, see page 125.

2. ESTABLISHMENT AND GROWTH OF THE NEW NATION 1787–1850

K E Y   W O R D S

Manifest Destiny—widely held belief among Americans that it
was America's destiny to occupy the entire continent

annexation—a country's incorporation of lands not originally a
part of it

sectionalism—the economic, political, and social differences
among regions of the U.S.

Jacksonian Democracy—the period roughly corresponding to
the presidency of Andrew Jackson in the 1830s during which
there were important political reforms

abolitionist—member of the antislavery movement prior to the
Civil War

The New Nation Establishes Itself

In the years immediately after the Constitution was adopted (1787)*,
George Washington, the first president, had to organize the various government departments, establish taxes to finance them, and organize the federal
judiciary. Great political disagreements emerged over how much power the
central government was to have in comparison to the states.

---

*There is additional material in the political science section of this book
concerning the U.S. Constitution.

Struggling to organize itself internally, the new nation also faced formidable external problems from England and France. Britain still had Canada and outposts on the Great Lakes. Likewise, France, thrown out of North America in 1763, had obtained the Louisiana Territory from Spain in 1800 and now controlled the Mississippi River.

In 1803, the United States, under President Thomas Jefferson, purchased the huge western Louisiana Territory from the French for the sum of fifteen million dollars. The area doubled the size of the young United States, which previously had occupied most of the territory east of the Mississippi. American ownership of the new territory also secured the Mississippi River from both French and English control.

In 1812, the United States declared war on England in order to stop the harassment of American merchant ships. The war ended nearly three years later with no clear military victor and prewar boundaries unchanged.

However, the conflict actually represented an important victory for the United States in two respects. First, it helped unite the American people and temporarily made national interests more important than sectional concerns. Second, the war proved to Europe that the United States was militarily strong enough to remain an independent country. With the availability of new land in the West and the removal of the threat by a foreign power, the road to westward expansion was finally open.

Directions: Based upon what you have just read, fill in the circle that corresponds to the correct answer.

10. Based on America's experience in the War of 1812, you could conclude that governments facing a divided nation have used a war against external enemies to
   (1) permanently heal differences
   (2) temporarily unite the country
   (3) cause more divisions
   (4) prevent the growth of nationalism
   (5) institute a military draft

10 ① ② ③ ④ ⑤

For answers and explanations, see page 125.

American Expansion

During this era of rapid expansion (1800–1850), Americans believed that it was their **Manifest Destiny** to occupy the continent from ocean to ocean, and they quickly gained control of the remaining land. The United States acquired Florida from Spain and Texas from Mexico.

American settlers had originally received grants from the government of Mexico to settle in the Mexican province of Texas during the 1820s. Later, after citing their grievances against Mexican rule in Texas, Anglo-American settlers revolted against Mexico in 1836 and declared Texas an independent republic. The Texans won their independence after a brief but fierce war that became famous for the battle fought at the Alamo mission in San Antonio.

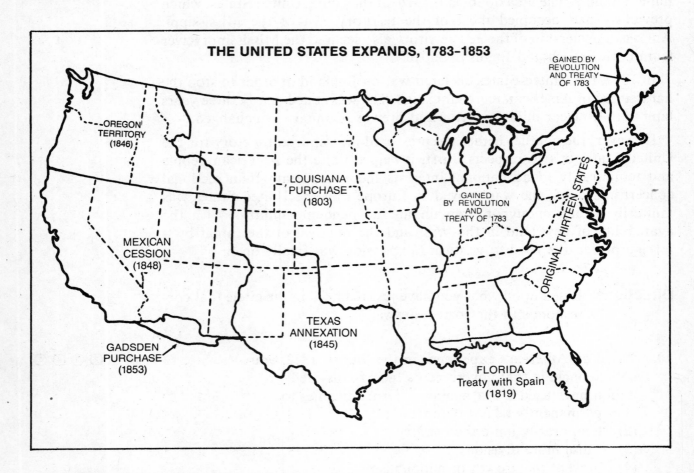

THE UNITED STATES EXPANDS, 1783–1853

In 1845, the United States annexed Texas as a state. The **annexation** of Texas, when combined with American offers to buy even more land from Mexico, angered many Mexicans and created an atmosphere of distrust. These factors and a move by American troops to occupy a border region claimed by Mexico led to the Mexican-American War. The United States won the war and took possession of more than one-half of the territory of Mexico. This area now consists of the states of California, New Mexico, Arizona, Nevada, Utah, Texas, and parts of Colorado. At about the same time, the United States also acquired the Oregon Territory.

In acquiring these lands, the United States gained access to great natural resources. The new lands contained rich farmlands, vast pasture lands for cattle and sheep, boundless forests, and rich stores of gold, silver, and other minerals and metals. They contributed greatly to the economic growth of the United States.

Economic Development and Sectionalism

Economic development was rapid during this period. Transportation improvements helped to push the economy forward. An upsurge in canal-building and the development of the steamboat gave a big boost to water travel for trade and transportation.

In the 1820s, a truly revolutionary transportation development began when railroads were introduced. Railroad building became a major economic activity, and by 1860, there were 30,000 miles of track in the United States.

Cotton cultivation also became important to the overall expansion of the United States economy (especially that of the southern states), bringing in more money than all other exports combined. This boom began with Eli Whitney's invention in the early 1800s of the cotton gin, which mechanically cleaned large amounts of cotton to be used for manufacturing. At the same time, the Industrial Revolution resulted in the mechanization of textile mills in England, creating a large demand for increased cotton production in the South. Cotton, highly profitable and suited to plantation cultivation, helped to firmly establish slave labor as the basis of the economic system in the South.

Continuing territorial expansion and economic development created growing political problems. This led to the development of different economic regions. The South was based on slavery and the export of cotton; the West, on diversified agriculture and small farms; and the East, on shipping, financing, and industry. These differences led to growth of sectional feelings. Each section of the country organized politically to defend its own economic interests. The doctrine of states rights was developed, particularly by southern states, to defend the rights of states to do as they pleased without interference by the federal government. This growth in **sectionalism** was an important cause of the Civil War.

Directions: Based upon what you have just read, fill in the circle that corresponds to the correct answer.

11. Technological advancements are often credited with alleviating human misery. Which of the following nineteenth-century technological advances actually was used to perpetuate human misery?
    (1) Railroad
    (2) Telegraph
    (3) Cotton gin
    (4) Steamboat
    (5) Photography

11 ① ② ③ ④ ⑤

12. The current debate in American politics concerning the   12 ① ② ③ ④ ⑤
distribution of federal tax money between the Frost Belt
and the Sun Belt is
   (1)   something new in American politics
   (2)   an example of nationalism in American politics
   (3)   a demonstration that political parties are divisive
   (4)   similar to earlier sectional disputes over economic
         issues
   (5)   likely to be settled soon once and for all

13. The political history of this era would lead one to   13 ① ② ③ ④ ⑤
conclude that American national unity was
   (1)   firmly established with the Constitution of 1789
   (2)   continually being threatened by foreign aggression
   (3)   threatened because of economic stagnation
   (4)   never a serious political question in this period
   (5)   achieved through a constant process of balancing
         different sectional interests

For answers and explanations, see page 125.

Politics and Movements

Political parties as we now know them also developed in this period. By the late 1820s, they had come to resemble modern parties, complete with a national organization and a party press. Political parties began to represent the very real economic and political differences that were developing in American society.

Issues concerning democratic rights were also very important. Some of these rights were greatly expanded during Andrew Jackson's presidency (1829–1837). During this era of **Jacksonian Democracy**, universal manhood suffrage was established in most states. Prior to this time, most states had required people to own a certain amount of property in order to be eligible to vote. Property qualifications for voting were dropped, and all white male citizens over the age of twenty-one could vote. The extension of voting rights, profound as it was, was restricted to white males. Indians, women, and blacks were still left out.

Other political innovations of the period included the ratification by popular vote of state constitutions and the use of elections, rather than appointment, to fill public offices. A movement led by Horace Mann firmly established free public education as a basic right in a democratic society.

National growth brought increasing conflict with the Indians as they sought to retain their homelands. The federal government followed a systematic policy of Indian removal, forcing the Indians to move west of the Mississippi River. The military marched 15,000 Creeks out of Georgia and Alabama to the Oklahoma Territory in 1836. Two years later, 17,000 Cherokees were forcibly removed from the Carolinas and marched to Oklahoma on what has become known as the Trail of Tears.

The institution of slavery came under increasingly bitter attack. The **abolitionist** movement attacked the system that held more than four million blacks in slavery in the South. The members of the antislavery movement wanted the total abolition of slavery. Abolitionists set up the Underground Railway—a secret network of people who aided slaves in their escape. While the abolitionists never gained widespread support as a political party, they helped create an antislavery climate in the North and West that paved the way for popular support for the Union position in the Civil War.

Women were also denied many rights, including the right to vote. Women took an active part in the early antislavery societies and used this experience to begin their own organizations to fight for women's suffrage. The first national organization was formed at Seneca Falls, New York, in 1848, where Elizabeth Cady Stanton presented the Declaration of Sentiments, modeled after the Declaration of Independence.

Directions: Based upon what you have just read, fill in the circle that corresponds to the correct answer.

14. The extension of voting rights during Andrew Jackson's presidency
    14 ① ② ③ ④ ⑤
    (1) was limited to white males
    (2) was unimportant window dressing
    (3) included women with property
    (4) ended the three-fifths rule for counting slaves
    (5) has not been expanded upon since then

15. The emergence of protest movements for social change as far back as the 1830s suggests that such movements are
    15 ① ② ③ ④ ⑤
    (1) a very important part of American history
    (2) inspired by a handful of radicals
    (3) very shortsighted and only achieve limited goals
    (4) not very important to the two-party system
    (5) a threat to the democratic way of life

For answers and explanations, see page 125.

HISTORY EXERCISE 2——————————————————————————

Directions: Read the following passage and fill in the circle that corresponds to the correct answer.

This passage is excerpted from an original letter written by a party of settlers heading west in 1852. The letter, never before published, should give you an idea of what people faced during preparation for their long journey across the prairie.

To make your reading easier, some spelling and punctuation changes have been made by the editor, but otherwise, the letter has not been changed.

Letter from A. H. Wilson to A. H. Evans, St. Louis, Missouri
In camp 4½ Miles above St. Joseph
April 25th, 1852

Dear Sir:

We arrived here (St. Jo) on the 14th. All in good order or as good as could be expected. Some of our animals were stiffened by standing on the boat. I arrived at Weston a little before the

5   company and joined them there. The weather was very disagreeable and cold until yesterday. We put up in town one week to recruit our animals. They are all in good condition and look well with some exceptions. We bought two mules at St. Jo for $120.00. They are as good or better than an average of our other ones.

10   After our arrival here, we concluded to sell one of our wagons and only take three. We sold it to some advantage. We are going to put four mules to two wagons and two mules to one.

Mules, oxen, corn, and oats can be had to some better advantage than in St. Louis but nothing else. They put the screws

15   very tight to emigrants for all small jobs and articles the emigrants are obliged to get, and upon the whole, I think outfits can be had as cheap in St. Louis excepting livestock. . . .

There has been teams starting for several days past, heavy loaded with feed. The grass is very backward, and from what

20   information I can get for some distance on the prairies, little or no old grass to be had as it has been eat and burned off. My intention is to haul feed to do us about 12 or 14 days. Consequently I want to see whether it is warm enough for grass to grow while we have feed, so that when our feed is out we can have some grass. There

25   has not been any here yet but it begins to start or make appearance this morning since the rain.

Some of the men got cold on the boat but are all doing well at this time. My health is good at this time and has been since I left. I will write the first opportunity after leaving this Port. I have
30 concluded not to go to Council Bluff as the season is late and that point so much north of this. There is at least 10 days difference in vegetation between this place and St. Louis. I have nothing of much importance more to write to you at this time. There is large quantity of cattle starting and emigrants fitted out in every way,
35 but their wagons are generally heavier than ours. We have as light wagons as any that I have seen and our teams look as well as any. There is some better and many not half as good. Give my best respects to all inquiring friends.

From yours respectfully,

A. H. Wilson

16. From the passage, you can infer that the route these settlers planned to take
    (1) was unexplored
    (2) was very lightly traveled
    (3) was not well known
    (4) crossed very rough terrain
    (5) was well known

16 ① ② ③ ④ ⑤

17. Why did the group have to bring feed for its animals?
    (1) The animals got sick from eating prairie grass.
    (2) The old grass had been eaten and burned off.
    (3) They planned to sell it to other settlers.
    (4) They needed it for their first winter.
    (5) They planned to use some of it for seed.

17 ① ② ③ ④ ⑤

18. What can we infer about merchants and craftsmen in St. Joseph?
    (1) For most jobs and articles, they charged more than merchants in St. Louis.
    (2) They earned more money from local townspeople.
    (3) They charged much less than merchants in St. Louis.
    (4) Their businesses were barely surviving.
    (5) Their businesses could not handle the settlers.

18 ① ② ③ ④ ⑤

For answers and explanations, see page 126.

3. CIVIL WAR AND RECONSTRUCTION 1850–1877

Dred Scott case—the controversial 1857 decision in which the Supreme Court ruled that slaves were not citizens and that Congress could not prohibit slavery in the territories

secession—the act of a state or province leaving (seceding from) a country or federation of which it is a member

impeachment—the bringing of formal charges of a crime or misdemeanor against an officeholder

Background to the Civil War

Sectional economic and political differences (sectionalism) continued to deepen in the years 1820 to 1860. The northern manufacturing interests wanted to forge ahead in building an industrial country based on manufacturing, free (not slave) labor, and a diversified agriculture. The southern plantation owners were content to develop a single-crop export economy based on slave labor and huge plantations owned by a small aristocracy.

Confrontation over slavery was at the heart of these sectional differences. The confrontation grew sharper as the sections competed for control over the new western territories. A victory for either side in the western territories could tip the political balance in the U.S. Congress and determine the whole future development of the United States. A perilous peace was kept through a series of compromises.

"Free soil versus slave soil" was the main issue in settling the Louisiana Territory during the early 1800s. Antislavery forces wanted slavery banned in the territory. Proslavery forces claimed that the future states should decide their own fate on the slavery question. The Missouri Compromise (1820) settled an immediate crisis by admitting Missouri as a slave state and Maine as a free state and by limiting slavery to below the Missouri border in the area of the purchase. One controversial result was that large new areas were opened to the possible expansion of slavery.

The decision in the **Dred Scott case** in 1857 marked the high point for supporters of slavery. In this case, the Supreme Court ruled that slaves were not citizens, they were merely the "personal property" of their masters and that slave owners' property rights were protected by the U.S. Constitution. Therefore, Congress could make no law prohibiting slavery in the territories. The Scott decision created great anger against the South and generated fear that slavery would be expanded further.

Meanwhile, other events helped to build a strong antislavery movement. In 1853, Harriet Beecher Stowe published the novel *Uncle Tom's Cabin,* a stirring indictment of slavery that became a best seller. In 1859, John

Brown, a long-time militant abolitionist, attacked the federal arsenal at Harpers Ferry, Virginia (now part of West Virginia). Brown sought to capture firearms so that he could arm slaves for rebellion. His rebellion was crushed by federal troops, and he and other participants were later hanged. Brown became a martyr to the antislavery cause. Finally, Frederick Douglass, an ex-slave and eloquent spokesman against slavery, toured the North, raising substantial support for the abolitionist cause.

The newly formed Republican Party soon became a leading force against the spread of slavery. This position, combined with its program advocating economic growth, helped the young party to grow rapidly. In 1860, Abraham Lincoln, the Republican presidential candidate, won the presidency running on a platform that opposed the expansion of slavery.

Directions: Based upon what you have just read, fill in the circle that corresponds to the correct answer.

19. Which of the following best states the main idea of the essay?
    (1) The Dred Scott decision led to the Civil War.
    (2) The confrontation over slavery was a major issue between the North and the South.
    (3) There was little economic difference among the sections of the country.
    (4) The Republican Party was responsible for the economic problems of the South.
    (5) The antislavery movement received many votes in the election of 1860.

    19 ① ② ③ ④ ⑤

20. In the period before the Civil War, slaveholders won their biggest victory as a result of
    (1) John Brown's rebellion
    (2) Uncle Tom's Cabin
    (3) the Kansas-Nebraska Bill
    (4) the "free soil" controversy
    (5) the Dred Scott decision

    20 ① ② ③ ④ ⑤

21. During the period described in this essay, "Free Labor, Free Soil" became a popular slogan. Based on the reading, you could assume that this was a slogan that
    (1) the South supported
    (2) took hold after the Civil War
    (3) was the slogan of communists and socialists
    (4) was used to unite the North and West
    (5) was used to unite the South and West

    21 ① ② ③ ④ ⑤

For answers and explanations, see page 126.

The Civil War

The rapid growth of northern political and economic strength during the 1850s (three new states were admitted to the Union—California, Oregon, and Minnesota) and Lincoln's election to the presidency convinced the South that the balance of power had been permanently tipped against it. Now, it was only a matter of time before there would be a large enough majority of free states to vote for a constitutional amendment abolishing slavery. The southern leaders feared Lincoln and quickly moved for **secession** from the Union. The secessionists formed the Confederate States of America and started the war with the northern states in 1861.

During the Civil War, Lincoln's Emancipation Proclamation (1863) freed slaves behind rebel lines. This, as well as the recruitment of ex-slaves into the Union army, helped to undermine the southern economy and war effort. The proclamation also strengthened northern support for the war effort and turned a war to save the Union into a crusade against slavery.

The war lasted four years, until the vastly superior ability of the industrial North to arm, feed, and transport a modern army had ground down the industrially backward Confederate states. The conflict all but ended with General Robert E. Lee's surrender in the spring of 1865.

Directions: Based upon what you have just read, fill in the circle that corresponds to the correct answer.

22.   A major reason that southern leaders chose to secede from the Union was because
   (1)   they underestimated Lincoln
   (2)   they believed they could win the conflict
   (3)   they feared a growing majority of free states would vote to abolish slavery
   (4)   they thought it would stop abolitionists such as John Brown from provoking slave rebellions
   (5)   they wanted to extend slavery to the North

22 ① ② ③ ④ ⑤

23.   According to this essay, President Lincoln's Emancipation Proclamation
   (1)   helped to mobilize the North to support the war effort
   (2)   was unnecessary to the war effort
   (3)   had little effect on the Confederacy
   (4)   was made just to appease the British
   (5)   was welcomed by the Confederacy

23 ① ② ③ ④ ⑤

For answers and explanations, see page 126.

Reconstruction

Following the Civil War, the nation faced a time of rebuilding. This has become known as the Reconstruction era.

President Lincoln, assassinated in April 1865, and Andrew Johnson, his successor, sought to rapidly reunite the torn nation. They were willing to let the southerners, including former Confederate officials, decide most questions of race relations in the defeated states. Lincoln and Johnson supported an amnesty for the rebel officers and politicians, many of whom assumed office in newly formed state legislatures in 1865. Many of the southern legislatures passed new laws known as Black Codes that severely restricted the rights of former slaves.

Radical Republicans, such as Thaddeus Stevens, who controlled Congress at this time, were enraged by the actions of state legislatures in the South. These Congressmen wanted far-reaching social changes in the South and sought to protect the rights of freed slaves. They also opposed President Johnson's conciliatory moves and sought to limit the influence of former Confederate officials. The Congressional plan for Reconstruction was eventually adopted.

The Radicals' conflicts with President Johnson became so heated that, in 1868, the House impeached him; however, he was not convicted in his **impeachment** trial before the Senate. The only other president to face possible impeachment proceedings was Richard Nixon, who resigned from office in 1974.

The Radicals sponsored many important reforms, and several important constitutional amendments were passed. These included the Thirteenth Amendment (1865), which abolished slavery. The Fourteenth Amendment (1868) established that blacks were citizens and had the right to equal treatment under the law. Finally, the Fifteenth Amendment (1870) granted blacks (actually black men) the right to vote. Congress was given the right to enforce these three amendments.

In the southern states, the Radicals' plan for Reconstruction also temporarily forced many former Confederate officials out of office. For the first time, blacks were elected to statewide offices and to the U.S. Senate. The Freedman's Bureau set up the first schools that blacks were allowed to attend in the South.

Reconstruction ended in 1877, when a coalition of conservative Republicans and southern Democrats took control of the federal government. They had elected Rutherford B. Hayes president in the disputed Hayes-Tilden election of 1876. As part of the compromise agreement that gave Hayes the crucial southern Democratic support he needed for election, the remainder of U.S. Army troops were pulled out of the South.

Reconstruction fell far short of changing underlying economic and social relations in the South. Despite some promising beginnings, no real program of land reform was carried out. Ex-slaves did not receive the "40 acres and a mule" that they had been promised, and the large plantations remained. Thus, the freedmen had little land and no economic base from which to defend their newly won freedom. Many fundamental issues of justice and equality remained unresolved for the next hundred years.

Directions: Based upon what you have just read, fill in the circle that corresponds to the correct answer.

24. From this passage, one can conclude that the civil rights movement of the 1950s and '60s had its roots in
    (1) the failure of Reconstruction to establish legal freedom for ex-slaves
    (2) the excesses and corruption of the carpetbaggers
    (3) the failure of Reconstruction to establish an economic base for equality
    (4) the uncompromising attitude of the North during the period of Reconstruction
    (5) the former slaves' unreasonable expectations about equality

24 ① ② ③ ④ ⑤

25. According to the essay, the major reason the Radical Republicans opposed President Andrew Johnson was that
    (1) he was too lenient toward former Confederate officers and politicians
    (2) his economic programs were too conservative
    (3) he was a Democrat and they were Republicans
    (4) he wanted to redistribute southern landholdings
    (5) he had opposed the Emancipation Proclamation

25 ① ② ③ ④ ⑤

For answers and explanations, see page 126.

Directions: Look at the table below and fill in the circle that corresponds to the correct answer.

COMPARISON OF RESOURCES BETWEEN NORTH AND SOUTH IN 1860		
	North	South
Population	71%	29%
Railroad Mileage	72%	28%
Iron & Steel	93%	7%
Farm Output	65%	35%

26. This table illustrates
    (1) that by the time of the Civil War, the South had a superior railroad system
    (2) equal regional economic development before the Civil War
    (3) the great agricultural wealth of the South
    (4) the economic advantages of the North
    (5) the agricultural weakness of the South

For answers and explanations, see page 126.

HISTORY EXERCISE 3

Directions: Read this letter and fill in the circle that corresponds to the correct answer.

This is a letter sent by an ex-slave to his former master in 1865.

To My Old Master

Sir:

I got your letter, and was glad to find that you had not forgotten Jourdon, and that you wanted me to come back and live with you again, promising to do better for me than anybody else can. I
5 have often felt uneasy about you. I thought the Yankees would have hung you long before this, for harboring Rebs they found at your house. I suppose they never heard about your going to Colonel Martin's to kill the Union soldier that was left by his company in their stable. Although you shot at me twice before I
10 left you, I did not want to hear of your being hurt, and am glad that you are still living. It would do me good to go back to the dear old home again. . . . I would have gone back to see you all when I was working in the Nashville Hospital, but one of the neighbors told me that Henry intended to shoot me if he ever got
15 the chance. I want to know particularly what the good chance is you propose to give me. I am doing tolerably well here. I get 25 dollars a month, with victuals [food] and clothing; have a comfortable home for Mandy, the folks call her Mrs. Anderson, and the

children go to school and are learning well. . . . We are kindly
20 treated. Sometimes we overhear others saying "Them colored
people were slaves" down in Tennessee. The children feel hurt
when they hear such remarks. . . . Now if you will write and say
what wages you will give me, I will be better able to decide
whether it would be to my advantage to move back again.

25 As to my freedom, which you say I can have, there is nothing
to be gained on that score, as I got my free papers in 1864 from
the Provost-Marshal-General of the Department of Nashville.
Mandy says she would be afraid to go back without some proof
that you were disposed to treat us justly and kindly; and we have
30 concluded to test your sincerity by asking you to send us our
wages for the time we served you. This will make us forget and
forgive old scores, and rely on your justice and friendship in the
future. I served you faithfully for thirty-two years, and Mandy for
twenty years. At twenty-five dollars a month for me, and two
35 dollars a week for Mandy, our earnings would amount to eleven
thousand six hundred and eighty dollars. Add to this the interest
for the time our wages have been kept back, and deduct what you
paid for our clothing, and three doctor's visits to me, and pulling
a tooth for Mandy, and the balance will show what we are in
40 justice entitled to. Please send the money by Adam's Express, in
care of V. Winters, Esq., Dayton, Ohio. If you fail to pay us for
faithful labors in the past, we can have little faith in your promises
in the future. We trust the good Maker has opened your eyes to
the wrongs which you and your fathers have done to me and my
45 fathers, in making us toil for you for generations without recom-
pense. Here I draw my wages every Saturday night; but in
Tennessee there was never any pay-day for the Negroes any more
than for horses and cows. Surely there will be a day of reckoning
for those who defraud the laborer of his hire.

50 In answering this letter, please state if there would be any safety
for my Milly and Jane, who are now grown up, and both good-
looking girls. I would rather stay here and starve—and die, if it
come to that—than have my girls brought to shame by the
violence and wickedness of their young masters. You will also
55 please state if there has been any schools opened for colored children in your neighborhood. The great desire of my life is to give
my children an education, and have them form virtuous habits.

Say howdy to George Carter, and thank him for taking the
pistol from you when you were shooting at me.

60   From your old servant,
                                      Jourdon Anderson

27. This letter demonstrates that some ex-slaves
    (1) were miserable as freemen and wanted to return to their former homes
    (2) were easily attracted by the appeals of their old masters
    (3) had just as hard a time in the North as in the South
    (4) had little regard for the future
    (5) clearly understood how slavery had exploited them

28. The letter expresses the view that slavery
    (1) had been beneficial to blacks
    (2) had reduced human beings to the level of animals
    (3) was preferable to the life Anderson had found in the North
    (4) had given respectful treatment to young black women
    (5) had provided a good education for Anderson's children

29. Why is Anderson grateful to George Carter?
    (1) Carter taught him to read and write.
    (2) Carter opposed slavery.
    (3) Carter probably saved his life by taking the gun away from Anderson's master.
    (4) Carter hid Union soldiers in his stable.
    (5) Carter helped Anderson's wife and children escape to freedom.

For answers and explanations, see page 126.

4. SOCIETY CHANGES   1865–1900

KEY WORDS

industrialization—the development of large-scale industries and mass-production techniques

urbanization—the growth of large cities, with a population shift away from rural areas

sharecropper—a tenant farmer who must pay a portion of his crop as rent for his land

Jim Crow Laws—racially segregationist laws passed in the South during the late nineteenth and early twentieth centuries

An Era of Change

The time from the end of the Civil War to the turn of the century witnessed some great changes, both in the East and West, that completely altered the face of America. This was a time when the foundations of modern America were laid in the factories, mills, mines, and smoke-filled cities of the Midwest and the East. It was also the time when widespread settlement of western lands meant the end of the frontier.

In the West, migration greatly increased after the Civil War, and vast lands were settled. The rush for land brought great resistance from the Indians who were pushed off their lands. A war-trained cavalry fought the Indians, and from 1865 to 1890 there was open warfare against the tribes who inhabited the western lands. Between 1869 and 1875 alone, the army fought more than 200 battles with Indians. This war finally came to an end in 1890 following the tragic massacre by federal troops of more than 200 Sioux men, women, and children at Wounded Knee, South Dakota. At about the same time, the frontier also drew to a close as the last of the western lands were settled and the westward rush subsided.

Meanwhile, in the East, the U.S. was rapidly becoming an industrial urban society. Northern businessmen had gained wealth and experience from the Civil War. After the war, they moved quickly to revolutionize civilian production. In doing so, they launched America on the road to **industrialization**, as the development of large-scale production dominated American economic growth.

Technology, Industrialization, and Urbanization

Invention after invention also revolutionized all areas of life. During this time, a national railroad system was built, expanding from 35,000 miles of track at the end of the Civil War to 200,000 miles by 1900. National communications were established with the telegraph. Industrial production surged when the invention of the Bessemer and open-hearth smelter processes led to the creation of a giant steel industry. Explosive growth in energy resources took place with the opening of new coal fields, the invention of the electric dynamo, and the development of oil well drilling.

Technical advances also revolutionized agriculture by introducing mechanization to the farm. The McCormick Reaper allowed two farm laborers to do in one day what had previously taken eight or ten days. Mechanization of agriculture freed more farm laborers to work in the new factories in the cities, and it also meant that enough food could be raised to feed large and growing urban centers.

Industrialization also caused a gigantic growth in the population of cities and towns, as Americans moved to where the jobs were. The population shift from the rural areas to the cities is known as **urbanization**. Industry became centralized around sources of raw materials, energy sources for power, and transportation centers. Many smaller towns grew up around textile mills and shoe factories, and huge cities like Pittsburgh and Chicago began to take shape around steel mills and factories. The development of cities spurred the growth of even more new industry that was needed to build housing and transportation for these new urban areas. The rural to urban population shift continued, and by 1900, more than one-half of the U.S. population lived in urban areas.

Immigration from Europe also played an important role in the growth of American cities. American industry needed more labor, and some twenty-five million Europeans were recruited to work in American mines, mills, and forges. American industrialists and steamship lines sent agents to Europe to recruit immigrants. Millions of Europeans, facing economic hardship and often political repression in their homelands, flocked to the U.S. in search of a better life. A large number of Asians were also recruited to work on building the railroads in the West. The majority of the new immigrants settled in larger cities, where they encountered conditions of poverty and discrimination.

The process of industrialization was led by a powerful new ruling class of financiers and industrialists who have become known in history as the Robber Barons. Such men as Andrew Carnegie, John D. Rockefeller, J. P. Morgan, and Cornelius Vanderbilt invented the modern corporation and put together giant corporations that ruled American economic life. These monopolies centralized control of business in a few hands, and this power was often misused in order to keep prices high and wages low.

These corporate owners used their massive economic power to dominate American politics. They also gained legislation favorable to their businesses. One railroad owner reportedly received $200,000,000 in direct subsidies and millions of acres of public lands. Part of the land was used to build the railways, but a much larger part of it was sold back to the public and to land speculators.

The Impact on the South

In contrast to the dynamic growth of industry and cities in the North and West, the urban and industrial growth in the South was not as spectacular. Textiles and other industries expanded, and a start was made toward developing a modern iron and steel industry, especially in Birmingham, Alabama. Southern railroads also grew.

Large areas of the South were still characterized by a backward agricultural system of **sharecropping**. The situation was not much different from the old plantation, since tenant farmer sharecroppers—both black and white—did not own the land, had to pay part of their crop as rent, and were in constant debt to the large landowners.

After the collapse of Reconstruction, a new system of segregation, based on **Jim Crow laws** (these laws segregated blacks in nearly all phases of public life), destroyed any lingering hopes for racial equality. Poll taxes and literacy tests were used to deny the right to vote not only to blacks but also to poor whites. These abuses remained intact until the civil rights protests of the 1960s led to federal laws outlawing such practices.

Directions: Based upon what you have just read, fill in the circle that corresponds to the correct answer.

30. The impact of industrialization in America could best
be described as
   (1) affecting only industrial technology
   (2) influencing only where people lived
   (3) having little effect on the number of immigrants
   (4) revolutionizing the whole structure of society
   (5) affecting only agriculture

30 ① ② ③ ④ ⑤

31. Which of the following best describes the process of
urbanization in the United States?
   (1) Urbanization caused the industrialization of
America.
   (2) Urbanization was caused by the growth and
centralization of industry.
   (3) Urbanization took place faster in the South than
elsewhere in the country.
   (4) Urbanization was accomplished by simply moving
American farmers into the cities.
   (5) Urbanization met all the hopes of European
immigrants for a new life.

31 ① ② ③ ④ ⑤

32. You can infer from this section that
   (1) large-scale social change is usually very smooth
and free of conflict
   (2) changes in one important part of society, such as
the economy, create changes in all other areas
   (3) change can be isolated to one part of the society,
such as the economy
   (4) the settling of the Old West was the most
important event of this period
   (5) immigration caused America to industrialize

32 ① ② ③ ④ ⑤

33. From this essay, one can conclude that a lasting result of the Civil War and Reconstruction was that

   (1) there were still substantial social and economic differences between the North and the South
   (2) the South underwent rapid economic development
   (3) the North helped develop southern industry
   (4) the expansion of railroads helped to develop the South
   (5) the South developed its own industrial base

For answers and explanations, see page 126.

The Workers and Farmers Respond

Rapid industrialization meant great growth in production and wealth, but workers and farmers saw very little of these new riches. Workers in the mines and factories and on the rails faced workdays of twelve hours or longer, for extremely low pay, in situations where the owner usually had absolute power over working conditions. In reaction to these conditions, workers began to organize.

Union organizing activity increased throughout this period, and the first truly national federation of trade unions was formed by the Knights of Labor. Local labor disputes were widespread, and the first nationwide strikes took place on the railroads. A railroad strike in 1877 led to a nationwide labor upheaval that affected much of the eastern half of the U.S. and resulted in street battles between troops and labor union supporters in Pittsburgh and Chicago.

The efforts of union organizers met with limited success, as a few skilled craft unions survived to form the American Federation of Labor (AFL); however, organizing drives by most of the large unions of unskilled and semiskilled laborers were defeated.

Organizing efforts and labor disputes were often met with violence. Time and time again, as in the 1894 Pullman strike in Chicago, unions were defeated by the combined violence of private police, state militia, and, in some cases, federal troops.

The corporation owners effectively used their political power to break strikes of the young labor movement. During the Pullman strike, 6,000 U.S. troops were sent to Chicago. Thirty strikers died, their leaders were jailed, and the strike was broken.

Meanwhile, the rural areas were swept by waves of protests over high credit costs and steep freight rates on the railroads. Mechanization had increased production, but the wealth was harvested by the bankers and the monopolies. Farmers were urged by their leaders to "raise less corn and more hell," and they did. Across the country, they organized the Farmers' Alliances to fight for farmers' interests.

In response to the storm of protests, the Interstate Commerce Act (1887) and the Sherman Anti-Trust Act (1890) were passed in an attempt to control price fixing and other manipulations. Nevertheless, the power and political influence of the monopolies were so great that the antitrust law was eventually enforced more against unions and farmers than against them.

The failure of the reform laws such as the Sherman Act created strong public support for the Populists (People's Party) and their wide-ranging program for controlling the monopolies. After some electoral success, the Populists and their demands were incorporated into the Democratic Party in the election of 1896. The corporate-backed candidate of the Republicans, William McKinley, defeated Democrat William Jennings Bryan. Later, parts of the Populist platform were adopted by both parties.

The last thirty years of the nineteenth century were ones of great and rapid change. Industrialization and urbanization changed America, and new economic institutions were created. Nevertheless, the social and political problems created by these changes were not solved. These problems would surface in larger political movements and conflicts in the twentieth century.

Directions: Based upon what you have just read, fill in the circle that corresponds to the correct answer.

34. The People's Party was formed to   34 ① ② ③ ④ ⑤
    (1)   protect the interests of the Robber Barons
    (2)   help establish more monopolies
    (3)   protect the rights of Indians
    (4)   control the power of monopolies
    (5)   be a union for free workers

35. Drawing on the experience of America, today's   35 ① ② ③ ④ ⑤
    underdeveloped countries that embark on the path of
    industrialization should expect
    (1)   a smooth transition to a new society
    (2)   to keep most of their population in the traditional
          villages
    (3)   to see little political turmoil
    (4)   to be able to modernize their societies one at a
          time
    (5)   widespread changes combined with political and
          social turmoil throughout their society

36. Workers' efforts to organize unions in this period

36 ① ② ③ ④ ⑤

   (1) were characterized by peaceful negotiations with owners

   (2) were limited to local areas

   (3) were often met with violent resistance

   (4) succeeded in establishing large, lasting unions of unskilled workers

   (5) were aided by the federal government

For answers and explanations, see page 127.

Directions: Read the graph below and then answer the questions by filling in the circle that corresponds to the correct answer.

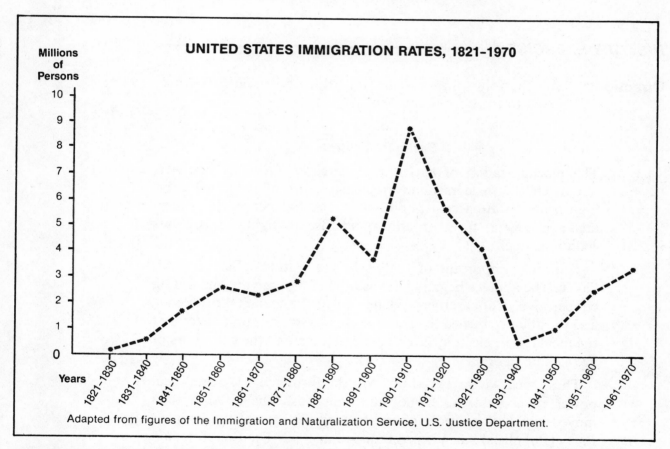

UNITED STATES IMMIGRATION RATES, 1821–1970

Adapted from figures of the Immigration and Naturalization Service, U.S. Justice Department.

37. During which decade did immigration reach its peak?

37 ① ② ③ ④ ⑤

   (1) 1921–1930

   (2) 1881–1890

   (3) 1901–1910

   (4) 1911–1920

   (5) 1871–1880

38. Which of the following generalizations best fits the
information in the graph and material you just read?

   (1)   Immigration was not an important factor in
         urbanization.
   (2)   Immigration was reaching its peak during the era
         of rapid urban and industrial growth.
   (3)   There appears to be no relation between
         urbanization and immigration.
   (4)   Most immigrants did not settle in the city.
   (5)   Although immigration reached its peak during the
         late 1800s and early 1900s, it was not related to the
         process of industrialization.

For answers and explanations, see page 127.

HISTORY EXERCISE 4 ——————————————

Directions: Read the following passage and fill in the circle that corresponds to the correct answer.

Farmers' Protests

The mechanization of agriculture increased farm productivity,
but it left the farmers impoverished because of increased debt,
high transportation costs, and low prices. Farmers were desperate, and several farm organizations rose to fight for a better
5   economic deal.

   The most important of these was the National Farmers' Alliance. The alliance began in Texas in 1877 as a buying and selling
cooperative. Cooperatives did not solve the farmers' problems,
and the alliance turned to electoral politics. It had some success at
10   the local levels, electing several congressmen and the governors of
Texas and Georgia.

   These local victories did not win the farmers enough political
power to control the banks and railroads. The alliance then
moved into national politics and formed the base of the People's
15   Party (Populists) when it was founded in 1892. The Populists had
a far-ranging program, advocating such things as a progressive
income tax, government control of the railroads and utilities, and
inflated currency so the farmers could pay off their debts at a
cheaper rate.

20   The People's Party candidate, General Weaver, polled more
than one million votes in the presidential election of 1892, which
was won by Grover Cleveland. In 1896, the Populists joined with
the Democrats in order to run William Jennings Bryan for the

presidency. Following his loss, the Populists rapidly faded away
25 as an organized force.

The Populists' rapid decline came as a result of both their inability to make an alliance with urban workers and the persistent racial prejudice of their leadership. Because of this, they failed to make an alliance with black farmers and field hands,
30 whom they could not win away from the Republican Party, the party of Lincoln and emancipation.

39. From the material in this passage, you could conclude
that for a political party to be successful, it must
    (1) build an alliance of different interest groups
    (2) be based on one interest group
    (3) be opposed to the regulation of business
    (4) be based on farmers
    (5) stay out of electoral politics

39 ① ② ③ ④ ⑤

40. The Farmers' Alliance formed the base for the
    (1) Republican Party
    (2) Democratic Party
    (3) Progressive movement
    (4) People's Party
    (5) Knights of Labor

40 ① ② ③ ④ ⑤

41. Which of the following increased farm productivity?
    (1) Transportation costs
    (2) Low prices
    (3) Mechanization of agriculture
    (4) The Populists
    (5) Cooperatives

41 ① ② ③ ④ ⑤

For answers and explanations, see page 127.

5. THE PROGRESSIVE ERA   1900–1917

KEY WORDS

Progressive Era—the years from 1900 to 1917, characterized by many social and political reforms

social class—group of people who share a common economic position in society

Muckrakers—writers who exposed corruption in business and politics during the early years of the twentieth century

Social Darwinism—the theory that the development of society is based on the survival of the fittest

Crisis and Change

The last quarter of the nineteenth century transformed America from a rural, agrarian society to a hard-driving industrial urban society. By 1900, the United States had replaced Great Britain as the leading industrial producer in the world. The country was poised for even greater growth, with the development of the first modern production line by Henry Ford.

However, the reform of worsening social conditions brought about by industrialization and urbanization became the main concern of many Americans. The level of social conflict, already high in the 1890s, showed no signs of lessening as the twentieth century began. Labor strife continued, abuses of child labor were widespread, and living and working conditions deteriorated in the cities.

At the same time, the economy became more concentrated in the hands of a small number of families. By 1904, the top 4 percent of businesses accounted for 57 percent of the total industrial production. Such concentrations of economic power failed to produce economic stability, as a serious depression in 1907 demonstrated.

This developing social and political crisis gave birth to a time known as the Age of Reform, or the **Progressive Era**, a period that lasted roughly from 1900 to America's entry into World War I in 1917. Political institutions that had proven adequate for a nation of farmers and small businessmen could no longer deal with the growing problems of a large-scale industrial society.

Industrialization had created a large new class of industrial workers as well as a far smaller class of very wealthy industrialists and financiers who owned the new industries. Industrialization, along with urbanization, had also created a large, new middle class composed of professionals—lawyers, doctors, engineers, teachers—and a rapidly expanding group of white-collar workers and small businessmen.

Each of these **social classes** had its own particular interests and ideas about how the country should confront the questions of reforms. Individuals from the growing urban middle class feared that the large corporations were stifling the American free-enterprise system and destroying competition. Many also suspected that wealthy bankers were working in collusion with the corporate owners.

A significant section of the working class, small farmers, and some segments of the new middle class were influenced by radical organizations and their vision of America's future. The Socialist Party, which called for public control of giant corporations, was the most influential radical political force. At one time, 1,200 Socialists were elected as public officials, including 79 mayors.

Far more radical than the Socialists, but lacking influence in electoral politics, were the Industrial Workers of the World (I.W.W.), or "Wobblies." They participated in several large and violent strikes and also demonstrated that there was a potential for unionizing many unskilled industrial workers.

The writings of radical journalists, **Muckrakers**, such as Lincoln Steffens and Upton Sinclair, also influenced many people. Steffens exposed in his books and articles the corruption, poverty, and boss-run political systems in the large cities. Sinclair exposed the horrifying conditions in Chicago's meatpacking industry in his novel *The Jungle* (1906). His exposé eventually led to federal passage of the Meat Inspection Amendment and the Pure Food and Drug Act.

Directions: Based upon what you have just read, fill in the circle that corresponds to the correct answer.

42. The main idea of this essay is best expressed by which of the following?
    (1) Different economic interests are often at the root of political conflict.
    (2) Control of the economy was not being exercised by the right people.
    (3) The survival of democracy is threatened during economic and social crises.
    (4) A third political party can decide an election.
    (5) The redistribution of wealth is one solution to an economic crisis.

42 ① ② ③ ④ ⑤

43. The great economic and industrial advances of this period also brought about
    (1) social classes
    (2) social conflict
    (3) economic stability
    (4) an end to agriculture
    (5) free enterprise

43 ① ② ③ ④ ⑤

For answers and explanations, see page 127.

Nature of Reforms

The growing strength of radicals and the influence of the middle class forced the Democratic and Republican parties to take reform seriously. The Progressive Era reforms, with strong middle-class support, were initially carried out at state and local levels. Some of the local reforms that were instituted included city manager forms of city government, sanitation laws, building codes, and child welfare laws.

Organized religion through the Social Gospel movement sought to bring the Christian religion to bear on urban evils. Many privately funded settlement houses, like Jane Addams's Hull House in Chicago, were established in poor urban neighborhoods. At these sites, some social and educational facilities were provided for the poor. Nevertheless, all of the local reforms as well as resources (public and private) were limited. Reformers therefore directed their attention to the national level where they sought government intervention to alleviate the most serious problems.

Society was deeply divided over what to do. One group supported **Social Darwinism**, the theory that society is based on the survival of the fittest. They believed that wealth was a symbol of survival and that nature intended for some to succeed and for some to fail. The Social Darwinists maintained that government should follow a policy of laissez faire—it should keep its hands off the economy and take no part in social reforms.

There were others who felt that reforms were necessary to keep the system from falling into economic anarchy. They found their spokesperson in President Theodore (Teddy) Roosevelt. Roosevelt thought that the excesses of big business had to be controlled, and he pushed for reforms to control its worst abuses.

Roosevelt, president from 1901 to 1909, did not run for reelection in 1908, but he did return to presidential politics in 1912. He felt that his party (the Republican Party) had turned its back on reform. He split from the Republicans and formed the Progressive (Bullmoose) Party. Roosevelt's third party split the Republican vote in 1912 and allowed the Democratic candidate, Woodrow Wilson, to win.

The Progressive Era produced a long list of legislative reforms, including regulation of railroads, the Meat Inspection Amendment, the Pure Food and Drug Act, the Federal Trade Commission, the Clayton Anti-Trust Act, child labor protection, and many others. The era came to an end as World War I approached and the country shifted its attention from domestic to international concerns.

The basic questions of the Progressive Era came to center on the dispute over what role the government should play in regulating economic and social conditions. The solution would not, as the Socialists wanted, place large segments of the economy under public control. It would not, as the conservative faction of big business wanted, let business do as it pleased. The ultimate answer was that private business was to rule the economy, with some government regulation to protect the general welfare. This solution has governed American society since then, although there has been ongoing conflict over extending or decreasing the protective and regulative role of the government.

Directions: Based upon what you have read, answer the following questions.

44. Teddy Roosevelt's 1912 candidacy resulted in
    (1) the end of the Progressive Era
    (2) Social Darwinism
    (3) the election of Woodrow Wilson
    (4) the end of the Republican Party
    (5) the Federal Trade Commission

    44 ① ② ③ ④ ⑤

45. If the political direction of the Progressive Era were applied to today's issue of environmental protection, what would be the most likely outcome?
    (1) Companies would be free to expand as they wanted and allowed to make all decisions about environmental protection.
    (2) Companies that pollute the environment would be taken over and run by their workers.
    (3) Companies that pollute the environment would be taken over by the federal government and run for the common good.
    (4) Polluting companies would be run by the communities in which they are located.
    (5) The worst abuses of the polluting companies would be regulated by the government, but control of the companies would remain in the hands of the present owners.

    45 ① ② ③ ④ ⑤

46. According to the essay, social reformers eventually turned to the federal government for aid in resolving problems because
    (1) reformers always believe in big government
    (2) they did not want to resolve the problems themselves
    (3) private and local resources were limited
    (4) the government demanded a voice in the situation
    (5) they thought the federal government would be more sympathetic

    46 ① ② ③ ④ ⑤

For answers and explanations, see page 127.

HISTORY EXERCISE 5

The passage below is taken from a speech delivered by Melinda Scott at a large meeting of women workers prior to a meeting with President Wilson. This meeting was part of the effort by American women to obtain the right to vote.

Directions: Read the following passage and fill in the circle that corresponds to the correct answer.

Women's Suffrage Movement

"No one could be serious when they maintained that the ballot will not help the working woman. It has helped the working man to better his condition and his wages. Men of every class regard the ballot as their greatest protection against the injustice of other
5   men. Women even more than men need the ballot to protect their especial interests and their right to earn a living. . . . We want a law that will prohibit home-work. . . . We hear about the sacredness of the home. What sacredness is there about a home when it is turned into a factory, where we find a mother, very often with
10   a child at her breast, running a sewing machine? Running up thirty-seven seams for a cent. Ironing and pressing shirts seventy cents a dozen, and children making artificial flowers for one cent. . . . These women have had no chance to make laws that would protect themselves or their children.

15   Men legislating as a class for women and children as a class have done exactly what every other ruling class has done since the history of the world. They discriminate against the class that has no voice. Some of the men say, 'You women do not need a ballot; we will take care of you.' We have no faith in man's protec-
20   tion. . . . Give us the ballot, and we will protect ourselves."

Inez Hayne Irwin, *Uphill With Banners Flying*

47. In this passage, the writer takes the position that   47 ① ② ③ ④ ⑤
(1)   the ballot will not help the working woman
(2)   men cannot be depended on to protect women and children
(3)   men should protect the well-being of women and children
(4)   children should work at home
(5)   giving women the right to vote will destroy the sanctity of the home

48. Which of the following opinions of the Equal Rights   48 ① ② ③ ④ ⑤
Amendment (ERA) would you expect the speaker in this passage to have?
(1)   The ERA is irrelevant because laws will do no good to help women.
(2)   The ERA should not be passed because women have already been given too many rights.

(3) The ERA should be passed because legal rights are necessary to gain economic rights.

(4) The ERA is not necessary because women can rely on men to protect their interests.

(5) The ERA should not be passed because it will destroy the American home.

49. The law "that will prohibit home-work" specifically refers to putting an end to

49 ① ② ③ ④ ⑤

(1) work on one's home

(2) family life

(3) factorylike production at home

(4) sewing

(5) schoolwork

For answers and explanations, see page 127.

6. U.S. FOREIGN AND DOMESTIC POLICY TO 1945

KEY WORDS

imperialism—the extension of one nation's control over other nations

gunboat diplomacy—American practice, especially during the early years of the twentieth century, of sending troops into Latin American and Caribbean nations when the U.S. believed that its interests were threatened

isolationism—limited involvement in foreign affairs characteristic of U.S. foreign policy during the 1920s and 1930s

industrial unionism—the organizing of unskilled and semi-skilled factory workers into trade unions undertaken by the Congress of Industrial Organizations (CIO) during the 1930s

America Pursues a Policy of Expansion Overseas

In 1823, while Latin American countries were locked in their struggle for independence from Spanish rule, President James Monroe announced that the United States would not tolerate future European interference in the affairs of the Western Hemisphere. From the time of the announcement of the Monroe Doctrine until the 1890s, the U.S. played a limited role in world affairs.

During the 1890s, several factors converged to launch the United States on a course of expansion and the acquisition of overseas possessions— **imperialism.** A severe economic depression from 1893 to 1898, caused in part by an overproduction of goods and a home market that could not absorb them, convinced American businessmen and farmers that they needed foreign markets in which to sell their goods. They hoped this would improve the economy, which would, in turn, help calm growing domestic unrest. The U.S. also feared being left empty-handed as European powers carved up spheres of influence in Africa, China, and the Middle East.

Cuba provided the United States with its doorway to empire. In 1898, the United States took advantage of the crumbling Spanish empire when it intervened in the Cuban independence struggle against Spanish rule. The United States declared war on Spain. The Spanish-American War lasted barely three months and resulted in the U.S.'s gaining control over Cuba. Cuba received its independence (with strong American controls), and the U.S. also annexed the former Spanish possessions of Puerto Rico, the Philippines, and Guam. The Philippines continued its struggle for independence, but was defeated by U.S. troops after a bloody struggle (1898–1902).

During the 1900s, the U.S. sent troops on several occasions to Latin American and Caribbean countries (Nicaragua, Mexico, Haiti, and the Dominican Republic) when it felt American interests were threatened by local political situations. American **gunboat diplomacy** of this era is still remembered and resented in Latin America.

At the same time, anti-imperialist sentiment was growing among many segments of the American public. Most Americans agreed about the need for increased foreign trade, but many disagreed with American military intervention and did not want the U.S. to become a colonial power like the European nations. The Anti-Imperialist League, founded in 1898, included senators, intellectuals, and some big businessmen among its members. American humorist and writer Mark Twain, best known for his novels *Tom Sawyer* and *Huckleberry Finn*, was a prominent critic of the new American imperialism and an outspoken member of the league.

World War I and Its Aftermath

Meanwhile in Europe, a thirty-year conflict among European powers for world empire led to the outbreak of World War I in 1914. Germany and the Austro-Hungarian empire battled against England, France, and Russia.

The United States government, feeling strong antiwar pressure from the American people, stayed out of the war until 1917. However, this did not prevent American banks from lending billions of dollars to hard-pressed Britain and France to finance their purchase of war materials.

Finally, unrestricted German submarine warfare resulted in attacks against unarmed merchant and passenger ships, forcing the U.S. to enter the war. The United States intervened on the side of the British and French and, by the conclusion of the war in 1918, had become one of the major powers of the world.

Following World War I, the United States had limited international involvement. American foreign policy during the 1920s and 1930s is often called **isolationism**. The U.S. Congress refused to join the League of Nations that was set up after World War I to ensure peace and collective security. The United States did not want its hands tied by European alliances, but in response to general antiwar sentiment took part in the Washington naval disarmament conference (1921) and also signed the Kellogg-Briand Pact (1928), which renounced war as a means to settle international disputes.

Directions: Based upon what you have read, fill in the circle that corresponds to the correct answer.

50. Which of the following best characterizes American foreign policy from the 1890s through the 1930s?
    (1) The U.S. alternated between periods of foreign involvement and periods of isolation from foreign affairs.
    (2) The U.S. generally did not pay much attention to foreign trade.
    (3) The U.S. followed only a policy of isolationism.
    (4) The U.S. did not use the military in expanding its influence.
    (5) The U.S. opposed entangling alliances with other powers.

50 ① ② ③ ④ ⑤

51. If a diplomat rose in the United Nations today to criticize America's sending troops to intervene in a Central American country, he would most likely refer to such action as a continuation of
    (1) gunboat diplomacy
    (2) isolationism
    (3) appeasement
    (4) the Good Neighbor Policy
    (5) entitlement

51 ① ② ③ ④ ⑤

For answers and explanations, see page 128.

The Twenties and the Great Depression

If the international situation was somewhat subdued in the 1920s, the domestic situation was just the opposite. This was the time known as the Roaring Twenties or the Jazz Age.

The main business of this decade was business. The giant corporations developed and expanded modern forms of production and marketing. Scientific management was applied to mass production. Henry Ford taught American businessmen how to build assembly lines and run them faster and faster. The mass market for consumer goods was created, as the chain store and the large, all-purpose department store replaced the small shops. The consumer age was born.

Industrial productivity increased a whopping 64 percent between 1919 and 1923. Workers shared in some of this prosperity, as real wages rose 24 percent. Dividends to corporate stockholders increased by 100 percent.

More women entered the labor force as the growth of giant corporations and mass marketing created new jobs for secretaries and other clerical workers. Women also won the right to vote with passage of the Nineteenth Amendment in 1920.

There was strong antiforeign sentiment during the 1920s, and it was fueled by the rebirth of racist groups such as the Ku Klux Klan. Immigration into the U.S. was sharply restricted by the Immigration Act of 1924.

New sources of labor opened up with increased migration of black workers from the South. The black migrants responded to racial discrimination in the North in a variety of ways, including supporting the development of Black Nationalism, most notably through the Universal Negro Improvement Association founded by Marcus Garvey.

The era of economic prosperity ended suddenly when the stock market crashed in 1929 and the Great Depression began. The productivity boom of the 1920s had flooded the markets with unsold goods, and now, the factories stood idle. In the large industrial centers such as Cleveland, Akron, and Chicago, the unemployment rate soared as high as sixty percent. In the countryside, thousands of small farmers and sharecroppers were thrown off the land.

At the time the Depression began, there was no unemployment insurance, very little public welfare, and no social security. Private relief agencies soon exhausted their meager resources. The victims of the Great Depression were on their own, with their very lives at stake.

The crisis led to direct action on the part of those most affected. While the unemployed in the cities faced starvation, farmers slaughtered livestock and destroyed crops and milk supplies rather than lose more money by selling at the extremely low prices that had been forced upon them. In the cities, many unemployed people joined in protests and later formed councils of the unemployed. These councils forcefully prevented the evictions of many unemployed homeowners and renters who could not pay their debts. Thousands of unemployed World War I veterans marched on Washington, D.C., in 1932 and camped out in the capital, demanding early payment of a bonus owed to them by the government. The "Bonus Army" was finally driven from the capital by federal troops.

Directions: Based upon what you have read, fill in the circle that corresponds to the correct answer.

52. Initially, those most affected by the Depression   52 ① ② ③ ④ ⑤
    (1) were aided by various forms of government assistance
    (2) organized themselves to protest their plight
    (3) lived mostly in large cities
    (4) were able to survive through private charity
    (5) were recent immigrants to the U.S.

53. According to the essay, the main business of the 1920s was   53 ① ② ③ ④ ⑤
    (1) automobiles
    (2) department stores
    (3) jazz
    (4) business
    (5) mass production

Base your answer to question 54 on the graphs below.

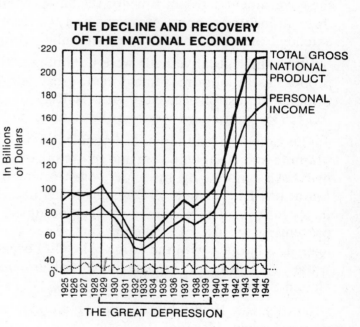

UNEMPLOYMENT

The Unemployed as a Percent of the Civilian Labor Force

THE GREAT DEPRESSION

THE DECLINE AND RECOVERY OF THE NATIONAL ECONOMY

TOTAL GROSS NATIONAL PRODUCT

PERSONAL INCOME

In Billions of Dollars

THE GREAT DEPRESSION

54. These graphs show that   54 ① ② ③ ④ ⑤
    (1) unemployment increased from 1929 to 1933 and the gross national product declined
    (2) unemployment decreased from 1929 to 1933 and the GNP decreased in the same period
    (3) movement in employment figures and the GNP are not related
    (4) unemployment has continuously declined since 1933
    (5) unemployment and the GNP both began a large increase in 1938

For answers and explanations, see page 128.

The New Deal

Franklin Delano Roosevelt (FDR) took the presidential oath in 1933, facing both a country close to economic collapse and a rising storm of protest from the victims of the Depression. Roosevelt launched a strong series of legislative reforms, known as the New Deal, to get the economy moving.

Over the next few years, federal legislation established many new programs. These included Social Security, Federal Unemployment Insurance, the National Labor Relations Board, and the Works Progress Administration (WPA). The latter provided tens of thousands of public works jobs for the unemployed.

The New Deal did not get the country out of the Depression; it took World War II to do that. However, the New Deal did establish the idea that the government is responsible for the basic economic security of its citizens through income support programs and the creation of jobs. It also further extended the government's role in regulating and directing the economy.

While the legislative halls were humming with debate on the New Deal proposals, the labor movement made great gains. New Deal legislation, the National Industrial Recovery Act (NIRA) in 1933, and later the Wagner Act (1935) guaranteed workers the right to collective bargaining.

The Congress for Industrial Organizations (CIO) was formed in 1935 to promote **industrial unionism** and to organize industrial workers, a task that had been ignored by the older, craft-oriented American Federation of Labor (AFL). The new CIO unions relied heavily on the new tactic of the factory sit-in. The striking workers occupied the factory from within, preventing the use of strikebreakers. They remained until the company agreed to bargain with the union. The CIO organized four million workers between 1935 and 1937, and industrial unionism was established in the United States.

During the 1930s, blacks played an increasingly visible role on the national scene. Many of the newly organized members of the CIO unions were black workers, especially in the northern factories. Blacks were also active in building successful nationwide campaigns against lynching and in defense of the Scottsboro boys.

Directions: Based upon what you have read, fill in the circle that corresponds to the correct answer.

55.   What has been the most lasting effect of the New Deal?   55 ① ② ③ ④ ⑤
      (1)   It brought the U.S. out of the Depression.
      (2)   It established a policy against government
            interference in labor-management relations.

    (3)   It established the idea that the government was responsible for the basic economic security of its citizens.

    (4)   It established the policy of creating economic growth by cutting back on social welfare and subsidizing business.

    (5)   It established the policy of letting citizens suffer from the effects of economic depressions in order to cut inflation.

56. During the Great Depression, American industrial workers   56 ① ② ③ ④ ⑤
    (1)   depended entirely on FDR's New Deal programs
    (2)   took direct action to organize unions
    (3)   ignored the call of the CIO to organize unions
    (4)   were not affected too much by the Depression
    (5)   were not willing to strike

For answers and explanations, see page 128.

The Road to World War II

On the eve of World War II, much had been accomplished in easing the people's pain and in organizing new institutions. But the effects of the Depression were still hanging heavily on the country. War production from 1940 onward would lift the country out of the Depression.

While the United States was trying to emerge from the Depression, an even more desperate battle was taking place in Europe and Asia. In both places, Fascist movements had used the turmoil of the worldwide Depression to rise to power in Germany, Italy, and Japan. These dictatorships, backed by strong military power, were now determined to solve their economic problems through military expansion and world conquest. In 1936, the three nations formed an alliance called the Axis.

In Germany, Adolf Hitler and his National Socialist (Nazi) Party had come to power in 1933. They jailed or murdered their political and labor opponents, destroyed democratic government in Germany, and began a systematic persecution of German Jews. The Nazis, backed by German industrialists and military power, began to rebuild the German armed forces.

Hitler began his expansion in the mid-1930s, taking the Rhineland in 1936, Austria and Czechoslovakia in 1938. The initial response of England and France was one of appeasing Hitler; they tried to keep peace in Europe by giving in to Nazi aggression. The French and English policy ended in complete failure as the Nazis continued seizing territory. Finally, in

September 1939, after Hitler's invasion of Poland, England and France declared war on Germany. The Soviet Union entered the war against Nazi Germany following a German invasion of that country in June 1941.

In Asia, Japan embarked on a campaign of conquest by seizing Manchuria in 1931 and invading China in 1937. On December 7, 1941, the Japanese carried out an attack on the U.S. Pacific fleet stationed in Pearl Harbor, Hawaii. Following this "Day of Infamy," the U.S. declared war on Japan, and Japan's Axis allies in Europe declared war on the U.S.

War raged in Europe until May 1945, when a combined assault by the Allied forces, which included the Soviet Union from the East and American-British forces from the South and West, defeated Germany. In the Pacific, Japan surrendered after the U.S. dropped atomic bombs on Hiroshima and Nagasaki in August 1945.

Directions: Based on what you have read, fill in the circle that corresponds to the correct answer.

57. English and French policy toward Nazi Germany's military expansion prior to September 1939 was one of
    (1) active military opposition
    (2) surrender
    (3) alliance with Axis countries
    (4) appeasement
    (5) isolationism

57 ① ② ③ ④ ⑤

For answers and explanations, see page 128.

HISTORY EXERCISE 6

Directions: Read the following passage and fill in the circle that corresponds to the correct answer.

The following is a description of the forty-four-day Flint sit-down strike against General Motors in 1936. This was the turning point in American unionism that established the United Auto Workers (UAW).

The Flint Sit-Down Strike of 1936

The Flint sit-down happened Christmas Eve, 1936. I was in Detroit playing Santa Claus to a couple of small nieces and nephews. When I came back, the second shift had pulled the plant. It took about five minutes to shut the line down. The
5   foreman was pretty well astonished.

We had guys patrol the plant, see that nobody got involved in anything they shouldn't. If anybody got careless with company property . . . he was talked to. You couldn't paint a sign on the wall or anything like that. . . . They'd assign roles to you. When
10 some of the guys at headquarters wanted to tell some of the guys in the plant what was cookin', I carried the message.

The soup kitchen was outside the plant. The women handled all the cooking, outside of one chef who came from New York. . . . Mostly stews, pretty good meals. They were put in containers and
15 hoisted up through the windows. The boys in there had their own plates and cups and saucers.

Most of the men had wives and friends come down, and they'd stand inside the window and they'd talk. Find out how the family was. If the union supplied them with enough coal.

20 We had a ladies auxiliary. They'd visit the homes of the guys that was in the plant. They would find out if there was any shortage of coal or food. Then they'd maneuver amongst themselves until they found some place to get a ton of coal. Some of them even put the arm on Consumer Power if there was a
25 possibility of having her power shut off.

Finally we got the word: THE THING IS SETTLED. My God, you had to send about three people, one right after the other, down to some of those plants because the guys didn't believe it. Finally, when they did get it, they marched out of the plants with
30 the flag flyin' and all that stuff.

When Mr. Knudsen put his name to a piece of paper and says that General Motors recognizes the UAW-CIO—until that moment we didn't even exist. That was the big one.

Studs Terkel, *Hard Times: An Oral History*
of the Great Depression

58. The Flint sit-down strike demonstrates that   58 ① ② ③ ④ ⑤
- (1) workers were helpless in face of business resistance to unionism
- (2) workers were manipulated by a small handful of outside agitators
- (3) workers in the plant were capable of organizing a complicated strike
- (4) workers' families were opposed to union strikes
- (5) the companies usually gave in very quickly

59. This passage reveals that the workers had what kind of attitude toward company property?
   (1) They treated it carefully.
   (2) They treated it with disdain.
   (3) They were very destructive.
   (4) They neglected it.
   (5) They made no effort to protect it.

59 ① ② ③ ④ ⑤

60. You might infer from this passage that the company did not attempt to remove the strikers because
   (1) there was public support for the strike
   (2) the strikers threatened to destroy the plant equipment
   (3) it preferred to ignore the strikers
   (4) it thought the strikers could be starved out
   (5) it thought the strike would be over quickly

60 ① ② ③ ④ ⑤

For answers and explanations, see page 128.

7. U.S. FOREIGN POLICY (1945 TO THE 1980s)

KEY WORDS

Cold War—the period of confrontation following World War II between the United States and its allies on the one hand and the Soviet Union and its allies on the other

containment—the foreign policy of the U.S. following World War II, the object of which was to block the further expansion of Communism

arms race—the development of huge military establishments and nuclear weaponry by the major world powers

Third World—the newly independent (since World War II), underdeveloped nations of Asia, Africa, and Latin America

détente—a policy that called for more peaceful cooperation between the United States and the Soviet Union

The Cold War

The U.S. emerged from World War II as the strongest world power. Western Europe and Japan were in ruins. America had become the leader of the Western alliance, facing the other major world power—the Soviet Union.

These two superpowers looked at each other through glasses clouded with a history of hostility. World War II forged a temporary alliance between the two nations with a common interest in defeating Hitler. As the war ended, hostility between the two nations again came to the forefront. This was a confrontation between two different social systems and between two giants competing for spheres of influence. The period of confrontation, lasting from the late 1940s until the 1970s, was called the **Cold War**.

By 1948, pro-Soviet governments, aided by the presence of Soviet occupation forces, had come to power in several Eastern European countries. Meanwhile, a revolutionary civil war in China had brought the Communists to power in 1949.

The American leadership feared the further progress of Communist influence and adopted the policy of **containment** of Communism to areas in which it was already established. To support this policy, the U.S. and Western Europe formed the North Atlantic Treaty Organization (NATO) as a military alliance. The U.S. also developed the Marshall Plan, which provided extremely important economic aid for the reconstruction of Western Europe.

The Soviet Union countered these moves by helping to form the Warsaw Pact alliance with its allies in Eastern Europe.

These moves and countermoves ushered in a long period of open hostility, confrontation, and an **arms race** between the two superpowers. Both spent billions of dollars to build up military arsenals. The Cold War occasionally turned "hot" during the Korean and Vietnam Wars, but the two nations managed to avoid direct military confrontation.

The Emergence of the Third World

While the Soviet Union and the U.S. tried to gain an edge on each other, Africa, Asia, and Latin America were aflame with political battles. Nationalist movements in colonial territories that had been dominated by European countries sought political independence (for example, the movement led by Mahatma Ghandi in India). In many cases, there were also movements against wealthy local elites who had helped maintain unjust social and economic conditions. Out of these battles emerged newly independent countries. The **Third World** developed as an independent political entity caught between the competition of the two superpowers but pursuing independent political and economic goals.

The American government viewed these developments in the Third World with a combination of fear and anxiety. Many of the governments that America had supported were being challenged by these movements. America's chief adversary, the Soviet Union, was also trying to gain influence in these areas by supporting the opposition forces. American business leaders feared that their involvement in the Third World economies would be hindered if governments favorable to them were replaced. Opposing Third World movements became an integral part of the official policy of containing Communism.

The U.S. government's worst fears were realized in Cuba when the ouster of dictator Fulgencio Batista in 1959 brought a revolutionary government to power that became Communist. A U.S.-supported invasion of the island by Cuban exiles at the Bay of Pigs in 1961 failed to overthrow Fidel Castro's government.

The U.S. Intervenes in Vietnam

Similar attitudes and fears toward the Third World led to America's involvement in Vietnam. Vietnam, a former French colony, had been partitioned into North and South Vietnam following the departure of the French in 1954. By the late 1950s, internal opposition in the South against both official corruption and American support for that government had escalated into a guerilla war against the South Vietnamese government.

Over a period of time and under a series of presidents from Eisenhower through Nixon, the United States became more and more involved by supporting the South Vietnamese government's war against its internal opposition and, eventually, the government of the North. The fateful Gulf of Tonkin incident during the presidency of Lyndon Johnson signalled an all-out escalation of American involvement. American troop strength in Vietnam reached a peak of 543,000 in 1969. By the time of America's withdrawal in 1973, more than 50,000 Americans had been killed and 155,000 had been wounded.

During this period, America's involvement also spread to the neighboring countries of Laos and Cambodia. In 1975, the government of South Vietnam fell, and the country was reunified under the government of the North.

The trauma of the war forced some in the U.S. to reevaluate the policy of opposition to Third World independence. It also led to several congressional resolutions limiting the power of U.S. presidents to commit troops to undeclared wars. The War Powers Act was the most important piece of legislation to result from the Vietnam conflict.

Directions: Based upon what you have just read, fill in the circle corresponding to the correct answer.

61. The principal aim of U.S. foreign policy in the period of the Cold War was to
    (1)   pursue the appeasement doctrine
    (2)   build the independence of the Third World
    (3)   seek détente with the Soviet Union
    (4)   contain the spread of Communist influence
    (5)   return to isolationism

61 ① ② ③ ④ ⑤

62. According to the passage, American foreign policy toward the Third World during the Cold War

   (1) stressed peaceful coexistence with nationalist movements

   (2) perceived nationalist movements as linked to Communist expansion

   (3) sought military intervention whenever possible

   (4) was only concerned with protecting business interests

   (5) sought to avoid situations like Vietnam

62 ① ② ③ ④ ⑤

For answers and explanations, see page 128.

Détente, the Beginnings of a New Cold War, and the Future

The war in Vietnam led both superpowers to see the danger of direct confrontation. President Nixon visited Russia in 1972 and 1974, and the two countries worked out a policy of **détente**, calling for more peaceful cooperation despite the fundamental differences in the two social systems. This policy led to a thawing of the Cold War and more open exchange between the two countries. A notable first step in possible arms control was taken with the Strategic Arms Limitation Talks (SALT I).

As the 1980s began, the U.S.–Soviet conflict was reemerging more openly. In 1979, the Soviet Union invaded Afghanistan. Polish workers, led by the Solidarity movement, rebelled against the pro-Soviet government in Poland. The U.S. elected Ronald Reagan as president in 1980. He promised a huge military buildup to overtake the military power of the Soviet Union. The atmosphere for a new era of Cold War developed as both countries traded charges and built up their military might.

Tensions also remained high between the U.S. and the Third World during the early 1980s as the U.S. began to take an interventionist role in the affairs of Central American and Caribbean nations. At the same time, it supported the minority white government in South Africa. American differences with the Third World also continued over issues of economic aid and political independence.

Directions: Based upon what you have just read, fill in the circle that corresponds to the correct answer.

63. If U.S.–Soviet relations during the 1980s follow the pattern that has developed since World War II, we might expect relations between the U.S. and the Soviet Union to   63 ① ② ③ ④ ⑤
    (1) become friendly with all conflict resolved
    (2) become openly hostile and move toward war
    (3) be of little concern to American foreign policy
    (4) alternate between open hostility and limited cooperation
    (5) have little or no influence on Third World affairs

64. According to the essay, the period of increased peaceful cooperation between the U.S. and the Soviet Union during the 1970s is referred to as   64 ① ② ③ ④ ⑤
    (1) détente
    (2) containment
    (3) peaceful coexistence
    (4) the Cold War
    (5) the space race

For answers and explanations, see page 128.

HISTORY EXERCISE 7

Directions: Look at the cartoon below and fill in the circle that corresponds to the correct answer.

65. Which of the following best states the main idea of this cartoon?

65 ① ② ③ ④ ⑤

(1) Military personnel can now practice warfare by using video games.

(2) War games are more realistic with video.

(3) Future wars will be fought with video games.

(4) Technological advances will make a nuclear war seem like a video game to those pushing the buttons.

(5) You need a lot of patience to play a video game properly.

For answers and explanations, see page 128.

8. U.S. DOMESTIC HISTORY (1945 TO THE 1980s)

KEY WORDS

McCarthyism—the indiscriminate and careless use of accusations concerning a person's political loyalties

Brown vs. the Board of Education (1954)—the unanimous Supreme Court decision that struck down racial segregation in public schools

Great Society—the name given to the social legislation put into effect during the administration of Lyndon B. Johnson

national debt—the debt undertaken by the U.S. government to make up the difference between the revenue it collects and the money it spends

Themes in Domestic History

There are several important themes that characterized much of the domestic history of the United States from World War II to the 1980s. These themes include the impact of American foreign policy on politics at home, the emergence of mass movements for social change, the continuing debate over government's role in meeting social needs, and the role of the government in the economy.

Impact of Foreign Policy

The Cold War and fear of Communism were accompanied by a "red scare" in the 1950s. Senator Joseph McCarthy and his followers made many unproven charges of widespread Communist subversion. Thousands of Americans lost their jobs on mere suspicion of being "subversives." The congressional House Un-American Activities Committee probed into the political beliefs and associations of many Americans. Senator McCarthy was finally censured by the Senate in 1954, and the Un-American Activities Committee was disbanded during the 1960s.

Later, during the late 1960s and early 1970s, foreign policy again had a significant impact on domestic events. The escalation of American involvement in the war in Vietnam and the inability of the U.S. government to justify the war and its enormous casualties created a large antiwar movement. Hundreds of thousands of youths protested the war and the military draft. Some left the country rather than serve in the military.

The movement spread beyond the young to the point where the majority of Americans opposed the war. Popular pressure to end the war was so great that it forced President Johnson not to seek reelection in 1968. Partly because he claimed to have a plan to end the war, Richard Nixon was elected president in 1968. The conflict dragged on until early 1973, when Nixon, under heavy pressure, withdrew U.S. forces.

Movements for Social Change

This era witnessed the emergence of several large protest movements seeking basic changes in society.

In 1954, a historic Supreme Court decision, **Brown vs. the Board of Education**, banned segregation in public schools. The court ruled that separate, or segregated, schools could in no way be considered as equal treatment under the law. This decision opened the floodgate for protest against segregation and discrimination in America.

Protests against segregated public transportation led to a successful bus boycott in Montgomery, Alabama, in 1955. Out of the experience in Montgomery rose a young preacher, Dr. Martin Luther King, Jr., to a position of leadership in the growing civil rights movement. Dr. King went on to mobilize black and significant white support throughout the nation into a massive, nonviolent protest against racial segregation and discrimination. The movement, which often engaged in nonviolent disobedience of discriminatory laws, helped to produce some significant results, including the 1964 Civil Rights Act and the 1965 Voting Rights Act. Dr. King's life came to a tragic end when he was assassinated in 1968 in Memphis, Tennessee, where he had gone to aid striking sanitation workers.

Black leadership made use of the Voting Rights Act and moved into electoral politics. By the early 1980s, there were hundreds of black elected officials, including mayors of such cities as Atlanta, Detroit, Los Angeles, Chicago, and Philadelphia.

Two other major movements for change emerged in the 1970s. Many Americans became concerned with issues involving the environment. This led to the establishment of the Environmental Protection Agency (EPA) and to legislation such as the Clean Air and Water Act. The growing use of nuclear power and the safety problems associated with it became a related issue. This gave birth to an antinuclear power campaign, which became part of a broader movement against nuclear weapons by the early 1980s.

The women's movement was revitalized in the 1960s and 1970s. More women had gone to college, and many had taken part in the 1960s protests. Now, unwilling to accept an inferior role in American society, many women fought to end discrimination in jobs and education. In the 1970s and 1980s, the movement focused its attention on the Equal Rights Amendment to the U.S. Constitution.

Directions: Based upon what you have just read, fill in the circle that corresponds to the correct answer.

66. The conflicts over the rights of women and minorities during the 1960s and 1970s
    (1) were new developments in American history
    (2) were an evolutionary development of long-standing conflicts
    (3) led to creative solutions that put an end to discrimination
    (4) really involved only a few Americans
    (5) caused a lot of harm and produced no change at all

66 ① ② ③ ④ ⑤

67. You could assume that court-ordered busing of school children to achieve desegregation in public schools had its roots in the
    (1) Equal Rights Amendment
    (2) Montgomery bus boycott
    (3) Voting Rights Act of 1965
    (4) Brown vs. the Board of Education decision
    (5) separate but equal doctrine

67 ① ② ③ ④ ⑤

For answers and explanations, see page 129.

Government's Responsibility in Meeting Social Needs

The continuing debate over government's role in organizing society, especially in the maintenance of necessary social programs, was to be of great importance during the administrations of John F. Kennedy, Lyndon B. Johnson, and Ronald Reagan.

President Kennedy came into office on a wave of youthful idealism. He promised Americans a "New Frontier," but his major social programs, including federal assistance for education and medical care for senior citizens, were blocked by a hostile Congress. During a trip to Dallas, Texas, in November 1963, Kennedy was gunned down as he rode through the streets. A grief-stricken nation turned to Kennedy's successor, Lyndon Johnson, vice-president and former Senate majority leader from Texas.

President Johnson continued most of the Kennedy programs and increased American military involvement in Vietnam. Under Johnson, the country saw widespread governmental attempts to wipe out poverty through massive job training programs and an increase in other forms of government assistance to needy Americans. More civil rights legislation was also passed. Johnson's antipoverty programs were collectively known as the **Great Society,** or War on Poverty.

The question of government's role in maintaining social programs again became a major issue during President Reagan's administration. Federal spending on social programs had increased sharply during the 1970s. Many programs called for cost-of-living increases for recipients, and serious inflation caused the costs of the programs to rise at a rapid rate.

In 1980, President Reagan campaigned on a platform that advocated weakening the governmental regulatory structures for business and curtailing federal income support programs for the needy and elderly. Many federal social programs were cut back to reduce a mushrooming budget. These cuts provoked opposition, partly because the budget still continued to rise as a result of a massive increase in military spending. The national debt, increasing at a fast rate since the early 1970s, soared to a record level.

Government's Role in the Economy

The 1950s and 1960s were a time of relative prosperity in the United States. The U.S. emerged from World War II in a very powerful economic position. Relatively mild recessions occurred, but there were no serious economic problems until the early 1970s.

During the 1970s, the United States economy faced new problems, including a large jump in inflation heavily influenced by the spending on the war in Vietnam and rising oil prices. Heavy government spending on both the war and necessary social services had caused a great increase in the **national debt**. The American economy had also been running on extremely cheap imported oil. In 1973, the oil-exporting countries (OPEC) significantly raised the price of oil and ended the days of cheap energy. Finally, both Japan and West Germany had made remarkable economic recoveries following the war, manufacturing products by powerful industries that gave the U.S. and its aging industrial plants very serious competition.

Increasingly deeper recessions and the inability of a series of presidents to deal with them effectively have brought into question certain political principles concerning government intervention in the economy and aid to citizens. These questions date back to the Progressive and New Deal eras. How much of our present troubles are due to too much government aid? Are our people entitled to government-guaranteed minimum economic security? Should we return as much as possible to the unregulated business environment of 1900?

It appears that, despite wide differences, there still exists a consensus for government's providing a degree of economic regulation as well as some form of economic security and protection to its citizens.

Directions: Based upon what you have just read, fill in the circle that corresponds to the correct answer.

68. Which of the following reflects the outlook of the New Deal and Great Society eras?
    (1) Deregulation of businesses
    (2) Prayer in the schools
    (3) Cutbacks in social security
    (4) Cutbacks in military spending
    (5) Increases in federal support to the needy

    68 ① ② ③ ④ ⑤

For answers and explanations, see page 129.

HISTORY EXERCISE 8

The following graph shows the national debt for the United States from 1930 to 1980.

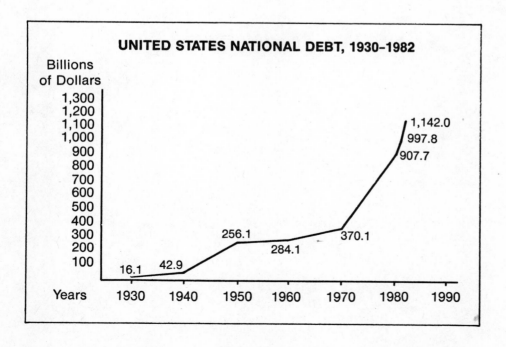

UNITED STATES NATIONAL DEBT, 1930–1982

Directions: Look at the graph and fill in the circle that corresponds to the correct answer.

69. During which ten-year period did the national debt   69 ① ② ③ ④ ⑤
     show the largest increase in dollar amount?
     (1)   1930–1940
     (2)   1940–1950
     (3)   1950–1960
     (4)   1960–1970
     (5)   1970–1980

70. Spending on which of the following probably accounted   70 ① ② ③ ④ ⑤
     for the rapid growth of the national debt between 1940
     and 1950?
     (1)   The New Deal
     (2)   World War II
     (3)   Social security
     (4)   Food stamps
     (5)   The Korean War

For answers and explanations, see page 129.

ANSWERS AND EXPLANATIONS

1. EXPLORATION AND DEVELOPMENT OF THE NEW WORLD   1492–1783

Main Idea	**1.**	(3)	This is stated in the first sentence of the section.
Applying Ideas	**2.**	(2)	*Mercantilism* refers to a system in which there is an unequal economic and trade relationship benefiting the larger, dominant country.
Finding Details	**3.**	(4)	This is mentioned in the essay.
Finding Details	**4.**	(4)	This is stated in the final paragraph of this section.
Drawing Conclusions	**5.**	(3)	The passage of the various laws of the 1760s and, finally, the Intolerable Acts strengthened the determination of the colonists to resist. From this, you can draw a more general conclusion.
Finding Details	**6.**	(5)	The colonists began by asserting their rights as Englishmen, and only after they had exhausted other means of protest did they turn to revolution.

HISTORY EXERCISE 1

Making Inferences	**7.**	(3)	See lines 18–20. The passage mentions 700 American ships engaged in slave trading and 100 distilleries that made rum for the slave trade.
Drawing Conclusions	**8.**	(4)	The Yankee ship owners were making money from slave trade, and you could conclude that they would probably agree to political compromises to keep the trade alive.
Applying Ideas	**9.**	(1)	The passage mentions that a significant portion of profits from the slave trade was used to finance the Industrial Revolution in England.

2. ESTABLISHMENT AND GROWTH OF THE NEW NATION   1787–1850

Drawing Conclusions	**10.**	(2)	Governments have used wars against a foreign power to unite a nation, encouraging people to bury their differences in a common war effort.
Drawing Conclusions	**11.**	(3)	The cotton gin made large-scale production of cotton possible and profitable and increased the demand for plantation slaves who were used to raise the crop.
Applying Ideas	**12.**	(4)	The debate reflects the economic differences between the Sun Belt states with their rapidly expanding economies and the Frost Belt states, which have experienced a decline in industry. Sectional political differences have a long history in the United States.
Drawing Conclusions	**13.**	(5)	Since politics were based heavily on sectional interests, you can conclude that there would have been a continuing need for compromises to maintain national unity.
Finding Details	**14.**	(1)	The passage states that voting rights were limited to white males.
Making Inferences	**15.**	(1)	Based on your reading of the passage, your earlier reading on colonial protests in Section 1, and common knowledge, you can see that movements for social change have played an important role in American history.

HISTORY EXERCISE 2

Making Inferences	16.	(5)	The letter mentions "teams starting for several days." The writer also notes that he got information from "some distance on the prairies."
Finding Details	17.	(2)	The writer mentions this in lines 20–21.
Making Inferences	18.	(1)	They appear to be charging a lot for necessities. The writer mentions that some things are cheaper but "They put the screws very tight to emigrants for all small jobs and articles the emigrants are obliged to get."

3. CIVIL WAR AND RECONSTRUCTION 1850–1877

Main Idea	19.	(2)	In the second paragraph, it is stated that the "confrontation over slavery was at the heart of these sectional differences."
Finding Details	20.	(5)	The decision left slave owners free to take slaves to all areas.
Making Inferences	21.	(4)	The essay points out that the North wanted free (not slave) labor for its factories and wanted new western territories to be free soil.
Finding Details	22.	(3)	They believed that if they did not secede, then slavery would certainly be abolished when more free states were admitted to the Union.
Finding Details	23.	(1)	The passage states that the Emancipation Proclamation strengthened northern support for the war effort.
Drawing Conclusions	24.	(3)	This can be concluded from material in the last paragraph of the essay. The essay points out that Reconstruction fell short of achieving equality and left many issues unresolved.
Finding Details	25.	(1)	They resented his easy amnesty for Confederate officers and politicians, some of whom went right back into government positions in 1865.
Drawing Conclusions	26.	(4)	The table shows that the North was clearly ahead in all areas of economic development.

HISTORY EXERCISE 3

Main Idea	27.	(5)	Despite the humorous, satiric tone, the author's main point is that he knows how he was exploited in the past and has no intention of letting that happen again.
Making Inferences	28.	(2)	On lines 47–48, Anderson says, "there was never any pay-day for the Negroes any more than for horses or cows."
Finding Details	29.	(3)	He mentions Carter and the incident with the pistol in the last sentence of the letter.

4. SOCIETY CHANGES 1865–1900

Main Idea	30.	(4)	This is the main idea of the essay. The essay details how industrialization affected the economy, population distribution, class relations, and politics of this period.
Finding Details	31.	(2)	The growth and centralization of industry hastened the growth of cities.
Making Inferences	32.	(2)	This is an inference about how historical change occurs. Change in a major institution, such as the economy, affects all other areas of society.

Making Inferences	**33.**	(1)	According to the essay, there were substantial differences between the economic development of the North and that of the South. Also, the Jim Crow laws had a profound political and social influence on the South.
Making Inferences	**34.**	(4)	The passage points out that the workers and farmers were organizing against the power of the monopolies and that these groups formed the basis for the People's Party.
Applying Ideas	**35.**	(5)	The American experience showed that widespread change as social turmoil can accompany industrialization.
Finding Details	**36.**	(3)	The passage describes the use of private police, militia, and even federal troops.
Reading Graphs	**37.**	(3)	The graph shows the highest immigration levels from 1901 to 1910.
Drawing Conclusions	**38.**	(2)	The passages discuss urbanization and the growth of cities in the late nineteenth and early twentieth centuries. The graph shows a high rate of immigration at the same time.

HISTORY EXERCISE 4

Evaluating Logic	**39.**	(1)	The People's Party had a far-ranging program, but it did not build an alliance with other classes and groups. See lines 27–29.
Finding Details	**40.**	(4)	This is stated in lines 13–15.
Finding Details	**41.**	(3)	The first sentence in the passage mentions that mechanization was a cause of increased productivity.

5. THE PROGRESSIVE ERA 1900–1917

Main Idea	**42.**	(1)	The essay points out that the Progressive Era reforms were championed by groups representing the workers, small farmers, and middle class, who feared the combined power of the large corporations and wealthy bankers.
Drawing Conclusions	**43.**	(2)	The passage describes the political and economic conflicts that resulted from the poverty and corruption that accompanied industrialization.
Finding Details	**44.**	(3)	The passage states that Roosevelt's third-party candidacy split the Republican vote and allowed Wilson to win.
Applying Ideas	**45.**	(5)	The final paragraph of this passage explains how the outcome of the Progressive Era modified the demand for government to control the economy completely, but at the same time, did allow for some degree of government intervention. Only choice (5) reflects this outlook.
Finding Details	**46.**	(3)	The essay points out that limited resources at the local level influenced the reformers to look to the federal government for help.

HISTORY EXERCISE 5

Main Idea	**47.**	(2)	The speaker says, "We have no faith in man's protection. . . . Give us the ballot, and we will protect ourselves."
Applying Ideas	**48.**	(3)	The speaker maintains that women must have certain legal rights to ensure their economic rights and well-being. Therefore, it is most likely that she would support the ERA.

Making Inferences   49. (3)   Melinda Scott protests against the so-called "sacredness of the home" when it is turned into a factory. Women often worked on production tasks at home. It was cheaper for many employers because such work was not regulated as to conditions or hours.

6.   U.S. FOREIGN AND DOMESTIC POLICY   1890–1945

Main Idea   50. (1)   The essay discusses the alternating periods of American involvement and noninvolvement in international affairs.

Applying Ideas   51. (1)   The essay describes gunboat diplomacy as American military intervention in Latin America. Today, this term is still in use.

Finding Details   52. (2)   The last paragraph describes organized protests by farmers, the unemployed, and veterans.

Finding Details   53. (4)   This is stated in the second paragraph, which discusses business and economic activity during the 1920s.

Reading Graphs   54. (1)   You must look at both graphs for the period 1929 to 1933. They show that during the Great Depression, unemployment rose while the gross national product declined.

Making Inferences   55. (3)   The notion of government responsibility for economic well-being is still with us today.

Finding Details   56. (2)   The passage states that workers participated in direct action, including sit-ins, to unionize.

Finding Details   57. (4)   The essay points out that, until the Nazis invaded Poland in 1939, the initial response of the Allies (France and England) was appeasement.

HISTORY EXERCISE 6

Main Idea   58. (3)   This is the main idea and is demonstrated by the workers' organizing inside the plant to keep the peace and organizing the food distribution and the families' helping each other.

Finding Details   59. (1)   This information is found in lines 7–9.

Making Inferences   60. (1)   The strikers were receiving outside aid in the form of food, and their families were being cared for by sympathizers.

7.   U.S. FOREIGN POLICY   1945 TO THE 1980s

Finding Details   61. (4)   It is stated in the passage that the aim of American foreign policy in the period following World War II was the containment of Communism.

Finding Details   62. (2)   The passage points out that the American government perceived Third World movements as Communist inspired.

Applying Ideas   63. (4)   This choice reflects the essay's description of U.S.–Soviet relations since World War II. The relationship has shifted between open hostility and mutual toleration.

Finding Details   64. (1)   The essay points out that the policy of détente called for more peaceful cooperation between the two superpowers.

HISTORY EXERCISE 7

Making Inferences   65. (4)   The cartoon shows how technology has depersonalized war, making it seem like a big video game.

8. **U.S. DOMESTIC HISTORY 1945 TO THE 1980s**

Drawing Conclusions	66.	(2)	Based on your reading of U.S. history, you could conclude that the movements of the 1960s and 1970s had their roots in long-standing social issues.
Making Inferences	67.	(4)	The decision banned racial segregation in public schools because such practice denied equal treatment to minority children. Court-ordered busing to desegregate certain schools and achieve racial balance has its roots in the *Brown vs. the Board of Education* case.
Drawing Conclusions	68.	(5)	The reading passages have described the New Deal and Great Society eras as periods when the federal government has increased its involvement in providing the social welfare. Only choice (5) reflects this orientation.

HISTORY EXERCISE 8

Reading Graphs	69.	(4)	The graphs show the biggest increase in the national debt to have been from $370.1 billion in 1970 to $907.7 billion in 1980.
Making Inferences	70.	(2)	World War II (1941–1945) accounted for the increase in the national debt from 1940 ($42.9 billion) to 1950 ($256.1 billion).

Political Science

=====================================

1. INTRODUCTION TO POLITICAL SCIENCE

KEY WORDS

political system—the recognized method of organizing power relationships in any society

government—the institutions that formally make and administer society's laws

power—possession of control or influence over others

authority—a government's ability to exercise power because the citizens recognize it as legitimate

politics—the process by which people are mobilized to influence government decisions

Politics, Government, and Authority

Political science is the study of man's organization of power arrangements in society. Political scientists study activities that influence the organization and use of power: governmental structure and policy making, political parties, interest groups, individual political behavior, international relations, etc.

Political scientists use the term **political system** to describe the recognized method of arranging power relationships in a society. Man has devised a wide variety of political systems according to the level of economic and social development. These systems have evolved from simple tribal organizations to very complex nation-states like the United States. The earliest political systems lacked a formal governmental structure, and the important decisions were often made by one person or a council. As societies became more complex, people had to create more formal and complicated governmental structures.

A **government** is the institutional form of power arrangements that includes the bodies that make and administer laws. It is responsible for maintaining order in society through the use of the police and the courts. Governments also raise armed forces to provide security against aggression from other countries. Most governments provide some basic support for the general welfare in the areas of health, safety, and education. They may also provide direct relief and assistance to needy citizens.

Underlying all governments are three necessary functions. The control of these functions can be in the hands of one person, such as an absolute monarch or dictator, or it can be carried out by three separate branches of government, as in the United States. These functions are (1) executive, which administers the operations of government, (2) legislative, which makes the laws, and (3) judicial, which interprets the laws.

All governments possess power. **Power** is the ability to make decisions and to have decisions carried out. Some governments rule by direct force or by the threat of force against its citizens. Other governments maintain their rule because the citizens voluntarily give their support. Whatever the reasons, a government that is recognized by the people as the legitimate government is said to have **authority**.

Governments can experience a breakdown in authority when the people perceive it as working against their interests. In some cases, this results in a decline in respect and popular support. In more intolerable situations, a government can face widespread opposition to its continuation. If a government meets its opposition with the use of force, the struggle can escalate, and some governments have been overthrown by a popular revolution. The American colonists' fight against the English king was an example of this. As recently as 1979, such an escalation of opposition led to the overthrow of dictator Anastasio Somoza in Nicaragua.

Governments can also lose authority with special interest groups, such as the military. These governments may be overthrown by a small group, rather than by a popular uprising. Such an action is called a coup d'etat (meaning a "blow against the state").

Besides the form of government, a political system includes politics. **Politics** is simply the way people are mobilized to influence the government, often without being directly involved in the government. For example, the political parties are a part of the American political system but are not a part of government. Similarly, Political Action Committees (PACs) that raise money for election compaigns are political but not a part of government. The use of petitioning, demonstrating, and lobbying also demonstrates the avenues for citizen involvement in the American system.

Directions: Based upon what you have just read, fill in the circle that corresponds to the correct answer.

1. Which of the following is an institution of government?   1 ① ② ③ ④ ⑤
   (1) Political Action Committee
   (2) City Council
   (3) Republican Party
   (4) Civil rights protest
   (5) Democratic Party convention

2. When people see their government as legitimate and   2 ① ② ③ ④ ⑤
   representing their interests, the government has
   (1) a conflict of interest
   (2) a coup d'etat
   (3) repression
   (4) politics
   (5) authority

3. When the Supreme Court makes a decision that   3 ① ② ③ ④ ⑤
   interprets the law, this is an example of which of the
   following functions of government?
   (1) Executive
   (2) Judicial
   (3) Legislative
   (4) Coup d'etat
   (5) Power

For answers and explanations, see page 170.

Types of Political Systems

Below are descriptions of major types of political systems. You will notice that some descriptions place emphasis on economic characteristics. It is difficult to describe a political system without referring to its economic system.

You should also be aware that characteristics of a political system may be combined with characteristics of other systems. For example, Sweden is both a constitutional monarchy and a social democracy. That country has both a figurehead monarch and a democratic government that plays an extremely active role in supporting many social programs.

Monarchies

Absolute monarchies are political systems based on power held by a royal ruler (king or queen) and a class of nobles. The overwhelming majority of the people have no voice in government. An absolute monarch receives his authority from the widespread belief in the divine right of the king or queen to rule. Such monarchs rule in the name of God and pass this authority on to their children. Some absolute monarchies were overthrown by revolution (France in 1789 and Russia in 1917), while others, such as those in England and Sweden, gradually evolved into constitutional monarchies.

The constitutional monarchy differs greatly from the absolute monarchy. The monarch's powers are usually severely limited by law, and in most cases, the monarch is only a figurehead. A representative assembly, such as the Parliament in England, writes the laws for the country. Representatives to the assembly are elected by the people and are accountable to them. Constitutional monarchies have come to resemble representative democracies (described below) in many respects.

Representative Democracies

This type of political system originally arose in reaction to the tyrannical and rigid rule of absolute monarchs. Representative democracies have governments that are run by elected representatives of the people. The duties, responsibilities, and powers of such representatives are set forth in fundamental written laws and principles known as a *constitution*. These governments receive their authority based on the consent of the governed. Representative democracies have gradually extended the franchise (right to vote) to nearly all of their adult citizens. The American Revolution led to the establishment of a representative democracy that has served as a model for governments in many other countries.

The development of large-scale industry has resulted in demands for industrial and economic democracy in addition to political democracy. In some countries, the demand that government become fundamentally responsible for public welfare and take a very active role in a country's social and economic life has resulted in a particular form of representative democracy, the social democracy. As of the early 1980s, social democratic countries included India, Sweden, and Costa Rica.

Communism

Those countries with a Communist political system operate on the basis of rule by one political party and state ownership of the major economic institutions. A Communist government claims that the Communist Party represents the interests of the working class. Open opposition to the Communist Party's right to rule is not tolerated. While Communist nations include Yugoslavia, the Soviet Union, China, Cuba, Hungary, and Albania, they have vastly different political systems.

Fascism

This type of political system gained power in Germany (through the Nazi

Party) and in Italy prior to World War II. Unlike the Communist systems, a fascist government usually controls only some of the important economic institutions while most ownership remains in private hands. Fascist governments seek popular support through extreme nationalism, claims of racial superiority, and anti-Communism. A fascist system is characterized by strong-arm dictatorship.

POLITICAL SCIENCE EXERCISE 1 ——————————

Directions: Keep the preceding essay in mind as you read the following political statements. Then answer the questions that follow by filling in the circle that corresponds to the correct answer.

" . . it [the state] by no means believes in the equality of the races, but with their differences it also recognizes their superior and inferior values, and by this recognition it feels the obligation in accordance with the Eternal Will that dominates this universe to promote the victory of the better and stronger, and to demand the submission of the worse and the weaker. . . ."

Adolph Hitler

"The strongest is never strong enough, to be always the master, unless he transforms strength into right, and obedience into duty."

Jean Jacques Rousseau

". . . we may define a republic to be, or at least may bestow that name on, a government which derives all its powers directly or indirectly from the great body of the people, and is administered by persons holding their offices during pleasure for a limited period, or during good behavior."

James Madison

"But when a long train of abuses or usurpations . . . it is their right, it is their duty, to throw off such Government, and to provide new guards for their future security."

U.S. Declaration of Independence

4. When Rousseau states that governments must "transform . . . obedience into duty," he is saying that legitimate governments must develop
   (1) authority
   (2) repression
   (3) blind obedience
   (4) a parliament
   (5) a monarch

5. Hitler's concepts might be used to justify which type of political system?
   (1) Communist
   (2) Constitutional monarchy
   (3) Absolute monarchy
   (4) Representative democracy
   (5) Fascist

6. The excerpt from the U.S. Declaration of Independence is arguing that people who have been unjustly treated by their government have the right of
   (1) coup d'etat
   (2) authority
   (3) power
   (4) revolution
   (5) monarchy

7. Which of the following statements supports Hitler's outlook and contradicts Rousseau's?
   (1) The strong will always prevail.
   (2) Strength must be tempered by justice.
   (3) Never support an unjust government.
   (4) Racial equality is the basis of a strong government.
   (5) Government is subject to the will of the people.

8. James Madison is discussing a basic principle of which political system?
   (1) Fascism
   (2) Representative democracy
   (3) Absolute monarchy
   (4) Communism
   (5) Social democracy

For answers and explanations, see page 170.

2.   THE AMERICAN POLITICAL PROCESS

participatory democracy—a form of democracy in which people have a direct voice and vote in governmental procedings and decision making

plurality—the greatest number of votes in an election, even if it is not a majority

simple majority—50 percent of the votes plus a minimum of one vote

third political parties—traditionally any American political party that is independent of the two major parties

Democracy, Majorities, and Minorities

Barely four and one-half months had passed since more than 50,000 Americans had given their lives on the rolling Civil War battlefield in and around Gettysburg, Pennsylvania. On November 19, 1863, President Abraham Lincoln spoke at the dedication ceremonies for the National Cemetery established on the site of the battlefield. In his Gettysburg Address, Lincoln probably came closer than anyone to defining the central concept of democracy when he referred to it as "government of the people, by the people, and for the people."

Democracy, as Lincoln described it, exists when people govern themselves. It is from this concept that any discussion of the American political process must begin.

Democracy has deep roots in Western political tradition. It has been established in a variety of forms ranging from the personal and participatory democracy of a Greek city-state and New England town meeting to the larger but more impersonal representative democracy that is found in the U.S. political system.

In a smaller **participatory democracy** (such as the town meeting), people have a direct voice and role in decision making. However, in large nations, direct democracy is impractical so democratic government is exercised through the elected representatives of the people; thus the name—representative democracy.

At the heart of any democracy is the concept of majority rule and consent. Majority rule is probably the most practical way of achieving some form of consensus, or group agreement. Certainly, minority rule is less likely to truly represent a consensus, and a unanimous vote would be impractical if not impossible in many situations.

In a representative democracy, such as the United States, a majority is normally needed by a person seeking election to political office, although in some cases only a **plurality**, the greatest number of votes cast, is sufficient to win. In order to pass legislation, a **simple majority** (50 percent plus a minimum of one vote) of representatives is often needed. In some special cases, a number greater than a simple majority may be required, such as two-thirds or three-fifths majorities.

The importance of a majority in American politics should not lead you to believe that the minority viewpoint is totally ignored. Since the United States is a society of many different interests, compromise is often needed to attract even a simple majority of votes to pass a piece of legislation. Representatives must also be conscious of public opinion and of the fact that many minority viewpoints of yesterday have become majority viewpoints today.

Directions: Based upon what you have just read, fill in the circle that corresponds to the correct answer.

9. In the mayoral elections in Big City, Alfred Johnson was elected mayor. The final vote total in the field of three candidates showed

    9 ① ② ③ ④ ⑤

Johnson	101,700
Alvarez	93,201
Smith	45,718

    Mr. Johnson's vote total is best described as a
    (1) plurality
    (2) majority
    (3) simple majority
    (4) consensus
    (5) three-fifths majority

10. All of the owners of condominium apartments in a building meet each month to discuss and decide upon the business of that building. A vote of the majority of owners is necessary to approve any action. This meeting most closely resembles a

     10 ① ② ③ ④ ⑤

     (1) constitutional monarchy
     (2) participatory democracy
     (3) representative democracy
     (4) a court decision
     (5) a minority viewpoint

For answers and explanations, see page 170.

Interest Groups, Political Parties, and Social Movements

Since elected representatives play such an important role in the American political system, the obvious emphasis of the American political process is on electing representatives and influencing their decisions once they are in office. This becomes even more important when you consider that individuals, groups, and organizations have interests that can be aided by government decisions. Today, there are many stages of political activity between the desires and needs of citizens and final government decisions.

Interest Groups

Organized interest groups, such as unions, business groups, and PTAs, usually articulate their interests in an action-oriented political program. In recent years, single-issue groups such as those for or against abortion, prayer in schools, or nuclear disarmament have also become increasingly important. For example, a person deeply worried about the nuclear arms race may feel ineffective when he voices his concerns as an individual. To be more effective, he might join together with others with similar interests and concerns to formulate a program of political action on the issue of nuclear disarmament.

Interest groups do more than draw up political programs. They also increase the power of individuals by pulling them together and bringing their numbers and influence into the political system. They may do this by raising campaign funds to aid a candidate who is supportive of their position and by providing volunteers for that candidate's election campaign. They may also put pressure on officials (this is called *lobbying*) by writing letters, making visits, and carrying out demonstrations or publicity campaigns.

Political Parties

National political parties are the next level in the structure of American politics. The U.S. Constitution did not provide for political parties. However, the many conflicts over the direction of national policy in the 1790s made it necessary to have organizations that could harness the energy and efforts of different interest groups and channel these into political action.

Two major parties, the Republicans and Democrats, now dominate the U.S. political system and have done so since the 1860s. These two parties have been particularly effective in organizing coalitions of interest groups. To do this, they develop compromise programs that can unite a broad coalition and hold it together in order to campaign for the party's candidates.

Political parties use national conventions to select presidential candidates. The delegates to national conventions are elected at local levels in party caucuses or through primary elections preceding the conventions. The national party platform is also adopted at the convention. The platform is a statement of what the party stands for.

In a complex society like ours, the interest groups and political parties are very crucial to an effective democracy. The individual citizen cannot have much influence on the direction of politics without becoming part of an organized political group. Of course, the citizen can and should exercise her right to vote for candidates, but only through participation in the process of defining issues can citizens meaningfully affect what choices they will have at election time.

Professional politicians play an important role in the political process. The term *politician* has almost become a dirty word. However, politicians are the experts at building the coalitions necessary for getting things done, and they usually have finely tuned senses that detect which way the winds of public opinion are blowing. They are seldom heroes, even viewed by some as scoundrels, but they are indispensable to the American political process.

The American method of building political coalitions has led to a very slow-moving and stable political process. The majority of people vote repeatedly for the same party, and they generally vote for the same party their parents did. However, in recent elections, an increasing number of voters have come to consider themselves "independents," and many old voting patterns are breaking down. For example, recently, the Republican Party has been picking up strength among traditionally Democratic working class voters.

Social Movements

Besides the two major parties, there are a wide variety of other so-called **third political parties** in the United States whose interests represent a wide political spectrum. (These "third" parties include the Libertarian, Communist, American Independent, Prohibitionist, Socialist, Citizens, Peace and Freedom parties, etc.) Nevertheless, the two major parties have maintained their domination of American politics because they have incorporated some popular "third" party demands. The major parties have also articulated a far broader appeal to voters than the narrower interests usually represented by third parties.

Among the other forces at work breaking down traditional voting patterns are the activities of social movements. These movements have a long history in the U.S., from Shay's movement of rebellious debtor farmers in Massachusetts in the 1780s through the abolitionists, the Farmers' Alliance, and labor, civil rights, and women's, peace, and environmental movements, to the New Right.

These movements mobilize people who feel very strongly about a particular issue and who are willing to break up past electoral coalitions in order to get their ideas across. This willingness to disrupt the status quo either leads to the formation of new parties or forces the major parties to adopt some of their ideas. Usually, one of the two major parties absorbs a new coalition and confines these changes to the existing two-party structure. The last significant formation of a new party was the founding of the Republican Party in the 1850s.

It is through the activities of social movements and interest groups that the limits of American democracy have constantly been expanded to allow for more and more groups to participate. The American political process has been a ceaseless struggle to define interests, to articulate and gain support for them, and finally, to form election coalitions capable of winning power and acting on those interests.

Directions: Based upon what you have just read, fill in the circle that corresponds to the correct answer.

11. According to this essay, what role do politicians play in American politics?
    (1) They obstruct it to gain personal advantages.
    (2) They corrupt it with their ambitions.
    (3) They build coalitions to get things done.
    (4) They cause too many splits in coalitions.
    (5) They are all crooks.

    11 ① ② ③ ④ ⑤

12. American citizens can play an effective part in politics
    (1) by staying independent from interest groups
    (2) by refusing to take part in partisan politics
    (3) by staying clear of political parties
    (4) by participating in interest groups
    (5) by refusing to compromise any principles

    12 ① ② ③ ④ ⑤

13. The essay views the political role of American third parties as
    (1) a positive source of change in American politics
    (2) very disruptive to the American political process
    (3) comical because Americans will never elect Libertarians or Communists
    (4) a serious threat to the two-party system that is at the heart of American democracy
    (5) unnecessary when Americans' interests are already well represented by Republicans and Democrats

    13 ① ② ③ ④ ⑤

PARTY IDENTIFICATIONS, 1960–1976
(in percentages)

Party Identification	Presidential Election Year				
	1960	1964	1968	1972	1976
Strong Democrat	21	27	20	15	15
Weak Democrat	25	25	25	26	25
Independent Democrat	8	8	9	10	12
Independent	8	8	11	13	14
Independent Republican	7	6	9	11	10
Weak Republican	13	13	14	13	14
Strong Republican	14	11	10	10	9
Other	4	2	2	2	1
Total	100	100	100	100	100

14. What can you conclude about voter identification from
the data in this table?   14 ① ② ③ ④ ⑤
   (1) By 1976, the two major parties had grown
       tremendously.
   (2) By 1976, the Democrats had lost influence but the
       Republicans had not.
   (3) By 1976, the Republicans had lost influence, while
       the Democrats had grown.
   (4) By 1976, people were more likely to consider
       themselves independent than to identify strongly
       with a party.
   (5) Most people support a third political party.

For answers and explanations, see page 170.

POLITICAL SCIENCE EXERCISE 2

Directions: Read the following passage and fill in the circle that corresponds to the correct answer.

Voter Turnout

The significance of the low rates of electoral participation in this
country lies in the fact that a relatively small number of people
who vote can control elections. Only about 30 million votes are
required for a popular majority in a presidential election. Most
5 close congressional races are decided by less than 7,000 votes.
Primary elections and state and local races are often decided by

much smaller margins. In the 1982 elections, a shift of only 45,000 votes would have changed the outcome in five Senate races won by Republican candidates. Low-income people could wield sub-
10   stantial political power—if they exercised their voting rights.

Nearly 27 million citizens make less than $10,000 per year. The food stamp program alone—one of the programs slashed most drastically over the last two years—serves more than 10 million adults, including 7 million women and one-third of all minority
15   household heads. It is astonishing that the President proposed (and Congress readily agreed) a series of cuts in programs with such a massive constituency. Compare the protests that have greeted every hint of cuts in Social Security. There is a simple explanation: senior citizens vote; low-income citizens don't—and
20   our elected officials know it.

Self-reporting surveys taken after mid-term elections over the last decade show that only 25 to 35 percent of eligible low-income people even claimed to have voted. This figure would be substan- tially lower if we could separate out the "low-income-with-
25   substantial-assets" populations (principally elderly people whose incomes have fallen but who do not live as if they were poor). This turnout rate stands in sharp contrast to the 70 to 75 percent turnout among persons making over $25,000 per year. When low- income people fail to vote in numbers commensurate with their
30   presence in the population, their interests are ignored.

Sanford Newman, "Project VOTE!"

15. This passage points out that, as a result of voter turnout patterns,

15 ① ② ③ ④ ⑤

   (1)   the elderly do not have much influence
   (2)   the poor have too much influence on elections
   (3)   minorities have too much influence on elections
   (4)   higher-income people have little influence on elections
   (5)   poor people do not have much influence on elections

16. We can conclude, based on this passage, that if lower-income people voted in large numbers,

16 ① ② ③ ④ ⑤

   (1)   social welfare programs, like food stamps, would probably be expanded
   (2)   social welfare programs, like food stamps, would probably be decreased
   (3)   Social Security payments would be decreased
   (4)   Congress would not pay any attention to them
   (5)   inflation would become a big problem

For answers and explanations, see page 171.

3. THE UNITED STATES CONSTITUTION

K
E
Y

W
O
R
D
S

federal system—the sharing of power between the states and the central government

checks and balances—the arrangement among the branches of the federal government that prevents any one branch from dominating the other two

Bill of Rights—first ten amendments to the U.S. Constitution that enumerate the freedoms and rights of individuals

Reasons for the Constitution

During the American Revolution, the Continental Congress adopted the Articles of Confederation as the guiding constitution of the new country. The articles, adopted in 1781, emphasized decentralization of power and tied the states together in a loose confederation. A national congress was established with some duties but with almost no power to enforce its decisions on the states. This limitation of power was intended to stop the rise of a powerful central authority.

The postrevolutionary years (1783–1789) are often called the "time of troubles." The American economy was in a shambles after the disruptions of the war, and there was a serious economic depression. The national government had no power to tax or regulate commerce between the states. The articles did not provide for a national chief executive or judiciary and left judicial matters to the states. Interstate commerce was carried on with the greatest difficulty since there was no standard currency. This led to the use of a confusing variety of different currencies. To complicate matters further, states often charged their own taxes on goods.

Compounding these difficulties was the serious plight of the debtor classes, especially the farmers. In Massachusetts, armed farmers, heavily in debt, took part in Shay's Rebellion (1786) and forcibly took over court-rooms to prevent mortgage foreclosures. Although the rebellion was finally put down with little bloodshed, Shay's Rebellion pointed to the need for a strong central government that could deal with such internal uprisings. The problems facing the new American nation made it clear that the Articles of Confederation needed to be changed drastically or scrapped altogether.

In order to deal with some aspects of the economic crisis, especially problems of interstate commerce, meetings were held among some states in 1785 and 1786. These meetings eventually led to a call for a Constitutional Convention to amend the Articles of Confederation. The convention call was subsequently endorsed by the Confederation Congress, and the Constitutional Convention opened in Philadelphia in May 1787, with fifty-five delegates representing twelve states. Instead of merely revising the articles, the convention scrapped them and produced a new constitution that remains to this day the basis for our system of government.

Directions: Based upon what you have just read, fill in the circle that corresponds to the correct answer.

17. Which of the following was a major weakness of the Articles of Confederation?

17 ① ② ③ ④ ⑤

   (1) The articles provided for a central government that was too strong.
   (2) The articles put too much emphasis on the federal courts.
   (3) The articles provided for a central government that was almost without power.
   (4) The articles promoted laws that always helped the debtor class.
   (5) The articles based the economy on a gold standard rather than on paper money.

18. Which of the following was a major reason for calling meetings among states prior to the adoption of the Constitution?

18 ① ② ③ ④ ⑤

   (1) Raising an army
   (2) Regulating interstate commerce
   (3) Increasing export trade
   (4) Helping debtor farmers
   (5) Organizing Shay's Rebellion

For answers and explanations, see page 171.

Debate over the Constitution

A central issue in the Constitutional Convention concerned the division of power between the central government and the states. The final Constitution represented a victory of centralized power over states' rights. The government in Washington increased its powers and gained the right to tax, create an army and navy, control foreign trade, make treaties, and control currency. The states, however, still maintained substantial responsibilities. The particular kind of arrangement that divides power between a central government and the states is called a **federal system**.

The convention attempted to protect against overcentralization of power by basing the new government on the separation of powers. A legislative branch, made up of a House of Representatives and the Senate, was to enact laws. An executive branch, headed by the president, was to administer the government. A federal judicial (court) system was created to settle disputes and legal matters. Thus, a system of **checks and balances** was created in order to prevent any single branch of government from dominating the others.

Another crucial issue at the convention concerned the fair distribution of the power between large and small states. This was resolved by giving each state equal representation in the Senate and basing representation in the House of Representatives on the size of the state's population. In this way, the House protected the rights of large states and the Senate protected the rights of small states.

Slavery was another serious issue in the making of a new Constitution. Several clauses were added to protect the institution of slavery so as to gain crucial southern support. Slave-holding states were allowed to count slaves as three-fifths of their actual numbers when determining representation in the House of Representatives. As a concession to northern states, the three-fifths count was also used in determining the size of population for the purpose of direct taxation.

Together, these measures were known as the *Three-fifths Compromise*. The compromise meant that slaves were not considered citizens, only as pieces of property who had no rights. The Three-fifths Compromise substantially strengthened the power of slave states in the House of Representatives. The Constitution also granted protection to the slave trade until 1808 and required that fugitive slaves be returned to their masters.

The finished Constitution was sent to conventions in each of the thirteen states. In order to become the law of the land, it needed to be ratified by nine states. There was some popular opposition to the document since many Americans believed that it gave too much power to the national government. Many people also opposed the Constitution because it did not contain any guarantees for rights of individual citizens. The supporters of the Constitution, known as the Federalists, were led by Alexander Hamilton, James Madison, and John Jay. They wrote a series of articles, *The Federalist Papers*, in which they argued for ratification. A majority of the leaders of the Revolution, including George Washington and Benjamin Franklin, also supported the Constitution. After a very close struggle in some states and easy victories in others, eleven states ratified the Constitution, and it became effective March 1789.

Amendments to the Constitution

The issue of the protection of the individual citizen's rights dominated the first session of the new Congress in 1789. During the drive for ratification, the Federalists had been forced by popular pressure to promise their support for a Bill of Rights in the form of amendments to the Constitution. Congress submitted the first ten constitutional amendments to the states for ratification, and they were approved by 1791.

These first ten amendments, which became known as the **Bill of Rights**, form the basis of individual rights and liberties in American society. These amendments guarantee freedom of speech and the press, the right to assemble and petition the government for redress of grievances, the right to keep and bear arms, protection against unreasonable search and seizure, the right to trial by jury, the right to due process and protection against self-incrimination, the right to a public trial, the right to have an attorney, protection against excessive bail or unusual punishment, and separation of church and state.

Since the Bill of Rights, sixteen more amendments have been added to the Constitution. The procedure for changing the Constitution was made difficult to ensure that it would not be easily tampered with or abused. Amendments must be proposed by a two-thirds majority vote of both houses of Congress. Otherwise, two-thirds of the state legislatures can ask Congress to call a convention for proposing amendments. Any amendment must be approved by either the legislatures or special conventions in three-fourths of the states. Many proposed amendments have never been ratified because of this difficult procedure. For instance, the Equal Rights Amendment was defeated in 1982 because it fell several states short of the required thirty-eight states needed for ratification.

All amendments that have been adopted have originated in Congress and have been ratified by the state legislatures. Among the more important are the thirteenth (1865), abolishing slavery; the fourteenth (1868), granting citizenship to the former slaves; the fifteenth (1870), guaranteeing all citizens the right to vote; the sixteenth (1913), establishing the federal income tax; the nineteenth (1920), giving women the right to vote; and the twenty-sixth (1971), lowering the voting age to eighteen.

The actual Constitution, even with amendments, is a short document, probably shorter than the bylaws of many organizations. It has vague guidelines concerning the powers and functions of the different levels of government. However, its flexibility has allowed it to survive as a symbol of national unity, while the concrete meanings of its various paragraphs have constantly evolved as the country has grown and changed.

Directions: Based upon what you have just read, fill in the circle that corresponds to the correct answer.

19. All adopted amendments to the U.S. Constitution have originated in   19 ① ② ③ ④ ⑤
    (1) state legislatures
    (2) state constitutional conventions
    (3) the presidency
    (4) national referendums
    (5) the U.S. Congress

20. Legislation that proposed to make the Supreme Court   20 ① ② ③ ④ ⑤
    subordinate to Congress would go against the system of
    (1) consent of the governed
    (2) federalism
    (3) checks and balances
    (4) proportional representation
    (5) universal franchise

21. A proposal that would reduce each state government to   21 ① ② ③ ④ ⑤
    a branch of the federal government would
    (1) be called a federal system
    (2) mean an end to the federal system
    (3) be similar to the Articles of Confederation
    (4) go against the separation of powers
    (5) not be a constitutional question

22. A constitutional amendment to eliminate the House of   22 ① ② ③ ④ ⑤
    Representatives and keep the Senate would go against
    the interests of which states?
    (1) The most populous states
    (2) The least populous states
    (3) The newest states
    (4) The oldest states
    (5) The Sunbelt states

23. Which of the following rights is guaranteed by an   23 ① ② ③ ④ ⑤
    amendment to the Constitution?
    (1) Right to employment
    (2) Right to education
    (3) Right to decent medical care
    (4) Right to housing
    (5) Right to freedom of speech

For answers and explanations, see page 171.

POLITICAL SCIENCE EXERCISE 3 ━━━━━━━━━━━━━

Directions: Read the following passage and fill in the circle that corresponds to the correct answer.

Through a variety of Supreme Court decisions, many of the
freedoms in the Bill of Rights have been upheld as the court has
taken steps to define, limit, or expand upon the meanings of the
amendments. For example, we do know, as a result of one court

decision, that the freedom of speech does not guarantee the right to shout "Fire!" in a crowded theater, but it does guarantee the right to espouse unpopular beliefs. Below are some brief examples from the hundreds of episodes in the court battles over the amendments in the Bill of Rights.

From the First Amendment,

". . . Congress shall make no law
abridging . . . the right of the people
peaceably to assemble, and to petition
the government for redress of
grievances."

In 1937, the court clarified the meaning of *freedom of assembly*. One state had, in effect, limited the assembly of a political group, when the assembly was not for the purpose of petitioning the government. In the *DeJonge* v. *Oregon* case, the Supreme Court ruled that freedom of assembly was *not* limited only to those who wished to petition the government.

From the First Amendment,

". . . Congress shall make no
law . . . abridging the freedom of speech
or of the press."

The Founding Fathers could not have imagined that this amendment would become the central issue in the debate over the dissemination of what some perceive as obscene or pornographic materials. In 1946, the Supreme Court prevented the Postmaster General from denying second-class postal rates to *Esquire* magazine. In 1962, the court overturned a government practice of treating homosexual magazines as obscene matter and barring them from the mails. However, the Supreme Court has all but sidestepped the issue of what constitutes pornography and has left this up to what are called "community standards."

From the Fifth Amendment,

". . . No person shall be . . . deprived of
life, liberty, or property without
due process of law. . . ."

In 1964, the Supreme Court interpreted this to include a right that Americans cherish—the right to travel freely. In *Aptheker* v. *the Secretary of State*, the Supreme Court struck down federal laws that forbade American citizens who were members of the Communist Party from holding a passport. Prior to this ruling, a Communist could have been prosecuted for committing a felony by applying for a passport. In making this decision, the court linked the right to travel with the broader issues of free speech and association.

24. The main idea of this passage is that   24 ① ② ③ ④ ⑤
   (1) Supreme Court decisions have served to uphold the constitutional rights of people with controversial opinions or preferences
   (2) freedom of speech has always been favorably observed by governmental bodies
   (3) the government should stop persecuting Communists and violating their rights
   (4) the Bill of Rights should have clearly spelled out individual rights and freedoms
   (5) the courts have always ruled in favor of the Bill of Rights

25. The Supreme Court has stated that a person standing in   25 ① ② ③ ④ ⑤
   a crowded theater shouting "Fire!" at the top of his voice is
   (1) disturbing the movie being shown
   (2) playing a joke
   (3) exceeding his right to free speech
   (4) exercising his freedom of speech
   (5) probably drunk

26. The Supreme Court's decisions on obscene materials   26 ① ② ③ ④ ⑤
   have been based on its interpretation of freedom of
   (1) assembly
   (2) religion
   (3) political beliefs
   (4) sexual preference
   (5) speech and the press

For answers and explanations, see page 171.

4. BRANCHES OF GOVERNMENT

K E Y   W O R D S

veto—the presidential power to refuse to sign into law a bill that has been approved by Congress; can be overridden by Congress

pocket veto—an automatic veto of a bill not signed by the president within ten days of a congressional adjournment

judicial review—the power of the Supreme Court to rule on the constitutionality of laws

As described in the previous essay, the new Constitution set up a national government with three different branches. In order to prevent an overaccumulation of power, it divided power and functions among the executive, legislative, and judicial branches. The Constitution also instituted a sophisticated system of checks and balances to ensure that one branch of government would be unable to accumulate enough power to dominate any other.

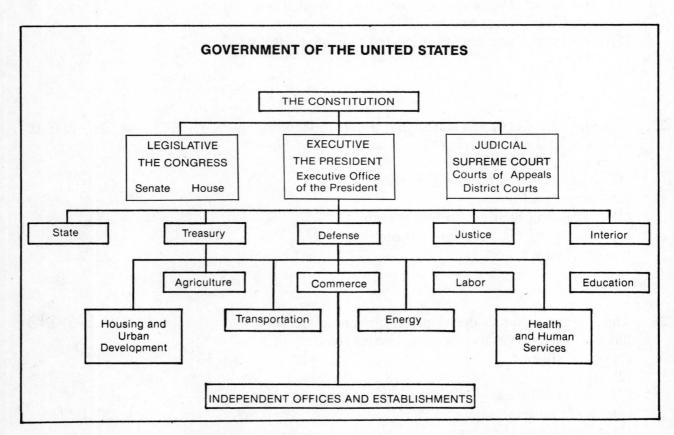

The Executive Branch

The executive branch is responsible for administering the day-to-day activities of the government. The president, who is the head of the executive branch, must be at least thirty-five years old and a natural born citizen of the U.S. The presidential term is four years, and any individual is limited to two terms by the Twenty-second Amendment.

The president has the responsibility of organizing the executive branch by appointing, with the advice and consent of the Senate, all of the major executive positions, including his own cabinet officers. The cabinet officers, called *secretaries*, are the heads of major government agencies, such as State, Defense, Justice, Agriculture, Labor, Housing, and Urban Development. The executive branch also includes federal agencies, such as the Environmental Protection Agency (EPA) and the Federal Trade Commission (FTC).

Article II of the Constitution gives the president the power to see that "the laws be faithfully executed." The executive branch is responsible for enforcing acts of Congress, court decisions, and treaties.

The president also can issue proclamations and executive orders. These are essentially legislative or lawmaking powers that have been delegated to the president either by law or by court decision. Lincoln's Emancipation Proclamation is one of the most famous examples of this power of the presidency.

All bills passed by Congress must be submitted to the president. If he signs the bill, it becomes law. However, he can refuse to sign the bill and return it to Congress; this is called a **veto**. Congress may override a veto by a two-thirds vote of both houses of Congress. However, if the president does not return the bill within ten days, it automatically becomes a law, unless Congress adjourns during that period. If Congress adjourns during that ten-day period and the president does not sign the bill, he has effected **a pocket veto**, which cannot be overridden by Congress.

Traditionally, presidents have used their constitutional responsibility to sum up the "state of the union" in order to present their views on where the country is going, where it should be, and how to get there. In so doing, the president develops his own legislative program, which he presents to Congress. This has given the president a measure of initiative in dealing with Congress because it is easier for him to develop a unified program than it is for a Congress that is divided along sectional and party lines.

The role of the president as commander in chief of the armed forces has strengthened the power of the executive in foreign and domestic affairs. In this century, the U.S.'s involvement in four major wars and in lesser military actions has been used to strengthen the office of the presidency. Recent presidents have also used appeals to national security interests to hinder congressional review of some foreign and domestic activities, such as in the Watergate incidents.

Another key figure in the executive branch is the vice president. It is expected that the vice president should have the same qualifications as the president, since the vice president would take over the office of the presidency if the chief executive should either die or become severely incapacitated.

Both the president and the vice president are chosen for office by the electoral college. This body is made up of electors from each state who have pledged to cast their votes for a certain candidate. When the voters cast a ballot for a presidential candidate and running mate, they are really choosing a slate of electors that is pledged to vote for the candidate in the electoral college in December. It is possible for an individual to receive more popular votes than his opponent but fail to be elected president by the electoral college. This has occurred three times in American history: when John Quincy Adams became president in 1824, when Rutherford Hayes was elected in 1876, and when Grover Cleveland became president in 1888.

Directions: Based upon what you have just read, fill in the circle that corresponds to the correct answer.

27. Which of the following is a lawmaking power of the president?
    (1) Judicial review
    (2) Joint resolution
    (3) Executive order
    (4) Writ of *habeas corpus*
    (5) State of the Union address

    27 ① ② ③ ④ ⑤

28. If the president should die in office, who is next in line to become president?
    (1) Speaker of the House
    (2) Chief justice
    (3) Senate majority leader
    (4) Vice president
    (5) Secretary of state

    28 ① ② ③ ④ ⑤

29. "The President of the United States is to have power to return a bill, which shall have passed the two branches of the legislature for reconsideration; but the bill so returned is not to become a law unless upon reconsideration, it be approved by two-thirds of both houses."

    Alexander Hamilton, *The Federalist Papers*

    To which of the following processes was Hamilton referring?
    (1) Pocket veto
    (2) Presidential veto and congressional override
    (3) Appointment of justices
    (4) Executive order
    (5) Confirmation of appointee

    29 ① ② ③ ④ ⑤

For answers and explanations, see page 171.

Legislative Branch

The legislative branch of the federal government, the Congress, is responsible for writing the basic laws of the country. The U.S. Constitution created a strong legislative branch.

The Congress is a bicameral legislature, meaning that there are two houses of Congress: the House of Representatives with 435 members and the Senate with 100 members. A representative in the House is elected for two years, must be at least twenty-five years of age, and also must have been a U.S. citizen for seven years. A senator is elected for six years, must be at least thirty years old, and must have been a U.S. citizen for nine years.

Powers

Congress has been granted a long list of specific powers by the Constitution. Perhaps the most important powers are those to levy taxes and appropriate government funds. While the president has the responsibility to submit a budget proposal, Congress has the authority to write and submit the actual budget to the president. All revenue bills must originate in the House, although the Senate must also consider them. In this way, Congress actually controls the purse strings of government.

Among other congressional powers is the power to override a presidential veto with a two-thirds vote of both houses. Congress also has a major role in the process of amending the Constitution. Congress has several judicial powers, including impeachment, and it also organizes the federal court system.

Some of the powers of Congress operate as a check upon the executive branch. Congress creates and defines the functions of the departments and agencies in the executive branch. Congress also controls the appropriations for those departments and has the power of investigation over numerous areas inside and outside of the government, including the executive branch. A congressional committee, like the court system, has the power to subpoena witnesses and can cite uncooperative witnesses with contempt of court. When Congress actually assumes a "watchdog" role over the executive branch, it can exert a great deal of influence.

Organization

The Speaker of the House presides over the meetings of the House of Representatives and is generally responsible for organizing its activities. The Speaker is a member of the majority party. The Senate is presided over by the vice president, who has little real power to direct the Senate and can cast only tie-breaking votes. The majority party elects a Senate Majority Leader, who is the main director of legislative activity in the Senate.

Both houses of Congress are organized into committees to carry out the task of researching, holding hearings, and writing legislation. All legislation must go through a committee before it can be considered for a vote. If a committee chairman strongly opposes a piece of legislation, he can use his power to prevent it from reaching a vote. If he supports it, he may be able to speed the legislation through the committee and onto the floor. Obviously, much of the real politics in Congress takes place at the committee level. Among the more important committees are the House Ways and Means Committee, which considers revenue bills, and the Senate Committee on Foreign Relations, which reviews all treaties.

The political party that has the majority in each house of Congress organizes the committees and other activities in its respective house. The majority party determines committee chairmen. For example, in the 98th Congress (1983–84), the Republicans used their majority in the Senate to organize that house, and the Democrats used their majority to organize the House of Representatives.

Directions: Based upon what you have just read, fill in the circle that corresponds to the correct answer.

30. The House of Representatives has the right to initiate   30 ① ② ③ ④ ⑤
    (1) treaties
    (2) all revenue bills
    (3) ambassadorial appointments
    (4) court appointments
    (5) cabinet officers' appointments

31. A period of international turbulence and the increased   31 ① ② ③ ④ ⑤
    use of American armed forces would probably most
    increase the power and influence of which of the
    following in foreign affairs?
    (1) The Senate
    (2) The House
    (3) The presidency
    (4) The courts
    (5) The cabinet

32. What power can Congress <u>not</u> use to influence the   32 ① ② ③ ④ ⑤
    work of executive departments?
    (1) budget appropriations
    (2) pocket veto
    (3) impeachment
    (4) subpoena
    (5) constitutional amendments

For answers and explanations, see page 171.

The Judiciary

The judiciary is the branch of the federal government that is responsible for interpreting laws. The primary responsibility of the federal court system is to hear cases involving federal law.

At the head of the federal courts is the Supreme Court in Washington, D.C., which consists of a chief justice and eight associate justices. These justices are appointed by the president with the approval of the Senate. They serve for life and can be impeached only for misconduct. The major function of the Supreme Court is to hear appeals of lower federal court decisions and from state courts when the questions may involve points of law or constitutionality. The Constitution gives the Supreme Court original jurisdiction (right to hear a case first) only in "all cases affecting ambassadors, other public ministers, and those in which a State shall be a party."

Below the Supreme Court are the federal circuit courts of appeals that hear appeals and review decisions of the federal district court and federal administrative bodies. At the lowest level are the federal district trial courts. All federal judges are appointed by the president.

Probably the single most important and controversial power of the Supreme Court is its power of **judicial review**—the power to rule on the constitutionality of laws passed by the legislative branch or on actions taken by the executive branch. The Constitution did not clearly give the Supreme Court this right, and it took several court decisions to clarify this power. The court determined that the framers of the Constitution believed that the courts had a right to decide on the constitutionality of laws, and Alexander Hamilton argued forcefully for this right in *The Federalist Papers*. Who would interpret the nation's fundamental law—the Constitution? The legislators? No! The executive? No! The judges? Yes! The power of judicial review was first used by the Supreme Court in 1803 in the *Marbury* v. *Madison* case when the court refused to enforce a law that it believed was unconstitutional.

The power of the Supreme Court to rule on the constitutionality of certain laws and practices has become an important part of our system of government. It has also enabled the judiciary to have the power to become an equal partner in the three-way separation of powers in the federal government. American law has evolved and changed over the years as a result of various Supreme Court interpretations of the law and the Constitution. The Supreme Court under Chief Justice Earl Warren (1953–69) was extremely active in expanding the powers of judicial review. However, in recent years, the Supreme Court has been gradually reversing that trend.

Directions: Based upon what you have just read, fill in the circle that corresponds to the correct answer.

33. The U.S. Constitution clearly gives what powers to the   33 ① ② ③ ④ ⑤
    Supreme Court?
    (1) Judicial review of congressional actions
    (2) Judicial review of presidential actions
    (3) Original jurisdiction in some cases involving
        ambassadors
    (4) Original jurisdiction over all state laws
    (5) Right to establish lower courts

34. Federal judges obtain their positions   34 ① ② ③ ④ ⑤
    (1) from the House of Representatives
    (2) by popular election
    (3) from the Chief Justice of the Supreme Court
    (4) by presidential appointment
    (5) by appointment by state governors

35. "The interpretation of the laws is the proper and   35 ① ② ③ ④ ⑤
    peculiar province of the courts. A constitution is, in
    fact, and must be regarded by the judges as, a
    fundamental law. It therefore belongs to them to
    ascertain its meaning as well as the meaning of any
    particular act proceeding from the legislative body."

    Alexander Hamilton

    Hamilton is presenting an argument in favor of which
    of the following?
    (1) Impeachment
    (2) Judicial review
    (3) Original jurisdiction
    (4) Executive privilege
    (5) Writ of *habeas corpus*

36. The Supreme Court's developing power of judicial   36 ① ② ③ ④ ⑤
    review shows that the U.S. Constitution
    (1) is an outdated document
    (2) is not open to interpretation
    (3) is open to significant interpretation
    (4) severely limits the power of the courts to review
        congressional action
    (5) severely limits the power of the courts to review
        presidential action

For answers and explanations, see page 172.

POLITICAL SCIENCE EXERCISE 4

Directions: Read the following passage and fill in the circle that corresponds to the correct answer.

The Supreme Court Reverses Itself

Men make the laws, and men interpret the laws according to their own beliefs and the influences of their society. Laws are always affected by changing conditions. What the Constitution "really means" is affected by such influences and is subject to judicial
5　review at any given time. The political and historical character of court decisions has led to some stunning reversals of previous Supreme Court decisions.

The influence of surrounding conditions has figured prominently in the Supreme Court's decisions on racial segregation. For
10　example, look at the two cases below:

1. In 1896, in the midst of a period of extreme white supremacist prejudice, the Supreme Court ruled, in *Plessy* v. *Ferguson*, that segregation in public facilities, including public schools, was constitutional so long as the facilities were "separate but equal."
15　At this time, many social scientists espoused theories extolling the superiority of whites and the inferiority of non-whites.

2. In 1954, the Supreme Court reversed the *Plessy* v. *Ferguson* decision in its new decision arising from the *Brown* v. *the Board of Education* case. In the Brown decision, the Supreme Court
20　declared that "separate but equal" schools were unconstitutional and violated provisions granting equal protection under the law. The written Constitution had not substantially changed since 1896, but the political situation in the U.S. and in the world had.

The court has reversed previous decisions in several other
25　areas, such as the rights of unions, of state and federal governments, and of suspected criminals. The fact that fundamental change is effected bloodlessly, through the courts, is representative of the stability of American politics.

37.　According to this passage, the decisions of the Supreme Court are

37 ① ② ③ ④ ⑤

(1)　influenced by politics and by historical developments
(2)　based entirely on the written Constitution
(3)　not subject to major revisions
(4)　very consistent over time
(5)　not influenced by politics and historical developments

38. The passage argues that the *Plessy* v. *Ferguson* decision
was very heavily influenced by
    (1) politicians
    (2) white supremacist beliefs
    (3) a need for separate schools
    (4) the end of the colonization movement
    (5) the civil rights movement

38 ① ② ③ ④ ⑤

For answers and explanations, see page 172.

POLITICAL SCIENCE EXERCISE 5

Directions: Read the following passage and fill in the circle that corresponds to the correct answer.

The Watergate Crisis

During the 1972 presidential campaign, President Nixon's Committee to Re-Elect the President (CRP) approved a burglary of the Democratic Party headquarters in the Watergate building in Washington, D.C. The burglars, ex-CIA men, had intended to
5 install a phone tap to overhear useful information on Democratic Party campaign strategy. After their discovery by a building security guard, the intruders were caught and arrested.

The Nixon administration engaged in two years of illegal and unconstitutional attempts to cover up the connection between the
10 burglary and the president's office. The president used protecting "national security matters" as the reason he could not provide information about the case. However, revelations by White House aides, such as John Dean, showed that the president had used the Internal Revenue Service to harass political opponents and that
15 presidential spying on political adversaries was common.

The discovery that the president had secret tapes of White House conversations set the final drama in motion. A Senate committee and the Watergate special prosecutor went to federal court to get the tapes. The president claimed he did not have to
20 surrender them because of "executive privilege" and "national security."

However, the Supreme Court ruled that claiming presidential privilege "cannot prevail over the fundamental demands of due process of law." Nixon had to give up the tapes, which revealed
25 his role in the cover-up of the Watergate investigation. On August 8, 1974, facing impeachment, President Nixon resigned from office.

The crisis was the direct result of the growth of the "imperial presidency." Evidence unearthed during Watergate and subse-
30 quent investigations showed a growing pattern in which U.S. presidents, from John Kennedy on, used the CIA and FBI for private spying and "dirty tricks" on domestic opponents. Presidents had also been using the CIA, without congressional oversight, for undercover international operations. The outcome of
35 the Watergate crisis reaffirmed the power of the legislative and judicial branches to exercise checks upon the powers of the presidency.

39. The author believes that President Nixon, like other presidents, used the claim of "national security"
    (1) for personal political purposes
    (2) to build bipartisan support for national defense
    (3) to build national support for arms increases
    (4) to work closely with Congress
    (5) to work closely with the federal courts

39 ① ② ③ ④ ⑤

40. Watergate was an institutional crisis that was resolved by reaffirming the principle of
    (1) executive mandate
    (2) federalism
    (3) bipartisanship
    (4) proportional representation
    (5) checks and balances

40 ① ② ③ ④ ⑤

For answers and explanations, see page 172.

5. STATE AND LOCAL GOVERNMENT

KEY WORDS

home rule laws—state laws that provide local governments with a great deal of self-government

direct initiative—allows citizens to draft laws by obtaining enough signatures on a petition to present the law directly to the voters

referendum—the mechanism by which voters can repeal legislation by voting on it in general elections

recall—permits citizens to vote an official out of office before his or her term is over

Under the American federal system, the central government and the states share political power. The central federal government has the power to tax, make war, and regulate interstate and foreign commerce. In addition, it has the right to "make all laws which shall be necessary and proper for" carrying out the powers granted to it under the Constitution. Those powers not specifically granted to the federal government are reserved for the states.

While the Constitution has set a general framework, the actual relations between local governments and the central government have been evolving continually. The general trend has been toward increasing power for the central government. The rise of a national economy, several major wars, the trauma of the Depression, complicated international relations, and serious urban problems have all helped to create a strong federal government.

State Governments

State governments follow an organizational form similar to the federal government. Each state has a written constitution and a governor who is the chief executive officer. All states have a bicameral (two-house) legislature, except Nebraska, which has a unicameral (one-house) legislature. All states have established state court systems. Nevertheless, there are wide variations among the states as to specifics of government operation. Although these differences cannot be summarized easily, one common trend is toward increased power in the hands of governors.

States provide a wide range of public services. They maintain highways, regulate intrastate commerce, and provide for both public education and public welfare.

One of the most important powers of the states is the creation of laws governing the formation and powers of local governments. Counties, towns, and cities are the legal creation of the states. Many states have strong **home rule laws** that provide the local governments with a great deal of freedom once they have been incorporated as legal bodies.

Many states also provide for initiative and referendum voting. The **direct initiative** allows citizens to draft proposed laws, and if they can obtain the required number of signatures on a petition, they can have the law decided on directly by the state's voters. The **referendum** allows voters to repeal legislation that has already been passed by voting on it in general elections. Several states also provide for **recall**, a special election that permits citizens to vote an official out of office before his or her term is over.

Local Governments

County governments usually have two functions. They enforce state law and perform whatever other duties the state may assign.

In county governments, power is usually vested in an elected board of supervisors or commissioners, which usually combines both legislative and executive powers. County governments take care of roads, police protection, some public schools, public health, and parks. They are usually financed by property taxes and by help from the state.

A city is governed under a charter that is granted by the state legislature. The most important forms of city government are (1) strong mayor–weak city council, (2) weak mayor–strong city council, and (3) city manager–city council. Under a strong-mayor form of government, the mayor has wide authority to run the local government, including the right to veto council actions. Under the strong-council form, the mayor is usually reduced to a figurehead, and the real authority lies with the council. The manager-council form usually has an elected council that appoints a city manager to be the head of city administration. The council retains the power to make all policy.

The development of great urban centers has caused tremendous growth in local government. In 1979, all state governments employed 2.9 million people, and local government employed 7.8 million. At the same time, the federal government employed 4.9 million people. The state governments had budgets totaling $257 billion in 1980, while the federal government was spending $579 billion.

Directions: Based upon what you have just read, fill in the circle that corresponds to the correct answer.

41. Local governments are established by home rule laws enacted by   41 ① ② ③ ④ ⑤
    (1) state governments
    (2) the U.S. Congress
    (3) the U.S. Constitution
    (4) federal courts
    (5) the president

42. A group of citizens became angered by a law that the state legislature passed. They circulated a petition to have the law put to a vote by the people of the state. This is an example of   42 ① ② ③ ④ ⑤
    (1) initiative
    (2) recall
    (3) referendum
    (4) home rule
    (5) local autonomy

43. A state legislator with two years left in her term goes
against overwhelming public opinion in her district and
votes for a state income tax. Voters who wish to remove
the legislator before the next general election could·set
in motion the mechanism for
(1) petition
(2) referendum
(3) impeachment
(4) initiative
(5) recall

43 ① ② ③ ④ ⑤

44. The mayor of the city tries to start a project to build a
new sports stadium, and the city council overrules him.
The form of local government is probably
(1) council-manager
(2) strong council–weak mayor
(3) strong mayor–weak council
(4) bicameral
(5) federal

44 ① ② ③ ④ ⑤

45. The number of people employed by local government
(1) has grown to be larger than the number employed
by the federal government
(2) is about half as large as federal employment
(3) has always been less than the number employed by
state government
(4) has not grown very much
(5) is less than the number employed by the federal
government

45 ① ② ③ ④ ⑤

For answers and explanations, see page 172.

POLITICAL SCIENCE EXERCISE 6 ─────────────

Directions: Read the following passage and fill in the circle that corresponds to the correct answer.

Metropolitan Government

Metropolitan forms of government and administration are a
relatively recent development in American local government.
They have developed in response to the growth of suburbs and
other forms of urban sprawl. Many metropolitan functions, such
5 as mass transit, are too big for one town to handle, so it has
become necessary to create new forms of organization.

The most common of these new forms are the various special districts. These are administrative agencies set up to handle a single function, such as fire protection or health planning, and to

10 administer these programs across several political boundaries. For example, the Regional Transportation Authority in Illinois crosses almost 100 political boundaries, including those of the suburbs and the city of Chicago.

Special districts have been criticized as undemocratic because

15 their governing boards are often appointed instead of elected. Many critics feel that this removes the districts from direct popular control. Those holding this view want democratically elected metropolitan governing boards.

While the creation of these single-function districts has helped

20 integrate the provision of separate services, there has been no movement to integrate all these services into metropolitan governmental structures. There are more than 7,000 special districts in the U.S., but only one metropolitan area, Dade County, Florida, has a metropolitan government. Local governments are reluctant

25 to give up power to a more centralized metropolitan government, and many citizen groups feel that such a form of government would be too large to influence.

The debate over the role and form of metropolitanwide government is sure to continue as a part of the ongoing debate over

30 centralization versus decentralization.

46. The growth of special districts has   46 ① ② ③ ④ ⑤
    (1) integrated metropolitan government into state government
    (2) integrated particular government functions on a local level
    (3) solved the problem of centralization
    (4) started a strong trend toward metropolitan government
    (5) established the power of city mayors over suburban areas

47. The author of this passage seems to believe that the   47 ① ② ③ ④ ⑤
    debate over centralization vs. decentralization
    (1) has been settled
    (2) will be settled soon
    (3) will probably always be with us
    (4) is not an important debate in this country
    (5) is a new development in American politics

48. A major reason given by people opposing special
    districts is a belief that they are
    (1) inefficient
    (2) too costly
    (3) too large
    (4) undemocratic
    (5) too centralized

For answers and explanations, see page 173.

6. INTERNATIONAL RELATIONS

K
E
Y

W
O
R
D
S

treaties—formal agreements among nations

diplomatic recognition—a government's formal recognition of
another country's government, including the exchange of
ambassadors

The U.S. Government and Foreign Policy

Today's turbulent world has made the entire field of international relations
more important than in any previous time. Different branches of the U.S.
government have important roles to play in making and implementing
foreign policy.

The Constitution grants the president three important foreign policy
responsibilities: he is commander in chief of the armed forces, he has the
power to make treaties, and he has the right to appoint ambassadors. Over
the years, many presidents have seized the initiative to expand the powers
of the presidency in foreign affairs.

The president can negotiate **treaties** (formal agreements with other
nations) requiring the approval of the Senate. The president can also make
use of executive agreements with other nations that do not require Senate
approval. These pledge the word of a particular president and do not bind
his successors to any agreement.

Presidents can also extend **diplomatic recognition** to new governments
or nations. In some cases, U.S. presidents have withheld diplomatic
recognition in order to show disapproval of a nation's system of government. For example, the U.S. government withheld recognition of the
Soviet Union for sixteen years.

The president also has the power to nominate ambassadors, subject to

Senate approval. In recent years, presidents have made use of special diplomats who do not require the Senate's approval. The use of such diplomats has become a very common method of conducting diplomacy on sensitive or important issues. Richard Nixon made such use of Henry Kissinger at the Vietnam peace talks and during the negotiations that eventually led to renewed ties between the U.S. and the People's Republic of China.

The chief executive's position as commander in chief of the armed forces has been used by presidents to order military intervention without a formal declaration of war by Congress. Without congressional authorization, President Truman sent troops into Korea in 1950; during the 1960s, Presidents Kennedy and Johnson sent troops to Vietnam; and in 1983, President Reagan sent troops to Grenada. In order to restrain presidential activities that could involve the country in an undeclared war, Congress passed the War Powers Act in 1973.

The Department of State is the section of the executive branch directly responsible for foreign affairs. The State Department is also responsible for the U.S. diplomatic service. Dominant secretaries of state can play an influential role in foreign affairs, but in recent years they have often competed with the head of the National Security Council for influence with the president.

In foreign policy matters, Congress exerts its influence through its ability to approve or disapprove appropriations, treaties, and ambassadors and by exercising its sole right to declare war. Many of the "domestic" bills that Congress reviews, including tariffs, immigration, and import quotas, can have far-reaching international effects.

Directions: Based upon what you have just read, fill in the circle that corresponds to the correct answer.

49. Which of the following requires Senate approval?   49 ① ② ③ ④ ⑤
    (1) Establishing diplomatic relations
    (2) Breaking diplomatic relations
    (3) Executive agreements
    (4) Treaties
    (5) Renouncing treaties

50. For which of the following reasons did Congress pass   50 ① ② ③ ④ ⑤
    the War Powers Act in 1973?
    (1) To make it easier for Congress to declare war
    (2) To give the president more power over the military
    (3) To restrain the president from actions that could
         involve the U.S. in an undeclared war
    (4) To reorganize the branches of the armed forces
    (5) To give the president the power to declare war

51. If the president wants to make an agreement with a
country and he feels it may be opposed by the Senate,
he can still

51 ① ② ③ ④ ⑤

   (1) make an executive agreement
   (2) negotiate a treaty with that country
   (3) have the State Department negotiate the agreement
   (4) seek the support of the House of Representatives
   (5) seek the approval of the Supreme Court

For answers and explanations, see page 173.

International Organizations

International organizations have played an increasingly important role in
the foreign policy of nations. Many countries, despite their differences,
have sought to work together on matters in which they have a mutual
interest, including the prevention of a global conflict. International organizations have tended to fall into three different categories: diplomatic,
economic, and military.

  1. Diplomatic international organizations have emphasized the promo-
tion of better understanding among nations and the prevention of serious
conflicts. The most important diplomatic organizations have been the
League of Nations (1919–1939) and the United Nations (1945–present). The
league was formed right after World War I as an organization of sixty-five
countries. The U.S. never joined the league because of political reasons,
including strong American sentiment favoring isolationism. The organization lacked any power to enforce its decisions and finally collapsed with the
onset of World War II.

  The league was succeeded by a stronger international organization, the
United Nations (UN), formed at the end of World War II. The real power
of the UN originally resided with the five major nations that were in World
War II—the United States, England, France, the Soviet Union, and
China—but some of this power has shifted away from those nations during
the past thirty years. In the General Assembly, the U.S. and the Soviet
Union now find themselves strongly vying for the support of nonaligned
Third World countries. Most of the UN's real decision-making power,
however, still resides in the powerful UN Security Council, where the
original five member nations have permanent seats and veto power.

  The United Nations has performed several important functions. It has
provided an international forum, though not always effective, at which
nations can air their disputes and grievances. Countries have used the
organization to line up world opinion on their sides. It has also provided a
means by which diplomats can communicate with each other and in some

cases has forced two parties in conflict to start discussing their differences. The UN has also organized international peacekeeping forces to oversee settlements of local disputes.

The United Nations has sponsored international agencies that cover a wide range of necessary international activities. These include: encouraging health (World Health Organization); stabilizing currencies and expanding world trade (International Monetary Fund); raising standards of living (Food and Agricultural Organization); providing education about different peoples and cultures (Educational, Scientific, and Cultural Organization); and regulating communications and assigning radio frequencies (International Telecommunications Union).

2. A second type of international organization is chiefly economic. These range from agencies such as the International Monetary Fund to cartels such as the Organization of Petroleum Exporting Countries (OPEC), the regional European Economic Community (the European Common Market), and the economic organization of the Soviet Union and its allies, the Council for Mutual Economic Assistance. There are many reasons that nations take part in an international economic organization, and they are as varied as the organizations themselves. These reasons include: encouraging world trade; finding loans for economic development; fixing prices on a certain commodity, such as oil; obtaining better markets for exports; etc.

3. The third type of international organization is the military alliance. These alliances are as old as war itself. Countries with common interests join military alliances for mutual defense and security reasons. There are two major military alliances today: NATO, the North Atlantic Treaty Organization, made up of the United States, Canada, and allied nations in Western Europe; and the Warsaw Pact, consisting of the Soviet Union and its Eastern European allies. Though there are other regional military alliances, NATO and the Warsaw Pact stand out as the most important and powerful on the international scene today.

Directions: Based upon what you have just read, fill in the circle that corresponds to the correct answer.

52. Which of the following nations does not have a permanent seat on the UN Security Council?
  (1) United States
  (2) England
  (3) Soviet Union
  (4) China
  (5) Japan

52 ① ② ③ ④ ⑤

53. Which of the following best describes the shift in power in the UN during the past thirty years?

53 ① ② ③ ④ ⑤

    (1) Nonaligned Third World nations have become a very large majority on the Security Council.

    (2) Third World countries that always support the Soviet Union and its allies now dominate the General Assembly.

    (3) There has been no real shift in power among the member nations.

    (4) Nonaligned Third World countries have become a very strong power in the General Assembly.

    (5) The Soviet Union and its allies now dominate both the General Assembly and the Security Council.

54. The most likely reason for a nation to join international organizations such as OPEC or the European Common Market would be

54 ① ② ③ ④ ⑤

    (1) political

    (2) economic

    (3) military

    (4) cultural

    (5) educational

For answers and explanations, see page 173.

POLITICAL SCIENCE EXERCISE 7

Directions: Look at the graph below and answer the questions that follow. Fill in the circle that corresponds to the correct answer.

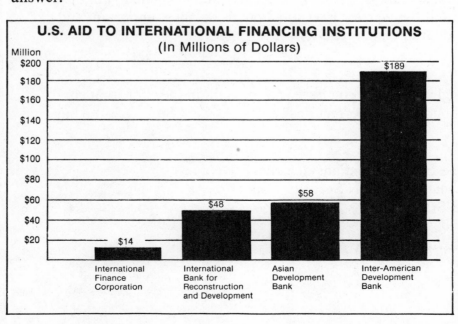

U.S. AID TO INTERNATIONAL FINANCING INSTITUTIONS
(In Millions of Dollars)

55. The greatest amount of U.S. aid to the foreign
institutions shown on the graph was to the

    (1)   United Nations

    (2)   International Financial Corporation

    (3)   International Bank for Reconstruction and
Development

    (4)   Asian Development Bank

    (5)   Inter-American Development Bank

55 ① ② ③ ④ ⑤

56. The total amount of money given by the U.S.
government to foreign financial institutions was
approximately

    (1) $14,000

    (2) $189,000

    (3) $310,000

    (4) $189,000,000

    (5) $310,000,000

56 ① ② ③ ④ ⑤

57. Which diagram most accurately represents the
information on the graph?

57 ① ② ③ ④ ⑤

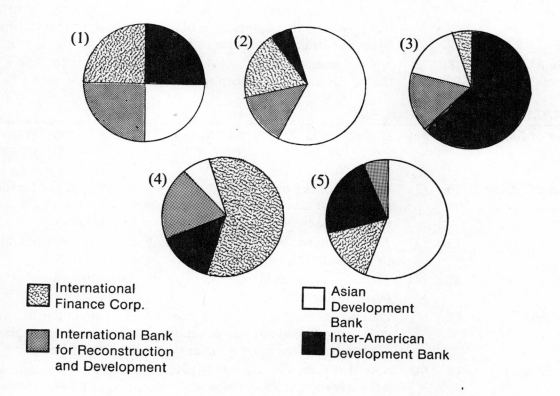

☒ International
Finance Corp.

▨ International Bank
for Reconstruction
and Development

☐ Asian
Development
Bank

■ Inter-American
Development Bank

For answers and explanations, see page 173.

ANSWERS AND EXPLANATIONS

1. INTRODUCTION TO POLITICAL SCIENCE

Application of Ideas   **1.**   (2)   A city council is the legislative branch of city government. All of the other responses are part of the political system but not of government.

Finding Details   **2.**   (5)   The essay says that when people recognize their government as legitimate, it has authority.

Drawing Conclusions   **3.**   (2)   According to the essay, the judicial branch of government interprets the laws.

POLITICAL SCIENCE EXERCISE 1

Application of Ideas   **4.**   (1)   Rousseau argues that mere strength is not enough and that a government must transform its power into a sense of duty. According to the preceding essay, the voluntary support of the people indicates that the government has authority.

Drawing Conclusions   **5.**   (5)   The statement by Hitler discusses his ideas of racial superiority and inferiority. The previous essay describes claims of racial superiority as a cornerstone of a fascist system.

Drawing Conclusions   **6.**   (4)   The Declaration of Independence talks about the right to overthrow a despotic government, that is, the right to revolution.

Evaluation of Logic   **7.**   (1)   Hitler describes a universe where an Eternal Will promotes a victory of the stronger over the weaker. Rousseau, on the other hand, believes that the strong is not strong enough to prevail until strength is transformed into right (justice).

Application of Ideas   **8.**   (2)   A government in a representative democracy is accountable to the people and derives its power from them.

2. AMERICAN POLITICAL PROCESS

Application of Ideas   **9.**   (1)   A plurality is the greatest number of votes cast when there are more than two candidates and no one candidate gets a simple majority.

Application of Ideas   **10.**   (2)   Since all of the owners are directly participating in the decision making and a majority vote is necessary to approve any action, this is an example of participatory or direct democracy.

Finding Details   **11.**   (3)   The essay views politicians' coalition building as "indispensable to the American political process."

Main Idea   **12.**   (4)   The essay discusses the effective role of interest groups and social movements.

Finding Details   **13.**   (1)   The essay notes that part of the reason the two major parties have maintained their dominant position is that they have been able to adopt some of the more popular demands of third parties.

Making Inferences   **14.**   (4)   Note that there are two trends being illustrated: that people are less likely to identify strongly with either party and that they are more likely to view themselves as independents.

POLITICAL SCIENCE EXERCISE 2

Main Idea	**15.**	(5)	The writer believes that poor people do not vote in proportion to their numbers in the population. As a consequence, they do not have as much political influence as other groups that tend to vote in proportion to their numbers.
Drawing Conclusions	**16.**	(1)	If lower-income people voted in significant numbers, elected officials would have to pay more attention to their interests. This would probably result in an expansion of programs serving the poor.

3.   THE UNITED STATES CONSTITUTION

Finding Details	**17.**	(3)	Under the Articles of Confederation, the central government was extremely weak. It had no national court system and no national chief executive and could not regulate interstate commerce.
Finding Details	**18.**	(2)	The essay states that problems of interstate commerce were a major reason for calling those meetings.
Finding Details	**19.**	(5)	This fact is mentioned in the second from the last paragraph.
Application of Ideas	**20.**	(3)	This would upset the balance that has been achieved among the executive, legislative, and judicial branches.
Application of Ideas	**21.**	(2)	Federalism is a system of shared power between separate national and state governments.
Application of Ideas	**22.**	(1)	The House was created to give the larger states a share of the vote based on population.
Finding Details	**23.**	(5)	This is the only answer choice that is guaranteed in the Bill of Rights.

POLITICAL SCIENCE EXERCISE 3

Main Idea	**24.**	(1)	The fact that certain rights are guaranteed by the Constitution has not meant that there is a unified viewpoint about what they mean. The Supreme Court has used its power to define certain rights to extend to those with controversial ideas.
Application of Ideas	**25.**	(3)	Freedom of speech does not imply the right to incite panic and create a dangerous situation.
Finding Details	**26.**	(5)	The cases concerning obscenity and pornography are discussed in terms of the right to free speech and a free press.

4.   BRANCHES OF GOVERNMENT

Finding Details	**27.**	(3)	Executive orders issued by the president have the effect of law.
Finding Details	**28.**	(4)	The vice president succeeds the president in the event of the president's death or a severe incapacity that prevents the president from functioning in office.
Application of Ideas	**29.**	(2)	Hamilton is describing the process of a presidential veto and the procedure for override.
Finding Details	**30.**	(2)	This is pointed out in the section on the powers of the legislative branch.
Making Inferences	**31.**	(3)	The essay makes the point that the U.S. has been involved in four major wars and other military involvements during this century,

and the president's role as commander in chief of the military has helped strengthen the power of the executive in foreign affairs. We can infer that periods of increased military activity might further strengthen the presidency.

Drawing Conclusions	32.	(2)	All of the other choices are tools that Congress can use to influence the executive. The pocket veto is a tool the president uses to reject legislation proposed by Congress.
Finding Details	33.	(3)	This is one of the few areas of original jurisdiction that the Constitution grants to the Supreme Court.
Finding Details	34.	(4)	The passage states that federal judges are appointed by the president.
Application of Ideas	35.	(2)	Hamilton is describing the rationale behind judicial review.
Drawing Conclusions	36.	(3)	The Supreme Court's power of judicial review shows that the meaning of the Constitution has been open to interpretation.

POLITICAL SCIENCE EXERCISE 4

Main Idea	37.	(1)	The passage points out that some Supreme Court decisions were heavily influenced by political and historical developments.
Finding Details	38.	(2)	The passage places the court's *Plessy* v. *Ferguson* decision in the context of white supremacist prejudice at home.

POLITICAL SCIENCE EXERCISE 5

Main Idea	39.	(1)	The author says that President Nixon used "national security" as an excuse to cover up political spying and harassment.
Drawing Conclusions	40.	(5)	The Watergate crisis involved questions about more than President Nixon's personal integrity. At issue was the growing power of the presidency and the need to reaffirm our system of checks and balances.

5. STATE AND LOCAL GOVERNMENT

Finding Details	41.	(1)	Counties, towns, and cities are legal creations of the state.
Application of Ideas	42.	(3)	The essay explains that legislation can be repealed by a referendum.
Application of Ideas	43.	(5)	The essay says that some states give their voters the right to recall unpopular elected officials.
Application of Ideas	44.	(2)	When the city council can overrule the mayor on key decisions, it indicates a strong council–weak mayor form of city government.
Finding Details	45.	(1)	The essay states that, in 1979, local government employed 7.8 million people while the federal government employed 4.9 million.

POLITICAL SCIENCE EXERCISE 6

Drawing Conclusions	46.	(2)	Special districts have integrated specific functions, but this has not generally led to metropolitan government.
Making Inferences	47.	(3)	The author believes that this controversy has been with us for a long time and will continue.
Finding Details	48.	(4)	The passage mentions this in lines 14–15.

6. INTERNATIONAL RELATIONS

Finding Details	49.	(4)	The Constitution gives the president power to "make treaties," but it also requires a two-thirds vote of the Senate to confirm the treaty.
Finding Details	50.	(3)	The War Powers Act forces the president to seek approval from Congress for any long-term commitment of the military to situations where combat is involved to prevent the recurrence of another war like the Vietnam conflict.
Making Inferences	51.	(1)	The president can conclude executive agreements with other nations. The agreements do not require Senate approval but remain in force only for the duration of that president's term.
Finding Details	52.	(5)	The five nations with permanent seats on the Security Council are the United States, the Soviet Union, England, France, and China. Japan is not one of these.
Drawing Conclusions	53.	(4)	The passage states that the power has shifted away from the five major nations and that now the U.S. and Soviet Union are vying for the support of the Third World nations.
Finding Details	54.	(2)	Both organization—OPEC (Organization of Petroleum Exporting Countries) and the European Common Market—are economic organizations.

POLITICAL SCIENCE EXERCISE 7

Finding Details	55.	(5)	The highest bar on the graph represents the Inter-American Development Bank.
Drawing Conclusions	56.	(5)	The graph title tells you that the amounts of money given are in millions of dollars. Add the totals of all of the bars represented and the answer will be close to $310 million.
Application of Ideas	57.	(3)	Only diagram (3) shows the Inter-American Development Bank with more than half of the total and the rest having unequal, but smaller, amounts.

Behavioral Science

=====

1. INTRODUCTION TO BEHAVIORAL SCIENCES

The behavioral sciences—psychology, sociology, and anthropology—are all based on applying the scientific methods of research, observation, and experimentation to the study of behavior. However, each behavioral science uses a different approach, and each studies different aspects of **behavior.**

Psychology studies individual behavior and concerns itself with a person's mental processes. How does a person think, learn, remember, and make decisions? What are a person's feelings or emotions? What affects a person's motivation, personality, and behavior?

For example, a psychologist may wonder why some students easily learn mathematics while other students have trouble and even develop mental blocks and anxieties The psychologist may question students and find out that those with problems had experienced early difficulties with math. The psychologist might also find that those who are successful with math are especially skilled at working with abstract ideas and manipulating information.

Behavioral scientists have also learned how a person's personality can affect his behavior in surprising ways. More than thirty years ago, Morris Janowitz and Dwaine Marvick studied the relationship between voting behavior and personalities. They found that people with intolerant and inflexible personalities seemed to favor isolationism in U.S. foreign policy.

Sociology is a behavioral science that concerns itself with the behavior of groups. Sociologists look at how people behave in families, in organizations, in institutions such as a church, and on the job. They look at the groupings in society that people identify with:

(1) social class: middle, upper, or lower

(2) occupational groupings: professional, blue collar, white collar— skilled or unskilled

(3) ethnic, racial, or cultural groups: Italian, Hispanic, black, Jewish, etc.

The sociologist studies the characteristics of these groups and how such groups behave and interact.

A sociologist may offer explanations about the characteristics and behavior of certain groups. For example, she might investigate the interrelationship of poverty, education, and employment. The sociologist might compare public aid recipients who have attended job training programs with those who did not. From such a study, the sociologist could make some observations about what effect training programs have on those considered to be "chronically unemployed."

Anthropology is the third behavioral science you will learn about. *Anthropology* literally means the "science of man," and it combines several different scientific disciplines in its study of physical, social, and cultural development.

Anthropologists study how cultures evolve slowly as well as how they change dramatically. Imagine the changes that took place in the reindeer-herding culture of the Laplanders when snowmobiles were introduced in place of dogsleds. The use of snowmobiles necessitated the construction of roads into the region for fuel delivery. The very existence of these roads brought in even more outside influences. Social relationships also changed because easier and faster travel brought about increasing contact between people at a village level. For instance, teenage boys now had the use of father's snowmobile, thereby dramatically changing dating patterns. The job of the anthropologist would be to study the impact of innovations (snowmobiles) on an aspect of culture (dating).

A Case Study

To better understand the uniqueness of each of these three behavioral sciences, let's look at how each one might approach a social phenomenon such as child abuse.

Sociology Looks at Child Abuse

A sociologist would look for a relationship between households with abused children and another social phenomenon, such as unemployment. The sociologist might ask: what percentage of households with abused children also has unemployed heads of household? If the sociologist finds that there is a relationship between the two—a high percentage of child abusers are unemployed heads of households—the sociologist might conclude that unemployment is a contributing factor in child abuse.

Psychology Looks at Child Abuse

The psychologist would look at the sociologist's study and say, "Yes, you have shown a relationship between the rate of child abuse and unemployed heads of households, *but* you have not explained why there is still significant child abuse in households where the head person is employed. Furthermore, there is no child abuse in many households where the head is unemployed. I'm interested in why certain people take out their frustations on their children."

A psychologist might then compare the personality traits of employed and unemployed people who are child abusers. From this comparison, the psychologist may draw the conclusion that those individuals who project blame for their personal problems onto other people are likely to abuse their own children.

Anthropology Looks at Child Abuse

The anthropologist will look at both the psychologist's and sociologist's studies and comment, "That's all well and good, but I'm really more interested in how different cultures handle economic hard times and how this in turn affects the family." She would then look at different cultures and their dominant type of family structure. These could include rural cultures based on agriculture and urban cultures based on industry. She might then conclude that different types of family structure respond in different ways to economic hard times.

For example, cultures with small, nuclear families (industrial cultures) may show more child abuse than cultures with large families that include several generations (agrarian cultures).

The three behavioral scientists reached conclusions based on different approaches. These conclusions do not conflict with one another and could be integrated into a more general understanding of child abuse.

All three behavioral sciences also share the use of the scientific method in their work. This means that individual behavior, group behavior, and cultures can be studied scientifically. Behavioral scientists use unbiased, systematic methods of observing or gathering facts on which they base their conclusions. Out of such research, the scientists develop a **generalization**, which is a general principle based on particular facts. When the behavioral scientist is able to bring together a system of scientifically tested generalizations, he has developed a **theory**—a belief that can explain a social phenomenon.

Practical Uses of Behavioral Sciences

It may be surprising to see how many of the findings and methods of the behavioral sciences have been put to practical use by both business and government.

Businesses have used behavioral scientists to study human motivation in buying. Behavioral scientists have actually designed packaging, shelf placement, lighting, and musical backgrounds to promote sales. Corporations have used behavioral studies to make their organization more efficient. They have also used the behavioral sciences to learn how to improve worker morale and forestall union organizing. Some companies even use personality testing to decide whom to hire.

The behavioral sciences have also significantly affected a wide variety of government programs and policies. During the 1960s, behavioral scientists were involved in designing and reviewing many of the War on Poverty programs. To take advantage of knowledge gained from studies of human perception, the space program has used behavioral scientists to design the interiors of space crafts and the instrumentation of cockpits. Intelligence testing, long used in schools, was also developed by behavioral scientists.

The behavioral sciences have also had an important impact on public policy. For instance, the 1954 Supreme Court decision to desegregate American schools was based heavily on the conclusions of studies by social scientists. These studies demonstrated that racially segregated schools were not only unequal but were actually harmful to black children. Behavioral scientists have also designed programs for the elderly and have taken part in city planning.

Perhaps the greatest achievement of behavioral scientists has been to help all citizens better understand the world they live in. They have aided people in understanding different people, cultures, and societies; and they have helped to break down many of the barriers that have traditionally separated individuals, groups, and cultures.

Directions: Based upon what you have just read, answer the following questions. Fill in the circle that corresponds to the correct answer.

1. "The higher the unemployment rate, the higher the rate of divorce" is a statement most likely made by a
   (1) sociologist
   (2) anthropologist
   (3) psychologist
   (4) economist
   (5) marriage counselor

1 ① ② ③ ④ ⑤

2. Which of the following would most likely be called into court to give <u>expert</u> testimony about a defendant's personal motivation?
   (1)   A bailiff
   (2)   His mother
   (3)   A court appointed psychiatrist
   (4)   A sociologist who studies the criminal justice system
   (5)   An anthropologist with expertise in criminal subcultures

3. The United Nations wants to study villagers in an underdeveloped country in order to get them to change their cultural habits and to accept the introduction of modern technology. What kind of social scientist would it send?
   (1)   A psychologist to conduct individual counseling sessions
   (2)   A sociologist to study the society's child rearing practices
   (3)   An economist to explain the financial advantages of credit cards over the barter system
   (4)   An anthropologist to understand the society's culture and values
   (5)   An agricultural specialist to increase crop production

4. According to the essay, the fields of behavioral science have
   (1)   had an inconsequential impact on American life
   (2)   had an impact only on national policy issues
   (3)   been used successfully only by private business
   (4)   no practical applications
   (5)   had a wide impact on institutions and individuals

5. "Children of alcoholics are likely to become alcoholics themselves" is an example of
   (1)   a fact
   (2)   a generalization
   (3)   a bias
   (4)   propaganda
   (5)   a case study

6. "We have come to conclude that, in most areas of
   employment, women are still discriminated against. This
   conclusion is based, in part, on the evidence that
   women earn 60 percent of what men earn in similar job
   categories." This statement is an example of

   (1) a fact
   (2) a generalization
   (3) a theory
   (4) a biased statement
   (5) propaganda

For answers and explanations, see page 206.

2. PSYCHOLOGY

**K
E
Y

W
O
R
D
S**

character—the values that influence a person's behavior

temperament—a person's emotional makeup

primary motives—biological bases for behavior

secondary motives—learned behaviors that can be encouraged
   through reward or discouraged through punishment

neuroses—emotionally based psychological disorders

psychoses—psychological disorders, often biologically based,
   that prevent a person from functioning on a daily basis

What Is Psychology?

Psychology is the study of individual behavior. In exploring the basis of
individual behavior, psychologists have developed specialized fields of
study. These range from the study of the functioning of the brain to
broader concerns, such as the mass psychology of groups.

Many of us feel that we already have some understanding of psychology—we can work out our own problems and help people to work out
theirs. At times, we may use a "little psychology" to calm someone down or
to get our own way.

In these and a hundred ways, we use "commonsense psychology" based
on the skills and the insights that we have developed. However, this is
vastly different from the organized practice of the field of psychology.

Although psychologists vary greatly in their approaches, they all use the
tools of research and objective observation. Very often psychologists use

experiments to observe the behavior of an experimental group versus a control, or unaffected, group.

Much of the work of psychologists extends beyond observation and experimentation to work with people and institutions on everyday problems. For example, guidance counselors are trained to help students with their educational and psychological problems, marriage counselors help couples who need assistance with communication problems, and industrial trainers use psychological practices to help business and industry better motivate their workers.

The field of psychology is diverse and complex. To get a glimpse of what psychology is concerned with, we will look at:

```
personality
motivation
abnormal behavior
```

Personality

Personality is a key concept for psychologists. It refers to the characteristics that show consistent responses by a person to his environment. Such characteristics range from extroverted (outgoing) to introverted (shy), from aggressive to passive, from curious to apathetic. A personality is defined by such characteristics and their integration into a whole.

Why do people have such diverse personalities? What makes people different? Psychologists have no one answer to this, but they look at a variety of influences:

Genetic

Many personal traits are based on inherited characteristics. For example, from birth babies show different temperaments. Parents are always fascinated that such characteristics remain with the child and develop through life. Inherited characteristics are said to be innate or inborn.

Childhood Experiences

Psychologists often trace a learning or behavior problem to negative childhood experiences—including neglect, abuse, or just poor parent-child communication.

Expectations of the Future

The expectations that people have of the future are often unfulfilled. Certain personality disorders are exhibited by people who feel inadequate or unable to live up to others' expectations.

When psychologists look at personality, they are considering two aspects of behavior: **character** and **temperament**. *Character* refers to the values that determine how a person acts in a certain situation. *Temperament*, what we usually identify as "what kind of person she is," consists of an individual's emotional makeup. Although a person's actions and attitudes may change over time, those characteristics that comprise one's personality are highly unlikely to change.

Motivation

Psychologists also study motivation. *Motivation* refers to those factors that start, maintain, or stop an individual's activity. An understanding of motivation answers the question "Why did she do that?"

Motivation can be divided into two main categories: primary motives and secondary motives. **Primary motives** are biologically based and include hunger, thirst, need for sleep, avoidance of pain, etc. For example, hunger is a motive to eat; once the hunger is alleviated, the motivation for eating is gone.

Secondary motives are drives that are learned. Secondary motives include such things as greed, desire for friendship, and the need for achievement. For instance, a person learns the joy of friendship, and this motivates the person to behave in such a way that maintains the friendship.

Motivation can be learned through either positive or negative reinforcement. Another term for a positive reinforcement is a *reward*. A child who is praised for a good report card is more likely to repeat the behavior that earned it than a child whose parents are indifferent.

Learned behavior can also be stopped or extinguished through negative reinforcement, commonly known as *punishment*. Psychologists claim it is more efficient to reward desired behavior than to punish undesirable behavior.

The debate over positive and negative reinforcement involves not just individual behavior but also social concerns. One focus of this debate is our criminal justice system. Some people believe that the emphasis in dealing with crime should be on negative reinforcement—to punish the individual offender to serve as a warning to other potential criminals. Other people put the emphasis on positive reinforcement, for all but the most violent offenders. They stress counseling, education, and training so that the individual is better suited to reenter society.

Abnormal Behavior

One of the most important areas of concern to psychologists is psychological disorders. Often referred to as *mental illness*, psychological disorders are characterized by behavior that is not considered normal.

Normal Behavior

This is hard to define. Certainly different people act in diverse ways and even contrary to the mainstream. Individuals who do not have a typical lifestyle, or who dress and think differently, are still considered to be psychologically normal. Psychologists describe people who exhibit normal behavior as those who have a good general sense of reality, are able to control their personal affairs, and can hold up in stressful situations.

Neurosis

This term is applied to a group of symptoms that a person exhibits when he has trouble coping with life. A neurotic person behaves in such a way that deteriorates his relationships with co-workers, friends, and family.

Neuroses are disorders that interfere with a person's goals or feelings of self-worth. A neurosis leads to a variety of symptoms that occur when a person finds it difficult to deal with pressure. For example, we all use defense mechanisms to cope with everyday problems. We use defense mechanisms to keep from being overwhelmed by anxiety and to keep a good self-image. However, defense mechanisms can become a severe problem when a person distorts reality but is unaware that he is doing this.

Another type of neurosis is a phobia—an intense and irrational fear of someone or something. For instance, people who panic at a closed elevator door because they are afraid of enclosed places are said to have claustrophobia.

While a neurosis impairs a person's ability to function on a daily basis, he can still manage his own affairs. Most psychologists believe that the causes of neuroses are emotional and not physical.

Psychosis

Psychoses are much more complicated and disabling than neuroses. **Psychoses** are not exaggerated forms of neuroses but qualitatively different kinds of behavior.

Psychotic behavior covers a wide range that can be divided into two general areas: organic and functional. Psychologists believe that organic psychosis is caused by a deterioration of some part of the nervous system (which includes the brain). Brain damage from illness, drugs, or alcohol can bring on such deterioration. People with functional psychoses show disturbed behavior, but there is no real evidence that there is physical deterioration.

Individuals who are psychotic are judged to be largely out of touch with reality. They are deemed unable to manage their own affairs and may be committed to a mental institution for treatment.

Directions: Based on what you have just read, answer the following questions. Fill in the circle that corresponds to the correct answer.

7. Which of the following is not a major factor in personality development?
   (1) Genetic makeup
   (2) Childhood experiences
   (3) Expectations of the future
   (4) Parental values
   (5) Primary motives

   7 ① ② ③ ④ ⑤

8. Ralph began playing the violin when he was three and was giving public concerts when he was seven. From this, you could conclude that
   (1) little Ralph is psychotic
   (2) Ralph has certain innate talents
   (3) Ralph has developed a defense mechanism
   (4) Ralph is an all-around genius
   (5) Ralph has strong primary motives

   8 ① ② ③ ④ ⑤

9. A corporation is trying to learn how to get its employees to cooperate better. It needs to get a psychologist who is a specialist in
   (1) human motivation
   (2) heredity
   (3) neuroses
   (4) psychoses
   (5) negative reinforcement

   9 ① ② ③ ④ ⑤

10. Sally comes home from school with her shirt torn from a fight. Her mother puts her to bed without supper. The mother's action is an example of
    (1) positive reinforcement
    (2) negative reinforcement
    (3) psychotic behavior
    (4) neurotic behavior
    (5) a defense mechanism

    10 ① ② ③ ④ ⑤

11. "I started taking drugs because you pressure me all the time" is an example of
    (1) an innate trait
    (2) commonsense psychology
    (3) psychosis
    (4) a phobia
    (5) a defense mechanism

    11 ① ② ③ ④ ⑤

12. According to the essay, one cause of a psychosis could be
 (1) stress
 (2) drug abuse
 (3) defensiveness
 (4) fear of heights
 (5) lack of sleep

12 ① ② ③ ④ ⑤

For answers and explanations, see page 206.

BEHAVIORAL SCIENCE EXERCISE 1

Directions: Read the following passage. Answer the questions by filling in the circle that corresponds to the correct answer.

Motivation to Work

What motivates people to study and to work? One school of thought argues that we work for outside rewards, such as money, grades, and prestige. But is this true?

5 According to McGregor, most institutions are structured around a set of assumptions about human nature. That set of beliefs, which he called Theory X, holds that people basically dislike work and will do anything to avoid it. Although people want security, they have little ambition and do not want responsi-
10 bility. Therefore, people have to be bribed or coerced to be productive.

There is an alternate set of assumptions that McGregor calls Theory Y. According to Theory Y, people are basically creative and responsible. The expenditure of energy in some form of work is a natural process. To the extent that work objectives can fulfill
15 personal needs (such as self-esteem, curiosity, creativity, etc.), people will be intrinsically motivated to do well and will have less need for rewards.

Most businesses function on the basis of Theory X. They usually try to increase the quantity or quality of production by
20 offering such standard inducements as extra pay or vacation time. However, some businesses have changed their operating procedures based on the principles of Theory Y. These companies have found dramatic changes in their employees' work performances.

Instead of being organized around assembly lines (where each
25 person makes only a small part of the final product), these companies have set up small work teams where each person works on some aspect of the final product from beginning to end. Not only do people have more pride in their work, but the chance to work in small groups allows them to develop close personal
30 relationships. The workers are more satisfied and productive, and there is less absenteeism, job turnover, and indifference to quality.

13. The basis of the difference between the outlooks of   13 ① ② ③ ④ ⑤
Theory X and Theory Y is a different view of
    (1) personality disorders
    (2) assembly lines
    (3) vacation time
    (4) increased pay
    (5) human nature

14. Based on the viewpoint of Theory Y, you could   14 ① ② ③ ④ ⑤
conclude that a classroom with the most learning, least
absenteeism, and fewest discipline problems would be
    (1) a "back to basics classroom" based on drill
    (2) a classroom motivated by fear of punishment
    (3) a classroom where students are motivated by
        grades
    (4) a classroom where the students work as a team on
        learning projects
    (5) a classroom where everyone works independently

For answers and explanations, see page 206.

BEHAVIORAL SCIENCE EXERCISE 2

Directions: Look at the graph and cartoon. Answer the questions by
filling in the circle that corresponds to the correct answer.

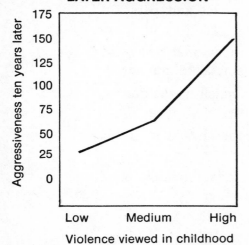

VIEWING TV VIOLENCE IN
CHILDHOOD AND ITS INFLUENCE ON
LATER AGGRESSION

"This will teach you to hit your
sister!"

15. The graph shows that those children who watched   15 ① ② ③ ④ ⑤
relatively little TV violence
    (1) never became aggressive as adults
    (2) were less likely to become aggressive adults than
        those children who watched more TV
    (3) were very likely to become aggressive adults
    (4) were likely to become strict disciplinarians
    (5) were not likely to watch TV when they were older

16. From the cartoon, you can tell that the cartoonist believes that
    (1) parents should physically punish their children
    (2) boys should not hit girls
    (3) parents must spare the rod and spoil the child
    (4) parents who use violence encourage their children to be violent
    (5) the child in the cartoon will never hit his sister again

16 ① ② ③ ④ ⑤

17. Taken together, the graph and the cartoon seem to indicate that violence and aggression are
    (1) learned behaviors
    (2) innate characteristics
    (3) primary motives
    (4) not influential on behavior
    (5) defense mechanisms

17 ① ② ③ ④ ⑤

For answers and explanations, see page 207.

3. SOCIOLOGY

KEY WORDS

primary group—a small, intimate group of people in which there is a great deal of face-to-face contact and personal interaction among members

secondary group—a formal and often impersonal group of people whose members interact in a businesslike manner

socialization—the process by which a person learns the norms, habits, and beliefs that govern his society

social stratification—the division of people by their status (ranking) in society

inconsistency of status—a situation in which factors affecting a person's status seem to contradict each other

What Sociologists Study

Sociology is concerned with the group behavior of individuals across a broad range of social activity. Sociologists study and explain various patterns of human activity, asking such questions as: What kinds of groups do people belong to? How do these groups relate to one another? What roles do individuals play in these groups? How is society organized?

In this essay, we will discuss certain concepts that sociologists work with. Two of the most important concepts are society and institutions.

A **society** is a large social group that perpetuates itself. Its members share certain fundamental values. Through their interaction, the members establish organized patterns of social relations that will be discussed later in this section. Each person conducts himself in accord with what he thinks is expected of him. When this is not the case, an individual's actions are seen as antisocial behavior. Some antisocial activities may be considered criminal behavior by the standards of the society.

When individuals' patterns of behavior are organized around a central point of interest, sociologists refer to this as an **institution** of society. For instance, the family is an institution in which behavior is organized around blood and marriage relationships. Religion, another institution of society, is organized around a systematic body of belief and worship.

Groups

Primary Groups and Socialization

As many philosophers have pointed out, humans are social animals, and interaction with others is an essential aspect of human life. Humans have the mental ability to solve problems and are also able to improvise so that social relationships tend to be very flexible and exhibit a wide variety of behavior. Human activity is extremely dependent on the experiences that we have as members of groups. Sociologists have determined that there are two fundamental types of groups to which people belong: primary groups and secondary groups.

A primary group is usually small and intimate. There is a great deal of face-to-face contact and personal interaction among its members. Primary groups include families, peer groups, street gangs, small cliques at work, or simply a small group of close friends. Most people belong to several primary groups. Emotional attachments tend to be strong in primary groups, and members mean a lot to each other. If a member leaves the group, he cannot be replaced easily, if at all.

The two most important primary groups are families and peer groups.

Family

The **family** is a special relationship among **kin** (people related through marriage or common ancestry). Families exists in different forms in many societies. In North American culture, the center of the family consists of the wife, husband, and unmarried children. This is called the **nuclear** (conjugal) family. In our society, a newly married couple normally detach themselves from their parents. In some societies, a newly married couple become part of an **extended** family (a household containing a nuclear family plus other relatives).

The family is probably the most important primary group because it is the group in which a person first undergoes socialization. **Socialization** is the process through which a person learns the norms, habits, and beliefs that govern his society.

A child is socialized through her participation as a family member. A child learns both his **role** (expected pattern of behavior in the group and in society) and **norms** (standards that govern how his role must be performed) from his contact with adults in his family. Socialization is normally an informal process through which the child picks up much of what he learns through discussions, explanations, overheard adult conversation, and the example set by his parents.

Of all the roles that children are socialized into, one of the most important is their sex role: What is expected of girls and women? What is expected of boys and men? Since the late 1960s, every aspect of American family and social life has been affected by changing expectations of traditional sex roles. Some individuals and families have changed dramatically, while others have stood their ground for traditional roles and values.

Peer Groups

A **peer group** is simply a group of people who share a similar status such as age, class, or rank or who have an equal standing with one another. Peer groups can consist of our closest friends or our co-workers who do similar types of work on our jobs. A team in a bowling or softball league could also be a peer group as could a group of friends in a classroom at school.

Secondary Groups

In contrast to the personal and intimate nature of a primary group is the formal and impersonal nature of a **secondary group**. Members of a secondary group tend to interact in a businesslike manner. Secondary groups include unions and political, religious, and business organizations. Relationships among members of secondary groups lack the strong emotional attachments and intimacy that are experienced in primary groups.

Because of their standardized form of relationships, members of secondary groups can be interchanged or replaced with little effect on the group. Unlike simpler societies, where primary group associations are dominant, secondary groups are very characteristic of our modern complex society.

A special type of secondary group is the **organization**. An organization is a group that has been formed to carry out a specific goal. Organizations cover a wide range, from corporations to armies to churches. All organizations are characterized by the following:

(1) leadership that gives overall direction to the group

(2) responsibilities and labor divided among members to utilize their efforts most efficiently

(3) easy transfer or substitution of members in carrying out various roles or tasks

Two of the major forms of organizations are voluntary associations and bureaucracies. These represent the two extremes of organizational forms.

Voluntary associations are organizations that people willingly join. They tend to be informal in their makeup, and they provide help and support to their members. People usually participate as a leisure-time activity and can quit when they like. Examples of such organizations are the PTA and the League of Women Voters.

At the other extreme of organizations are the bureaucracies that we all joke about. Bureaucracies are formal and complex organizations that are usually governed by detailed regulations. They are organized in a hierarchy or chain of command.. Despite widespread feelings against bureaucracies, they are often rational, efficient, and highly organized. It is probably these qualities that contribute to the feeling that bureaucracies sometimes seem inhumane or, at best, inflexible and impersonal. Bureaucracies are most often found in large corporations, large universities, highly organized religious orders, the armed forces, and the government.

Directions: Based on what you have just read, answer the following questions. Fill in the circle that corresponds to the correct answer.

18. Which of the following would be a member of a primary group of a thirty-five-year-old man?
    (1) His instructor
    (2) His employer
    (3) His daughter
    (4) His doctor
    (5) His precinct captain

    18 ① ② ③ ④ ⑤

19. "Like father like son" is a common phrase reflecting what sociological concept?
    (1) Social stratification
    (2) Socialization
    (3) Secondary group status
    (4) Peer group pressure
    (5) Ascribed status

    19 ① ② ③ ④ ⑤

20. A corporation calls a university sociology department and asks for someone who can help to integrate a new company into the corporate structure. The department will send out someone experienced in the study of
    (1) peer groups
    (2) sex roles
    (3) socialization
    (4) secondary groups
    (5) primary groups

    20 ① ② ③ ④ ⑤

For answers and explanations, see page 207.

Social Stratification

Social Class

We have looked at how society is organized into various groups. The social relationships in most of these groups exist among people of roughly equal standing. For lack of a more descriptive term, these relationships could be described as having a horizontal characteristic.

Sociologists have also looked at other aspects of social relationships that take into account how income, wealth, and power are distributed. The factors have a vertical aspect to them. Sociologists have found that society is divided into different social classes based on their relationship to power and access to financial resources. A person's class position is generally fairly rigid since the class one is born into determines one's friends, education, and opportunities. The division of society into broad social classes is called **social stratification**.

America's division into social classes is reflected in its unequal distribution of income and wealth (see Economics Exercise 6, page 240). There is a small class of very rich individuals who possess income far out of proportion to their numbers. There is also a significant-sized lower-income group, including the working poor, whose income and resources are so small that they live in conditions of poverty. Between the two extremes are more than two hundred million people whose income and resources place them somewhere in the very broad "upper," "middle," or "lower" middle class. Within this large middle group, there are substantial differences in income, education, and occupation. The existence of a large middle class has had an important impact on American social structure. It has given American society a sense of social stability that is not found in many other countries. The existence of a large middle class has obscured the sharp differences between the wealthy and the poor in American society.

Social Status

Americans rarely consider class when viewing their position in society. Instead, they look at themselves according to what they believe is their social status (relative position or rank in society).

There are two ways in which a person receives his status or position in society: ascribed or achieved. *Ascribed status* is based upon factors over which a person has no control, such as inherited wealth, ancestry, and racial or ethnic affiliation. *Achieved status* consists of those factors (voluntary) over which a person can take action. These include education, job performance, knowing the "right" people, etc.

Four major elements affect a person's status in American society: income, occupation, education, and race or ethnicity. Income is probably the most important. Occupation is also often very important in determining status. Certain occupations carry prestige and command honor and respect, while other occupations carry less prestige. Doctors, scientists, lawyers, and judges have more prestigious occupations than janitors, bartenders, or farmhands. This does not reflect the worth of the individual but rather how his position in society is perceived. Likewise, education is a factor in determining a person's social status; however, education and prestigious jobs often go hand in hand.

A fourth factor affecting a person's status is membership in a racial or ethnic minority. Skin color or particular cultural traits can result in a group's being singled out for different treatment or discrimination.

Race and Ethnicity

Racial and ethnic background have always significantly affected people's status in American society since immigrants from foreign lands have traditionally started at the lower rungs of the American social ladder. One of the most dramatic examples of race affecting status was the situation faced by Americans of Japanese ancestry during World War II. Although the U.S. was at war with Germany, Italy, and Japan, it was the Japanese-Americans who were perceived as a security threat. Rounded up by the government and deprived of their property and liberty, thousands of Japanese-Americans were forced to live in government detention camps.

Today a relationship still exists between social status and race. A case in point is the status of black Americans. In recent years, increasing numbers of blacks have moved into the middle class, but a great number still live at or below the poverty level. Unemployment has hit young blacks especially hard. The unemployment rate among black Americans has been two to three times greater than for the rest of the population. It is true that there have been gains since the civil rights protests in the 1960s, but the gains have not offset the great degree of inequality still experienced by many blacks in American society.

A relationship between social status and cultural identity also exists for millions of Hispanic people who live in the U.S. The proportion of Hispanics in skilled and professional jobs is very small when compared to the numbers of Hispanics in the general population. Many Hispanics also face a language barrier. They must learn English in order to have a chance to advance to most of the better-paying jobs. Some Hispanics face a further barrier, their legal status. In their desire to escape severe poverty, many Spanish-speaking people have left their homelands and have come to the U.S. in search of a better life. Those who have entered the U.S. illegally have often found themselves the victims of serious abuses and exploitation. Unscrupulous employers have paid them lower wages and given them fewer benefits.

Inconsistency of Status

Because several factors influence it, status is not always easily understood. This leads to a situation that sociologists call *inconsistency of status*— where several factors affecting status seem to contradict each other. Below are several examples of inconsistency of status.

—A manual laborer with a very high income but little education may view his status as relatively high because of the money he makes. However, other people may view him differently because of his low educational level and occupation with relatively low prestige.

—An attorney with an income that is not substantial still may carry a higher status because of the prestige of his job.

—A wealthy hoodlum who does not carry a high status because of his criminal activity might encourage his children to go into legitimate business pursuits so that they can attain the status that has been denied him by his peers.

—A black physician with a substantial income and an Ivy League education may find it difficult to buy a home in some affluent white areas.

Directions: Based on what you have just read, answer the following questions. Fill in the circle that corresponds to the correct answer.

21. A doctor from a foreign country comes to the U.S. expecting to pursue his medical career. However, his medical degree is not recognized as valid, and he must take a job doing manual labor while he studies. He is probably experiencing
    (1) inconsistency of status
    (2) peer group pressure
    (3) antisocial behavior
    (4) primary group association
    (5) socialization

    21 ① ② ③ ④ ⑤

22. An example of a factor affecting ascribed status, a factor over which the individual has no control, is
    (1) racial background
    (2) educational level
    (3) income
    (4) occupation
    (5) marital status

    22 ① ② ③ ④ ⑤

23. Which of the following does not influence social stratification?
    (1) Social classes
    (2) Government social programs
    (3) Income levels
    (4) Socialization
    (5) Race and ethnicity

    23 ① ② ③ ④ ⑤

For answers and explanations, see page 207.

BEHAVIORAL SCIENCE EXERCISE 3

Directions: Based on what you have just read, answer the following questions. Fill in the circle that corresponds to the correct answer.

Joe Jones and Society

One way to understand how an individual's personal life relates to society is to look at the way a sociologist would describe the relationship. In the reading passage below, there is a sociological interpretation of the major events of Joe Jones's life. This passage and the questions that follow should give you a clearer idea of how a sociologist interprets everyday events.

The Life of Joe Jones	A Sociologist Views the Life of Joe Jones
Joe Jones is born to Mike, a factory worker, and Sylvia, a housewife.	Joe is automatically a member of the working class—an *ascribed status* in the social structure.
Joe goes to Catholic church and parochial schools.	These are institutions where Joe undergoes *socialization* and learns *values* and *norms*.
Joe runs with a group of guys who call themselves the Steel City Blues.	This is a *peer group*, a type of *primary group*. Members are of roughly equal status and are personal friends.
Joe works hard and becomes an all-conference basketball player.	This is an *achieved status*—something that Joe has earned himself.
Joe has low grades in school and cannot get a college scholarship, so he ends up working in the local auto plant. Joe runs for union office and is elected.	He now has an *ascribed status* as a worker. He earns an *achieved status* as an official in the union, a *secondary group* (organization).
Joe gets married to Jill and has kids. Joe drinks on Friday nights, roughhouses with the kids, takes care of the car, fishes with his buddies, and loves Jill. Jill washes the clothes, feeds and dresses the kids, takes care of the bills, goes to Tupperware parties, and loves Joe.	The Jones family is part of an *institution*, the family, and their life is organized around traditional *sex roles* that define proper male and female behavior and division of labor in the home.

30	Jill, feeling something is missing in her life, joins a women's consciousness-raising group and challenges her marriage's traditional sex	A *peer group* helps *socialize* Jill to a new set of *values* and *norms*, so she challenges the *sex roles* and *stereotypes*.
35	roles. Joe is convinced to help more around the house.	
40	The auto industry is affected by technological change, and Joe's plant is closed.	Technological innovation leads to *structural unemployment*— the type of unemployment caused by a change in the structure of economic institutions.
45	The union tries to pass legislation helping auto workers, but it is blocked by a big business lobby.	This represents *power* in political institutions.
	Joe and other union members protest in Washington, DC.	The workers took part in *collective action* and *social conflict*.
50	A compromise bill is passed, giving auto workers some assistance with job training.	This represents *accommodation of conflicting interests*, leading to some *social change*.

24. Jill's activities in a women's consciousness-raising group were a cause of which of the following?
    (1) Joe's drinking on Friday nights
    (2) Jill's challenging her marriage's traditional sex roles
    (3) Jill's going to Tupperware parties with her friends
    (4) Joe's decision to run for a union office
    (5) Joe's trip to Washington for a protest

    24 ① ② ③ ④ ⑤

25. When Joe was running with the Steel City Blues, the police department had youth officers working to channel the activities of groups such as the Blues into peaceful pursuits. The officers needed a good knowledge of
    (1) peer groups
    (2) identifying drugs
    (3) secondary groups
    (4) institutional change
    (5) techniques of vandalism

    25 ① ② ③ ④ ⑤

26. Which of the following processes did Joe engage in during the protest march?

26 ① ② ③ ④ ⑤

(1) Socialization
(2) Ascribed status
(3) Peer group pressure
(4) Collective action
(5) Traditional sex roles

For answers and explanations, see page 207.

BEHAVIORAL SCIENCE EXERCISE 4 ——————————

Directions: Look at the graph and answer the questions below. Fill in the circle that corresponds to the correct answer.

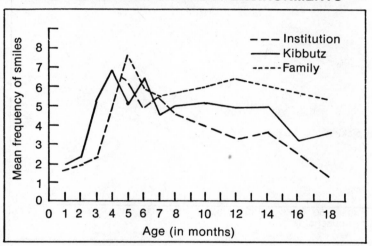

**FREQUENCY OF SMILING AMONG INFANTS
RAISED IN THREE DIFFERENT ENVIRONMENTS**

27. This graph demonstrates that the development of smiling behavior may

27 ① ② ③ ④ ⑤

(1) be an unchanging inherited characteristic
(2) not be influenced by the infant's social environment
(3) be related to the infant's physical health
(4) be influenced by social environment
(5) be dependent on infant's diet

28. We can conclude from the chart that the level of interaction with infants is

28 ① ② ③ ④ ⑤

(1) identical in the three environments
(2) very difficult for the child in the kibbutz
(3) unaffected by the institution
(4) probably different in all three environments
(5) higher in an institution than in a family

For answers and explanations, see page 207.

BEHAVIORAL SCIENCE EXERCISE 5

Directions: Look at the graph and answer the questions that follow. Fill
in the circle that corresponds to the correct answer.

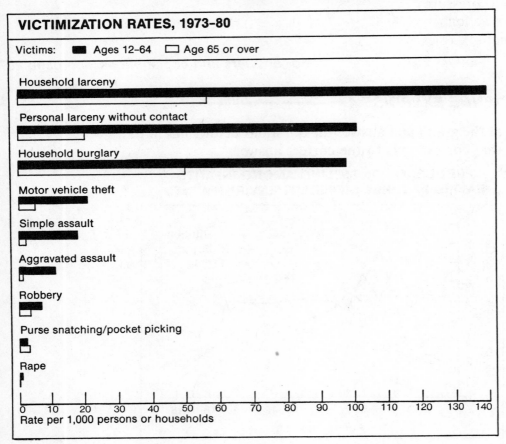

VICTIMIZATION RATES, 1973–80

Victims: ■ Ages 12–64   □ Age 65 or over

Household larceny

Personal larceny without contact

Household burglary

Motor vehicle theft

Simple assault

Aggravated assault

Robbery

Purse snatching/pocket picking

Rape

0 10 20 30 40 50 60 70 80 90 100 110 120 130 140
Rate per 1,000 persons or households

29. You can conclude from this graph that government
policy could have the largest impact on reducing crime
by concentrating on reducing
(1) assaults
(2) robberies
(3) crimes against households
(4) motor vehicle theft
(5) purse snatchings

29 ① ② ③ ④ ⑤

30. An elderly person is more likely than the rest of the
population to be a victim of which of the following
crimes?
(1) Motor vehicle theft
(2) Robbery
(3) Aggravated assault
(4) Household burglary
(5) Purse snatching/pocket picking

30 ① ② ③ ④ ⑤

For answers and explanations, see page 207.

4. ANTHROPOLOGY

**K
E
Y

W
O
R
D
S**

culture—the sum total of beliefs, values, ideas, customs, knowledge, and tradition shared by people in a society and transmitted from generation to generation

values—standards in a society that are viewed as being desirable for their own sake

norms—a standard or guideline that tells a person how he should behave in a particular situation

ethnocentrism—the practice of judging another culture by using one's own system of values

cultural relativity—the objectivity that an anthropologist must have in viewing societies with different moral standards

Physical and Cultural Anthropology

Anthropology means the "science of man." Anthropology is a behavioral science that studies mankind as a whole, in its physical, social, and cultural aspects. None of the other behavioral or social sciences studies all of the various aspects of human life and activity in such a unified way. Anthropologists utilize many of the concepts of other social sciences and even the natural sciences.

Anthropology is divided into two broad fields of study: physical and cultural.

Physical anthropology seeks to develop detailed scientific knowledge about the biological characteristics of man in both ancient and modern times. Physical anthropology is closely related to the natural sciences of zoology, physiology, and anatomy. Physical anthropologists study man by comparing anatomies of living people through observation and measurement.

The field of physical anthropology has traced man's physical evolution back over the centuries to his origins in lower-level animals. Much new fossil evidence, found recently in East Africa, leaves little doubt that modern man (Homo sapiens) can trace his history back through several stages to primitive ancestors who first walked erect more than three million years ago.

The other major branch of anthropology, *cultural anthropology*, studies the wide variety of cultural and social differences among humans. Cultural anthropologists study both past and present cultures. They often use evidence obtained by the field of *archaeology,* the study of man's ancient past. Archaeologists carefully dig and sift through layers of the earth to physically uncover the material remnants of ancient human culture.

Culture and Values

Anthropologists study **culture**, the sum total of beliefs, values, ideas, customs, knowledge, and traditions that are shared by people in a society and transmitted from generation to generation. Culture is a pattern of thinking and feeling that is shared by a group, and since it is transmitted from generation to generation, it is called *acquired behavior*. Anthropologists also study the physical aspects of a culture such as tools and pottery— the *material culture*.

A cultural anthropologist starts his research from the assumption that no part of a culture can be understood apart from the whole and that a culture as a whole cannot be understood without a thorough knowledge of its parts. Because anthropologists view a whole culture, their approach is different from that of a psychologist or sociologist who studies segments of a culture such as individuals or groups. Traditionally, cultural anthropologists have focused their attention on cultures that were relatively simple and undeveloped. Today, however, they are investigating modern cultures more and more.

Let's look at some of the various elements of culture.

All cultures have **values** or standards that are viewed as being desirable for their own sake. Values can be used to judge a person's behavior. For example, values may include honesty, equality, politeness, or belief in God.

Norms are another important cultural element that are based on society's values. **Norms** tell a person how he should behave in a particular situation. For example, a norm against lying is justified by a cultural value emphasizing honesty.

Folkways and *mores* are types of norms. Folkways are customs or common ways of doing things that are expected but not mandatory. You may be expected to say "thank you" to someone who does a favor for you, but you are not forced to do so. Mores (pronounced *mor-ays*) are customs that one is more or less compelled to carry out because they are considered to be necessary to "our way of life." For example, it is a custom of our culture to be married to one person at a time. This is a custom, or more, that is backed up by force of law.

Values become norms, folkways, or mores and thereby a part of a culture through the process of *institutionalization*. Institutionalization translates values into the norms of accepted daily practice. This is similar to a court's upholding a new law as constitutional. The customs of the culture are backed up by forms of social control. Every culture devises ways to enforce its rules and to punish or sanction deviations from the culture. The more developed a culture becomes, the more elaborate an informal social control system it has.

It is very common for people to judge other cultures by using their own system of values. This is referred to as **ethnocentrism**. Ethnocentric Americans might find it strange that men in Muslim societies may have more than one wife or that some societies view dog meat as a delicacy. Ethnocentric men from societies where women are placed in a subordinate position might feel very threatened by a society's practice of woman's equality. Ethnocentrism, unfortunately, has led to racial and cultural prejudice. It is only through breaking down barriers of ignorance among cultures and races that such prejudice can be overcome.

At the opposite end of the spectrum from ethnocentrism is **cultural relativity**. This is practiced by anthropologists who try to prevent their own values from influencing them when observing another culture with different moral standards.

For example, a wide variety of marriage customs, sexual practices, and taboos exist in different cultures. It is not the job of the anthropologist to pronounce moral judgments on cultural practices that she may personally disagree with, nor should she ever attempt to change a culture. This does not mean that inhumane or particularly offensive practices are justified, and it is easy to see that cultural relativity can occasionally conflict with certain moral and ethical considerations.

Changes in Cultures

Inventions and Cultural Diffusion
All cultures are changeable, although the rates of change may vary widely. Some cultures appear to change overnight, while others remain relatively unchanged for centuries.

One of the most important factors in cultural development is the level of a society's development or material culture. *Material culture* refers to the level of man-made tools and technology in a given society. It also encompasses the knowledge, applications, and values concerning these objects.

A change in a society's material culture usually comes about as a result of a new invention. The invention may have come from within the society, or it might have been borrowed from the outside. In primitive societies, most original inventions were not created systematically since rarely did man have time to tinker with gadgets. In our modern society, inventions are usually the result of a conscious scheme such as a research project.

Inventions must be accepted by a society. Such acceptance is largely dependent on a society's values. In simpler societies, an invention usually will have to satisfy a practical need such as making work easier or producing more needed goods. In modern industrial societies like the U.S., where technology is widely accepted, inventions have been adopted with minimum controversy and often little regard for possible social consequences. In recent years, many inventions have been subject to intensive scrutiny by various interest groups and by some government agencies.

Inventions are mostly introduced to societies through the process of **cultural diffusion**, the spreading of cultural elements to different societies.

Most societies can claim only a small number of original inventions. Different cultures have practiced a great amount of borrowing from other societies.

During the past fifty years, due to advances in transportation and communication, there has been a large increase in cultural diffusion. Modern technology has been spread to all parts of the Earth. For example, villages in underdeveloped lands that could not afford movie projection equipment are now viewing dubbed-in American movies on a television screen because of access to low-cost videocassette recorders. In North America itself, mass communications and increased mobility have blurred regional and national differences in food, music, and dress. You can now find Mexican snacks in popular fast food restaurants in Chicago and turn on your pocket-size FM stereo radio in Mexico City and listen to American rock music around the clock.

Cultural Evolution

Why do cultures evolve and change? Modern anthropologists have rejected any single theory of cultural evolution to explain this. However, they have accepted some partial explanations. These explanations demonstrate that some cultures show similar patterns of development and change while others do not. Likewise, they have argued that there are certain historical developments that must take place before others become possible.

For instance, two major elements in the advance of technology were the understanding of the concept of zero in mathematics and the practical application of the wheel for transportation and machinery. The concept of zero is necessary for the application of math to many aspects of everyday life. Many innovations, such as the thermometer, could not have been developed without the concept of zero. Likewise, modern machinery and production could not have been developed without the wheel. For example, the Aztec Indian civilization in Mexico was a generally advanced form of civilization, but the Aztecs never learned any practical application for wheels except placing them on children's toys. This limited their potential to grow technologically or economically.

Directions: Based on what you have just read, answer the following questions. Fill in the circle that corresponds to the correct answer.

31.   At a school board meeting, those supporting the teaching of evolution would seek the help of a specialist in
(1)   physical anthropology
(2)   cultural anthropology
(3)   monkeyshines
(4)   innovation
(5)   cultural relativity

31 ① ② ③ ④ ⑤

32. Laws against public nudity reflect
(1) a tradition
(2) a more
(3) an institution
(4) a change in material culture
(5) cultural diffusion

33. *Ethnocentrism* is another word for
(1) prejudice
(2) culture
(3) an anthropologist
(4) innovation
(5) evolution

34. According to the essay, most of man's original inventions were
(1) directly related to the discovery of fire
(2) the result of a conscious scheme
(3) not part of a systematic plan
(4) transmitted from one culture to another
(5) controversial

35. Which of the following is an example of cultural diffusion?
(1) The use of computers to diagnose illness
(2) The custom of June weddings
(3) Mandatory curfews for people under sixteen years of age
(4) The Aztecs' use of the wheel on children's toys
(5) The celebration of the Irish holiday of St. Patrick's Day in the United States

For answers and explanations, see page 208.

BEHAVIORAL SCIENCE EXERCISE 6

Directions: The following is an excerpt from an anthropological study of the rituals of the Nacirema culture. As you read through it, you may find that the Nacirema culture is one that you are quite familiar with. If you're still not sure about it, write the name of the cultural hero Notgnihsaw backward. Read the questions that follow the passage and fill in the circle that corresponds to the correct answer.

The Nacirema

Little is known of their origin, although tradition states that they came from the east. According to Nacirema mythology, their nation was originated by a culture hero, Notgnihsaw, who is

otherwise known for two great feats of strength—the throwing of
5   a piece of wampum across the river Po-To-Mac and the chopping
down of a cherry tree in which the Spirit of Truth resided. . . .

The fundamental belief underlying the whole system appears to
be that the human body is ugly and that its natural tendency is to
debility and disease. Incarcerated in such a body, man's only hope
10   is to avert these characteristics through the use of the powerful
influences of ritual and ceremony. Every household has one or
more shrines devoted to this purpose. The more powerful individuals in the society have several shrines in their houses, and, in fact,
the opulence of a house is often referred to in terms of the number
15   of such ritual centers it possesses. . . .

The daily body ritual performed by everyone includes a mouth-
rite. Despite the fact that these people are so punctilious about
care of the mouth, this rite involves a practice which strikes the
uninitiated stranger as revolting. It was reported to me that the
20   ritual consists of inserting a small bundle of hog hairs into the
mouth, along with certain magical powders, and then moving the
bundle in a highly formalized series of gestures.

In addition to the private mouth-rite, the people seek out a
holy-mouth-man once or twice a year. These practitioners have an
25   impressive set of paraphernalia, consisting of a variety of augers,
awls, probes, and prods. The use of these objects in the exorcism
of the evils of the mouth involves almost unbelievable ritual
torture of the client.

36. Who are the Nacirema?   36 ① ② ③ ④ ⑤
   (1) A prehistoric culture
   (2) An African tribal society
   (3) A group of anthropologists
   (4) Modern-day Americans
   (5) Dentists

37. What is the fundamental belief of the Nacirema?   37 ① ② ③ ④ ⑤
   (1) It is important to build religious shrines in every
       house.
   (2) Everyone must perform daily rituals with hog
       hairs.
   (3) The human body is ugly and its natural tendency
       is to debility and disease.
   (4) The hero Notgnihsaw was their god.
   (5) People must be exorcised by the holy-mouth-man
       once or twice each year.

38. The ritual shrine described here is probably located in
    (1)   some ancient village in the Middle East
    (2)   a medieval peasant's hut
    (3)   a West African village
    (4)   the western Pacific
    (5)   an American home

38 ① ② ③ ④ ⑤

39. With this passage, the author is trying to get us to
    (1)   see our own culture as an outsider might view it
    (2)   make fun of an obviously primitive culture
    (3)   see how cultural relativity is used in observing
        strange religious rites
    (4)   show understanding of an underdeveloped culture
    (5)   examine the roots of Nacirema religion

39 ① ② ③ ④ ⑤

For answers and explanations, see page 208.

BEHAVIORAL SCIENCE EXERCISE 7 ――――――――――

Directions: Read the passage and answer the questions that follow. Fill in
the circle that corresponds to the correct answer.

Cultures and Legal Systems

Have you ever thought about the wide variations of laws and legal
systems in different parts of the world? Below are examples of the
legal systems in two societies.

    1. An unusual form of legal system prevailed in Eskimo
5   societies in the harsh Arctic regions. Eskimo societies were organized into local groups that lacked any real form of government,
although they had a headman who led the group. The headman
had no legal or judicial authority, and there were very few laws in
these cultures. The Eskimos also recognized few crimes against
10 property because people did not own land. The custom of freely
borrowing goods from each other also discouraged stealing.

    In the past, certain Eskimo cultures sanctioned some forms of
homicide, including the killing of sickly infants, senile or sickly
elderly persons, and invalids. These actions were sanctioned so
15 that the society's resources could be used to support the healthy.
Access to modern transportation and medicine has greatly
changed this situation.

    In the Eskimos' cultures, wife stealing was not a crime, and it
was usually committed by a man who sought to outrank socially
20 the man whose wife was stolen. Legal disputes, such as wife

stealing, were settled by the murder of the offender (and the risk of a possible feud with the offender's relatives) or by a song contest during which each party insulted the other. The winner was determined by whoever received the most applause.

25   2.   The Ifugaos tribesmen of the Philippine Islands have a very different form of legal system from the Eskimos. Numbering more than 125,000, these headhunters live in the mountains of Luzon, where they have carved out enormous irrigated rice paddies from the walls of the mountains. The Ifugaos have virtually no
30   government; however, they do have a legal system in which offenses and punishments are stated with preciseness. It is up to the individual to prosecute wrongs since crimes against society are not even recognized.

An impartial "go between," a *monkalun*, is used as a judge. The
35   *monkalun* shuttles back and forth between the plaintiff and defendant in a very complicated display of diplomacy. He tries to force the parties to agree on acceptable terms for resolving the dispute. Both parties must agree on the offense and the terms of the settlement. While negotiations continue, both parties attempt
40   to raise a fighting force among their relatives. If a settlement is not reached, the *monkalun* backs out of the case and anarchy prevails as the plaintiff and his relatives feud with the defendant and his relatives.

40.   We can infer from the Eskimo experience that a society where there is little private ownership of property probably
    (1)   is run by socialists or communists
    (2)   has a low rate of crimes committed against property
    (3)   treats wives as public property
    (4)   has stiff penalties for crimes against property
    (5)   has a very strong government

40 ① ② ③ ④ ⑤

41.   The nature of the practice of wife stealing in an Eskimo society is an indication that
    (1)   women were in an inferior position and treated as possessions
    (2)   Eskimo society practiced women's liberation
    (3)   there was a surplus of women in the culture
    (4)   women held important positions in that society
    (5)   the family did not hold an important position as an institution

41 ① ② ③ ④ ⑤

42. The cultures of both the Eskimos and Ifugaos allow
    for feuds as one means to settle a legal dispute. This
    situation may reflect which of the following factors
    common to <u>both</u> societies?

    42 ① ② ③ ④ ⑤

    (1) No formal government structure to enforce
         settlement of legal disputes
    (2) A legal system with precise laws
    (3) A headman with strong judicial powers
    (4) The lack of private property
    (5) The use of a *monkalun* to mediate a dispute

For answers and explanations, see page 208.

ANSWERS AND EXPLANATIONS

1. INTRODUCTION TO BEHAVIORAL SCIENCE

Making Inferences   1. (1)   Sociologists are the behavioral scientists who study the impact of social developments on people's lives.

Applying Ideas   2. (3)   A psychiatrist would be the best choice to contribute expert testimony about a defendant's motivation and behavior.

Making Inferences   3. (4)   An anthropologist who specializes in understanding cultural values and traditions would be most helpful for observation and advice.

Finding Details   4. (5)   The last section of the essay describes the far-reaching impact of the behavioral sciences on society.

Applying Ideas   5. (2)   A generalization is a general statement based on a certain fact.

Applying Ideas   6. (3)   This is a belief—a theory—based on a systematic study of patterns of discrimination.

2. PSYCHOLOGY

Finding Details   7. (5)   In the section on personality, all of the choices except primary motives are mentioned as factors that affect personality development.

Drawing Conclusions   8. (2)   Innate traits are characteristics that a person is born with. It is safe to conclude that a child with such unusual talents was born with such tendencies.

Making Inferences   9. (1)   The essay described motivation as the factors that start, maintain, and stop an individual's activity. The company seeks to motivate its workers.

Applying Ideas   10. (2)   The mother is trying to stop her daughter's fighting by punishing her. Punishment is a form of negative reinforcement.

Applying Ideas   11. (5)   Blaming someone else for one's personal problems is one type of defense mechanism. According to the essay, defense mechanisms are used to help a person maintain a good self-image, but they can distort one's sense of reality.

Finding Details   12. (2)   The essay describes one root of psychosis as the physical deterioration of some aspect of the nervous system. Drug abuse is the only choice that could have such an effect.

BEHAVIORAL SCIENCE EXERCISE 1

Making Inferences   13. (5)   Each theory is based on vastly different assumptions about how people look at work and what motivates them to work.

Applying Ideas   14. (4)   Theory Y suggests that teamwork and involvement in all aspects of an endeavor encourage people to be more conscientious and productive. Applied to a classroom situation, this best fits choice (4).

BEHAVIORAL SCIENCE EXERCISE 2

Drawing Conclusions 15. (2) The graph shows that those adults who had been exposed to relatively less violence as children were less likely to show aggressive behavior than those who had watched more violence as children.

Making Inferences 16. (4) The cartoonist depicts a father using physical force to encourage the child not to "hit his sister." By illustrating such contradictory messages to the child, the cartoonist is showing that he believes that parents teach their children violent behavior.

Drawing Conclusions 17. (1) Both the graph and the cartoon show the influence that seeing or experiencing violence has had on the personality development of children. Together, they indicate that aggression and violence are learned behaviors.

3. SOCIOLOGY

Making Inferences 18. (3) A primary group consists of your closest personal relationships. Of the choices offered, only a daughter fits this definition.

Applying Ideas 19. (2) Socialization is the process by which a person learns the norms, values, and beliefs of his society. Most often, people learn these from their parents.

Applying Ideas 20. (4) A person knowledgeable in the area of organizations and bureaucracies—secondary groups—would be most helpful.

Applying Ideas 21. (1) A doctor is not used to doing manual labor for a living. This is an example of inconsistency of status.

Applying Ideas 22. (1) Racial background is something over which one has no control.

Finding Details 23. (4) This is the only point not mentioned in the section of the essay on social stratification.

BEHAVIORAL SCIENCE EXERCISE 3

Finding Details 24. (2) According to the chart, Jill's participation in a consciousness-raising group led both Joe and her to change their traditional sex roles.

Applying Ideas 25. (1) A group of friends is a peer group.

Finding Details 26. (4) According to the chart, Joe's participation with others in the protest march was an example of collective action.

BEHAVIORAL SCIENCE EXERCISE 4

Finding Details 27. (4) The title indicates that the graph compares the frequency of smiling in three different environments.

Drawing Conclusions 28. (4) The fact that there is such a difference in the frequency of smiling suggests that the level of interaction with infants differs greatly in the three environments.

BEHAVIORAL SCIENCE EXERCISE 5

Drawing Conclusions 29. (3) Together, the two sets of bars labeled "household larceny" and "household burglary" constitute the greatest number of crimes.

Finding Details 30. (5) Of all the areas shown, purse snatching and pocket picking affect those over 65 more than those under.

4. ANTHROPOLOGY

Drawing Conclusions	31.	(1)	According to the passage, physical anthropologists study human evolution.
Applying Ideas	32.	(2)	A more is a custom that you are somewhat compelled to carry out because it is expected of you.
Making Inferences	33.	(1)	According to the text, ethnocentrism represents a tendency to judge other people by one's own values. This type of thinking represents prejudice.
Finding Details	34.	(3)	According to the passage, most of man's original discoveries and inventions were not created systematically.
Applying Ideas	35.	(5)	Cultural diffusion is the spreading of elements of culture from one society to another. Of the choices given, only (5) is an example of this.

BEHAVIORAL SCIENCE EXERCISE 6

Making Inferences	36.	(4)	Several of the references in the essay are clues to lead you to this inference. For instance, Nacirema spelled backward is American, and Notgnihsaw is Washington. The description of the house shrines and the holy-mouth-man are also clues.
Finding Details	37.	(3)	This is stated directly in the essay.
Making Inferences	38.	(5)	Once you have inferred that the Nacirema are Americans, this follows naturally.
Making Inferences	39.	(1)	By describing an aspect of our culture in terms that seem unfamiliar and odd, the author is helping us to see how a society is viewed by outsiders.

BEHAVIORAL SCIENCE EXERCISE 7

Making Inferences	40.	(2)	According to the essay, the Eskimos owned little property and borrowed freely. This discouraged stealing and other crimes against property.
Drawing Conclusions	41.	(1)	If one man could steal another's wife, this is an indication that women held an inferior position and were treated as possessions.
Finding Details	42.	(1)	While these societies did have informal legal systems, neither had a formal governmental structure.

Economics

---

1. INTRODUCTION TO ECONOMICS

economy—the organized way in which a society produces, distributes, and consumes its goods and services

economics—the branch of social science that studies how economies work

market economy—the basis of the capitalist economic system, in which production, prices, and distribution of goods and services are determined by competition

commodities—goods for which ownership can be traded or exchanged

Economics and Economists

All human societies face the problem of producing, distributing, and consuming goods and services. An **economy** is the organized way in which a society carries out these tasks. **Economics** is the branch of social science that studies how these systems work.

Economics is mainly concerned with understanding how different types of economies work. Economics has many specialized areas of study. One important distinction in this field is between *macroeconomics* and *microeconomics*. Macroeconomics studies the workings of whole systems, like the U.S. economy. Microeconomics studies smaller parts of these systems; for example, the economics of retail trade in a particular city or state.

The growth of government activity in the economy has increased the importance of economic analysis, and the role of economists has expanded to deal with these needs. Economists are involved in government planning through such organizations as the President's Council of Economic Advisors, the General Accounting Office, and the Bureau of the Budget. The

Federal Reserve System uses economists to develop credit policies for the country.

Economists also have important roles in private business, planning long-range strategies. They are often involved in small-scale studies of corporate operations. Labor unions also hire economists to make forecasts and to evaluate contract proposals.

Economists, acting as social scientists, offer predictions about possible outcomes of specific economic decisions. For example, the president's advisors can offer ideas about the effect a specific jobs bill might have on inflation and unemployment. However, the final decision about whether to give more weight to fighting inflation or to fighting unemployment is a value judgment based on political views. Economists can advise, but elected political leaders and citizens must decide.

Directions: Based upon what you have just read, fill in the circle that corresponds to the correct answer.

1. The term *economy* is best defined as
   (1) the system of exchanging goods and services
   (2) the development of a division of labor
   (3) the system of producing goods and services
   (4) the system of investing and building a surplus for further development
   (5) the system of producing, distributing, and consuming goods and services

   1 ① ② ③ ④ ⑤

2. Macroeconomics is the study of
   (1) the food industry
   (2) individual parts of the economic system
   (3) how to develop production line efficiency
   (4) the workings of whole economic systems
   (5) the macrame industry

   2 ① ② ③ ④ ⑤

3. In what capacity might a power company employ an economist?
   (1) To analyze the safety of a nuclear reactor
   (2) To explain the functioning of a nuclear reactor to the public
   (3) To carry out the power company's billing procedure
   (4) To investigate claims that the reactor caused health hazards
   (5) To explain costs and cost savings to the power company's shareholders

   3 ① ② ③ ④ ⑤

For answers and explanations, see page 248.

Development of Economic Systems

Economists study past economic organization as well as today's economies. The study of earlier societies gives us a better understanding of modern economies and how economic organization has changed.

Early Economic Systems

Historically, the simplest economic system was that of the early hunting and gathering societies, which produced only for day-to-day subsistence. Nearly everything produced by economic activity was immediately consumed, leaving hardly any surplus product that could be stored or saved.

The development of settled agriculture (the raising of crops and animals) created more food than could immediately be eaten, and the resulting surplus was used to support people in jobs that were not directly involved in food production, including merchants, government officials, warriors, and priests. Part of the surplus was taxed, and the proceeds were used to build towns with centralized governments.

The feudal economy of medieval Europe (A.D. 600 to 1500) was based on settled agriculture. Peasant serfs, tied to the land, farmed the land that belonged to nobles and the Church. Craftsmen in the towns, organized into guilds, accounted for most of the small-scale nonfarm production of goods. Essentially, everyone was legally tied for lifetime to his economic and social position. Markets and all economic activity were strictly controlled by tradition, which greatly restricted economic growth and gave no incentive for technological change.

The discovery and conquest of the New World during the sixteenth century quickened the pace of economic development in Europe. Vast amounts of gold and silver, plundered by Spain in Mexico and in other New World possessions, flooded into Europe and helped to finance economic expansion. World trade began to flourish, partially as a result of the new slave trade. By the late eighteenth century, this great wealth was used to finance the rapid growth in industrialization that became known as the Industrial Revolution. These developments paved the way for capitalism to replace feudalism as the dominant economic system.

The Emergence of Capitalism

With the emergence of capitalism, the marketplace became the center of economic activity; all goods, services, and human labor became **commodities**—items for sale in the marketplace. The term **market economy** refers to a system based on buyers' and sellers' abilities to compete for land, labor, goods, and services based on their own best interests. The market replaced feudal traditions and the authority of the Church as the regulator of economic life.

Under capitalism, workers were no longer tied to a particular piece of land or to a specific landowner. Over a period of centuries, the former serfs (now laborers) became free to sell their labor in the factories, but lost the means to support themselves off the land.

The dissolving of the feudal economic system was accompanied by a breakdown in the rigid political and economic systems that had governed Europe for centuries. The new class of merchants and manufacturers led political revolts against the restrictions of the feudal system, paving the way for democratic political rights, religious reform, and the birth of modern nations.

From the 1600s through the 1900s, the process of industrialization and accumulation of wealth revolutionized the face of the Earth. Great amounts of wealth were accumulated and invested in transforming industry and agriculture. These investments, combined with rapid technological advancement, have brought an era of economic prosperity and growth to many in the industrialized nations. At the same time, challenges to unrestrained capitalism have arisen. Legislation in capitalist nations has been used to prohibit abuses of the system. Also, socialist systems have replaced capitalism in some parts of the world.

Types of Economic Systems

Today, there are three main types of economic systems—capitalist, socialist, and mixed. Capitalist economies base their economic activity on the maximization of private profit for owners of business enterprises. These economies are called *market economies* because economic activity is governed primarily by the workings of the market and not the decisions of centrally directed economic planning.

Socialist countries have planned economies. The central government takes over the function of the market and attempts to plan production, distribution, and investment. Economic activity is motivated by the pursuit of maximum production for use by that society rather than by private profit. Mixed economies combine some elements of market economies with some centralized planning.

No country's economy is purely of one type, but countries do clearly differ as to which type is predominant. The U.S. is capitalist, although highly modified, as we shall see later. The Soviet Union has a socialist economy but increasingly is using market mechanisms and individual incentives. Sweden is a country with a mixed economy.

Directions: Based upon what you have just read, fill in the circle that corresponds to the correct answer.

4. Under capitalism, labor is   **4** ① ② ③ ④ ⑤
   (1) restricted by the rights of nobles
   (2) regulated by Church traditions
   (3) controlled by central planners
   (4) a special category, not affected by markets
   (5) a commodity for sale in the marketplace

5. Based on the ideas in this passage, you could conclude that, in the future, the American economy will probably
   (1) not evolve anymore
   (2) remain based on serf labor
   (3) continue to evolve in new directions
   (4) remain a pure capitalist economy
   (5) continue as a noncommodity economy

6. Based on the material in this essay, you could conclude that a change in the American economy would have the following effect on American political structures:
   (1) It would have little effect because political systems don't change.
   (2) It would lead to changes in the political system because economics and politics are closely related.
   (3) It would lead to little change because political structures are not related to economic structures.
   (4) It would lessen the political role of the economists.
   (5) It would lessen the impact of macroeconomics.

For answers and explanations, see page 248.

ECONOMICS EXERCISE 1

Directions: Read the following passage and fill in the circle that corresponds to the correct answer.

Keeping an Eye on Statistics

You may have heard people complain that "statistics can be used to prove anything." While statistics are important in understanding the economy, you can be misled if you are not familiar with some of their common uses. To clarify this, look at an example

5 about economic growth in the United States.

The economic output of a country is measured in Gross National Product (GNP)—the total value of goods, services, and income. The dollar amount of the American GNP rose from $30 billion in 1900 to almost $3 trillion in 1980. This is an enormous

10 increase—a rise of 10,000 percent. However, this is called the *nominal GNP* and does not take into account price increases or inflation over time. The nominal GNP can be very misleading.

To determine the *real GNP*, economists adjust the nominal GNP for inflation. This is done by using prices from one base year

15 (such as 1972) to calculate the value of goods sold in all other

years. When this adjustment is made, the real GNP is said to have gone from $150 billion to more than $1 trillion (based on 1972 dollars) between 1900 and 1980. This increase of more than 700 percent is still large, but not as large as the change in the nominal

20 GNP would indicate.

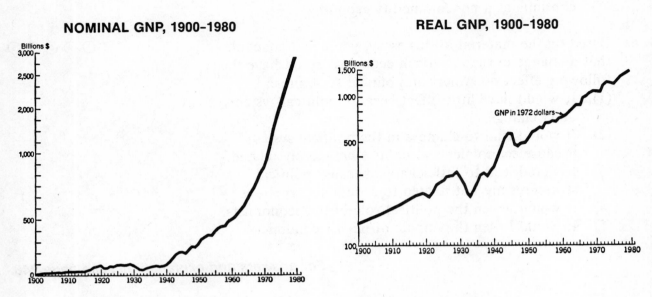

NOMINAL GNP, 1900-1980

REAL GNP, 1900-1980

How would average citizens know this? We wouldn't, which means that we must put some faith in those who put together and disseminate statistics. At the same time, we should be cautious, since statistics can be twisted to prove one point or another.

25 When you are reading comparisons of statistics, make sure that the same scales of measurement and the same time period are being used. Otherwise, you may be misled as to the significance of the statistics.

7. The main point of this passage is that   7 ① ② ③ ④ ⑤
   (1) you can never trust statistics
   (2) statistics are not really useful
   (3) you can never trust an economist
   (4) you should be aware of the basis for a statistical comparison
   (5) since statistics are facts, they can always be trusted

8. In warning about an increased national debt, a   8 ① ② ③ ④ ⑤
   newspaper editorial made the following observation:

   "The national debt has increased from $2 billion in 1880 to more than $1 trillion in 1984. This means that every man, woman, and child in this country is 500 times deeper in debt than their grandparents were, just a little more than a century ago."

In laying the groundwork for the editorial's description
of the growth in national debt, the writer
(1) has failed to indicate whether the same value is
     being used for 1880 and 1984 dollars
(2) has understated the growth in debt
(3) has deliberately misled the reader
(4) is arguing for large cuts in federal spending
(5) should also discuss the GNP

For answers and explanations, see page 248.

2. HOW THE OVERALL ECONOMY WORKS

K E Y   W O R D S

aggregate demand—the total demand for goods and services by individuals, business, and government

supply and demand—the process by which a market economy adjusts production and consumption

equilibrium—the point at which prices function to match supply and demand

Gross National Product—the value of an entire nation's production measured over a period of time

consumer goods—products bought for personal consumption

capital goods—goods used to produce other goods

Supply and Demand

The driving force in our economy is the demand for goods and services. **Aggregate demand** is the total amount of demand in the entire economy. The aggregate demand for goods by individuals, businesses, and government creates the conditions for business to behave productively.

Businesses do not produce in a vacuum; they must feel reasonably sure that their goods or services will be bought. At the same time, consumers must not only desire something; they must also be able to purchase it. This sets the basis for the relationship between **supply and demand**. This relationship is determined mainly by prices.

We see evidence of the impact of prices on supply and demand in our daily activities. If the prices for certain goods go up, demand will tend to fall, and if prices go down, demand will tend to rise.

Over the last decade, we have seen how changes in the price of gasoline have dramatically affected demand. In the days when gas was relatively "cheap," people thought nothing of using their cars for long trips and everyday use. When gas prices began to skyrocket, people began to find alternatives to driving long distances for vacations. They began to take economy measures such as driving in car pools or buying cars that get more miles to the gallon.

While price affects consumer demand, producers attempt to bring the supply that they produce under control. If there is an oversupply of a product, vast inventories will sit in warehouses and producers will take a big loss. If there is not enough supply, consumers will lose interest and potential sales will be lost.

How is all of this kept in line? No one has a crystal ball to project supply or demand. It is the competitive workings of the marketplace that help to keep relative order. Companies will try to sell products at a lower price than their competitors so that consumers will buy from them. This helps to keep prices from getting totally out of control.

The relation between supply and demand and prices is demonstrated by the graph below.

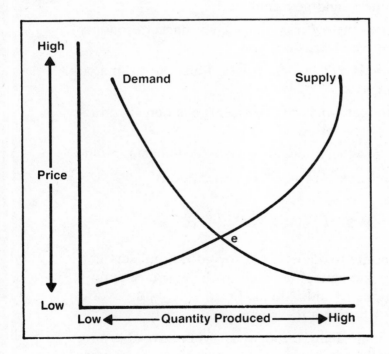

The curve labeled "demand" shows that there is low demand when prices are high but that demand increases as prices go down. The curve labeled "supply" moves in the opposite direction. Supply is low when prices are low, but supply increases as prices increase. The more income a producer gets from a product, the more he is encouraged to produce it.

Prices function to bring supply and demand into balance or equilibrium (this is labeled "e" on the graph). **Equilibrium** is the point at which supply and demand match exactly. If the producer tries to charge too much, demand will decline and he will be left "holding the bag." If he charges beneath this point, demand will escalate and a shortage will occur.

For each product, there is such a supply-demand relationship, and the function of the market is to constantly balance the economic interests of individuals, businesses, and government. If prices go too high, demand dries up and producers lower prices. If demand is high for an item and the supply is low, prices will tend to go up. However, other producers may take notice of high prices and begin to produce more of the item, ultimately forcing prices downward as the supply increases. In this way, the market works to balance out production and demand over the long run.

Directions: Based upon what you have just read, fill in the circle that corresponds to the correct answer.

9. Which of the graphs below shows the relationship between price and demand?

9 ① ② ③ ④ ⑤

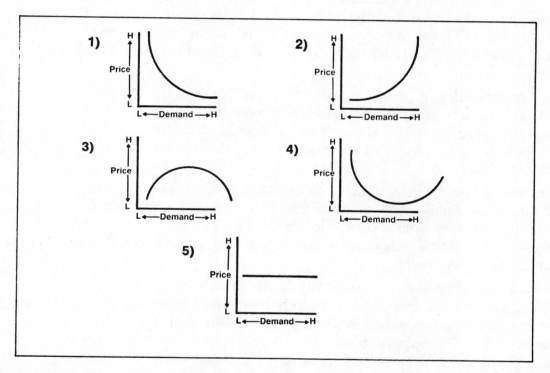

10. During Christmas 1983, there was a sudden upsurge in the popularity of a toy called the Cabbage Patch Kids. As Christmas drew near, the dolls became virtually unavailable, and people sold dolls for $50, $100, and even $1,000. In describing this phenomenon, an economist would say that

10 ① ② ③ ④ ⑤

(1) there was a surplus of the dolls and prices declined
(2) there was a surplus of the dolls and prices rose
(3) there was a shortage of the dolls and prices declined
(4) there was a shortage of the dolls and prices rose
(5) there was a shortage of the dolls, causing prices to stabilize

For answers and explanations, see page 248.

The Gross National Product, Spending, and Investment

The total value of the output of all economic activity in the country is measured as the **Gross National Product (GNP)**. The nation's production can be divided into two general categories: consumer goods and capital goods. **Consumer goods** are products and services that are purchased for personal consumption: cars, clothing, medical services, dry cleaning, etc. **Capital goods** are used to produce other goods: machinery, roads, power plants, etc. Capital goods are used to expand the productive capacity of the economy. In 1981, the GNP totaled three trillion dollars ($3,000,000,000,000).

Consumer spending makes up the largest single component of the GNP, about 70 percent. Changes in the levels of consumer spending are based mainly on fluctuations in consumer income, although they are also influenced by consumer debt, interest rates, and expectations about the future. However, as large as consumer spending is, it is not the dynamic force in the economy. Consumer spending is the cart, not the horse, of the economy.

Investment spending on capital goods is the horse that pulls the economy forward. This creates new jobs, higher total income, and more consumer spending. Investment spending also creates a multiplier effect—each dollar invested in new production creates several more dollars in investment and consumer spending.

Recessions and depressions result from declining investment in production. Reduced production leads to increases in unemployment, which means that fewer people have money to spend. This further discourages production and leads to a cycle of economic decline until something is done to stimulate new investment.

This kind of process contributed greatly to the Great Depression of the 1930s. The country did not recover entirely from the Depression until government spending for war production poured millions of dollars into the economy from 1941 onward. Since World War II, government spending has been a major factor in keeping recurrent recessions from becoming depressions.

While demand is the driving force in a market economy, fluctuations in investment are also critical and affect the ups and downs of the business cycle. Even though ours is considered a market economy, the government does intervene and has prevented economic disaster. A later essay in this section will describe in more detail the government's role in the economy.

Directions: Based upon what you have just read, fill in the circle that corresponds to the correct answer.

11. The largest component of the GNP is
    (1) government spending
    (2) consumer spending
    (3) investment spending
    (4) corporate spending
    (5) military spending

11 ① ② ③ ④ ⑤

12. The situation in which declining production leads to unemployment and lowered consumer spending is called
    (1) capital investment
    (2) a recession
    (3) overproduction
    (4) upward spiral
    (5) overconsumption

12 ① ② ③ ④ ⑤

13. The most likely result of a drastic decrease in investment on capital goods would be
    (1) a decline in production
    (2) an increase in consumer spending
    (3) a decline in unemployment
    (4) an increase in the GNP
    (5) a decrease in government spending

13 ① ② ③ ④ ⑤

For answers and explanations, see page 248.

ECONOMICS EXERCISE 2

Directions: Use the table below to answer the questions that follow. Fill in the circle that corresponds to the correct answer.

U.S. GROSS AND NET NATIONAL PRODUCTS (in millions of dollars) includes Alaska and Hawaii beginning in 1960				
	1950	**1960**	**1970**	**1980**
Gross National Product	286,172	505,978	982,419	2,633,108
Less: Capital Consumption Allowance	−23,853	−47,712	−90,827	−293,204
Equals: Net National Product	262,319	458,266	894,592	2,339,904
Source: U.S. Dept. of Commerce				

14. By 1980, the U.S. Gross National Product was

    (1)   more than $2½ trillion
    (2)   less than $2½ million
    (3)   less than the GNP in 1950
    (4)   double the GNP in 1950
    (5)   on the decline

15. To find the Net National Product, you

    (1)   add the GNPs for the thirty-year period
    (2)   add the Capital Consumption Allowance to the
          GNP
    (3)   subtract the Capital Consumption Allowance from
          the GNP
    (4)   divide the GNP by the Capital Consumption
          Allowance
    (5)   average the GNP over a thirty-year period

For answers and explanations, see page 248.

3.   HOW BUSINESSES BEHAVE

KEY WORDS

factors of production—the components required to make a commodity

productivity—the efficient use of the factors of production to produce goods

oligopoly—a market situation in which very few sellers account for a large proportion of sales of a product

monopoly—a market in which there is just one seller of a product (pure monopoly) *or* when one seller controls a dominant portion of the market

The beginning point for understanding business behavior is knowing that business exists for one purpose in a capitalist economy—to make profit. The president of General Motors once remarked that his company was not in the business of making cars, it was in the business of making profits, and making cars just happened to be the way it made profits. The profit motive is what makes the wheels of American industry turn.

Productivity and Profit

Businessmen make profits by skillfully managing the costs of the **factors of production**—land, labor, and capital. These factors are what are required for producing goods. In a capitalist economy, all three factors are for sale on the market as commodities.

Factors of production are used to keep the cost of production lower than the return on sales. The difference between the cost of production and the return on sales is the profit (or loss). To make a profit, the businessman tries to keep the costs of all three factors of production as low as he can by keeping down the costs of labor, raw materials, and machinery.

A major way of keeping down the cost of each item produced is to increase **productivity**. Productivity is usually measured in output per man-hour of labor.

Take the example of a group of workers that usually produces 60 cars per hour and is paid $1,000 per hour. If production increases to 120 cars per hour, productivity has increased 100 percent, but the workers are still being paid the same amount of money. In effect, the owner has saved money because he is paying less for the labor in each car. He can then take out or reinvest this money, or he can pass it along to the consumer in the form of lower prices or to the workers in the form of a wage increase.

Productivity can also be increased by raising the quality of the factors of production. A better trained work force is more productive; increased worker morale and motivation may also increase output. Investment in new technology and improvements in management planning and organization will also increase productivity. The Japanese have effectively combined several of these techniques in increasing productivity and improving quality. These changes have allowed them to make a better car for less money than the U.S. auto industry and to take away a substantial share of the auto market.

Besides making a product as cheaply as possible, the company must sell it in order to make a profit. The branch of business dealing with sales is called *marketing*. Companies develop marketing strategies for their products. They define target populations to sell to and plan packaging and advertising campaigns based on these targets. Advertising specialists select certain symbols that will appeal to their target population and choose the media that will reach that population.

Competition vs. Monopoly

Businessmen do not live in a vacuum. They must compete with other businessmen for sales. In areas of the economy where there are many small businesses, there is usually a great deal of price competition. For example, the service sector of the economy, which includes many small businesses, is highly competitive.

Other areas of the economy, such as aluminum production, are not very price competitive. They are dominated by a few giant corporations that create an oligopoly. An **oligopoly** is a market situation with just a few sellers of a product. There is usually little price competition between them, ensuring a steady rate of profit. In an oligopoly situation, the main competition is focused not on price, but on advertising, customer service, and other forms of nonprice competition.

The opposite extreme of a competitive market is a **monopoly** in which there is just one seller of a product. While a pure monopoly has never existed, the word *monopoly* has also come to mean a situation in which one seller controls a dominant portion of the market for one product. Prior to its breakup in 1984, American Telephone and Telegraph (AT&T) was considered to have had a monopoly, although not exclusive control, of telephone services. The closest thing to a real monopoly today would be a cartel. In a cartel, a group of producers divide up markets and set prices. The Organization of Petroleum Exporting Countries (OPEC) is an example of an international cartel. Cartels and monopolies are illegal in the U.S.

In summary, businessmen are in business to make profits. To make profits, they must combine the factors of production in such a way that the sale of their product brings in more money than costs take out. Businessmen try to accomplish this by: (1) paying the lowest possible amount for the factors of production, (2) increasing productivity, (3) using good marketing strategies, and (4) controlling or organizing the market to reduce price competition.

Directions: Based upon what you have just read, fill in the circle that corresponds to the correct answer.

16. If a company had a continuous increase in productivity, which of the following would be possible?
    (1) Prices could go higher and higher.
    (2) Prices could be reduced and wages increased.
    (3) The sales force would be cut.
    (4) Wages could go down and prices could go higher.
    (5) Layoffs would increase.

16 ① ② ③ ④ ⑤

17. Marketing is that branch of business activity concerned with
    (1) increasing productivity
    (2) controlling the cost of the factors of production
    (3) employee morale
    (4) planning sales campaigns
    (5) reducing unit costs

17 ① ② ③ ④ ⑤

18. A monopolistic market condition exists when
    (1) one seller dominates a market
    (2) a few sellers divide the market
    (3) there is only one buyer for a product
    (4) groups of producers get together to divide up markets
    (5) there are many small producers

19. Which of the following is a method that would best maximize profits?
    (1) Lower factor costs and raise productivity.
    (2) Raise factor costs and lower productivity.
    (3) Join a cartel.
    (4) Get a government subsidy.
    (5) Lay off more than half of the work force.

20. When a businessman says that "the bottom line determines everything," he is saying that his company judges things by
    (1) the quality of the product
    (2) the amount of employment it can generate
    (3) the amount of goods produced
    (4) the total profits it makes
    (5) the company's reputation for social service

For answers and explanations, see page 249.

ECONOMICS EXERCISE 3

Directions: Read the following passage and fill in the circle that corresponds to the correct answer.

The Multinational Corporation

Giant corporations have long dominated American business. The top 500 industrial firms account for more than 80 percent of all industrial sales, and the top 800 corporations employ as many people as the remaining 14,000,000 businesses.

5   A new trend has emerged in the last few decades: the growth of large corporations into multinational corporations with business spread all over the world. Ford, for example, has forty subsidiary corporations around the globe, accounting for one-third of its invested capital and 30 percent of its total work force. The foreign

10   growth of companies like Ford caused direct U.S. foreign invest-

ment to expand from $11 billion in 1950 to $213 billion by 1980. By 1980, more than 25 percent of the assets of our largest corporations were invested abroad.

15 This growth of foreign investment has caused a number of problems for U.S. domestic industry. Production in labor intensive industries, like electronic assembly, has been moved out of the U.S. to areas where labor costs are much lower. Much of the work has gone to Asian countries, but there has also been substantial investment in new plants and equipment in Western 20 Europe.

The growth of multinationals has also made it more difficult for the federal government to influence the national economy. Government plans either to slow inflation or to stimulate the economy can be thwarted by the multinationals' ability to move money 25 around the world to escape government control.

21. Based on the passage, you could infer that the continued growth of multinationals might have what effect on the power of trade unions?
    (1) Increase the power of unions because their workers would be part of bigger corporations
    (2) Decrease the power of unions because companies can seek nonunion labor abroad
    (3) No influence on U.S. labor-management relations
    (4) Increase the power of unions by decreasing the number of plants in the U.S.
    (5) Hurt U.S. unions because collective bargaining has been replaced by central planning

21 ① ② ③ ④ ⑤

22. According to the passage, approximately what percentage of the assets of the largest American corporations is invested abroad?
    (1) 5 percent
    (2) 10 percent
    (3) 15 percent
    (4) 20 percent
    (5) more than 25 percent

22 ① ② ③ ④ ⑤

For answers and explanations, see page 249.

4. FINANCIAL INSTITUTIONS

assets—total resources of a person or a business having a value for exchange

money—an asset that can be used immediately to purchase goods or services and is generally accepted as a means of settling debts

multiplier effect—the growth in value of an original deposit in a bank as it is, in turn, loaned and deposited by a succession of banks

monetary policy—the process by which the Federal Reserve System expands or contracts the money supply for the purpose of speeding up or slowing down economic growth

Money and the Money Supply

We all need it. We all use it. We all work for it. Some say it makes the world go 'round. But what is money? To understand this, let's start with wealth. Wealth is simply all those possessions we own that have a market value. Wealth is divided into financial **assets**—cash (bills and coins), savings, bank deposits—and real assets such as houses, cars, and machinery. **Money** (including cash) is made up of those financial assets that you can use immediately to purchase goods and services.

In economics, money means anything that is generally accepted as a means of settling debt. The term *money* includes cash but refers to more than coins and bills. To understand money, it is necessary to realize that most money exists only as a figure on paper in the form of bank accounts, loans, credit, etc.

The form of money most important to the growth of the economy is in checking accounts. These accounts are called *demand deposits* because you can obtain cash when you demand it. In 1981, the banks had checking accounts totalling $365 billion but had only $10 billion in cash. This makes sense if you remember that most of us are paid by checks that we deposit in the bank.

A bank takes in money from its depositors and loans out some of it. The money that is loaned then gets deposited in another bank. The second bank uses this new deposit as the basis for more loans that in turn can be deposited in yet another bank, which, of course, makes more loans. Each loan is the creation of new money. Through a series of these actions, the original deposit gets multiplied several times. This is called the **multiplier effect**. The money supply expands, and this is used to finance the growth of the economy.

You can see that money must circulate in order to keep growing. If we all demanded cash from our employers and then hoarded that cash by stuffing it in mattresses, the economy would grind to a halt. "Circulate or die" is the law of money expansion. Money that is not in circulation is not economically useful to society.

Directions: Based upon what you have just read, fill in the circle that corresponds to the correct answer.

23. If we all—individuals, government, and business—
adopted a policy of "not spending more than we have at
the moment," we would <u>ultimately</u> wind up
    (1)   much more secure financially
    (2)   with more debt and less money
    (3)   with a stagnant economy
    (4)   with long-run growth in the economy
    (5)   with less government spending but more economic
          growth

23 ① ② ③ ④ ⑤

24. The multiplier effect refers to the economic process
whereby
    (1)   the deeper in debt you get, the faster you go broke
    (2)   successive loans expand the supply of money
    (3)   you have more cash than demand deposits
    (4)   increased hoarding of money helps the economy
          grow
    (5)   government interference in the economy multiplies

24 ① ② ③ ④ ⑤

25. The fact that there is not enough cash in the banks to
cover all demand deposits means that
    (1)   you'd better run down and get yours while the
          getting is good
    (2)   the government will have to start printing enough
          money to cover them
    (3)   everyone is hiding cash at home
    (4)   the corporations are using the cash for foreign
          investment
    (5)   a modern economy is too complex to rely solely on
          cash

25 ① ② ③ ④ ⑤

For answers and explanations, see page 249.

Role of the Federal Reserve System

The money supply itself is controlled by a central bank, the Federal Reserve System (sometimes called "the Fed"). The Federal Reserve controls the amount of money available and has several techniques for controlling money expansion. By setting the reserve ratio, the percentage of deposits a bank must keep in cash, the Fed can raise or lower the amount that the banks have available to loan. If the Fed raises the ratio from 20 percent to 25 percent, it reduces the amount of money banks can loan and thereby reduces the growth in the money supply.

The Federal Reserve attempts to use many techniques to manipulate the money supply in order to slow down or stimulate the economy. Expansion of the money supply leads to economic growth. Restriction tightens the money supply and leads to a slowing down of the economy. This manipulation of the money supply is called **monetary policy.**

During the last years of the Carter administration and the first years of the Reagan administration, the Federal Reserve tightened the money supply in order to drive up interest rates to control inflation. The government hoped to discourage borrowing and thereby lead to an economic slowdown.

This successfully slowed business activity, but it also brought on the deepest recession since the 1930s. Inflation was reduced, at least temporarily. The Fed reversed its policy in 1982 and began to loosen up on the money supply in order to stimulate the economy. By 1984, the economy was recovering.

As you can see, there is far more to money than what meets the eye. The use of the money supply virtually lubricates the wheels of our economy, and without its controlled use, it is doubtful if our economy, let alone that of the world, would be going 'round.

Directions: Based upon what you have just read, fill in the circle that corresponds to the correct answer.

26. The country is in a recession. The Federal Reserve   26 ① ② ③ ④ ⑤
    wants to stimulate the economy. The Fed would
    probably
    (1) expand the money supply
    (2) sell more bonds on the market
    (3) increase interest rates it charges the banks
    (4) increase the income tax
    (5) tighten the money supply

27. *Monetary policy* refers to   27 ① ② ③ ④ ⑤
   (1) the Federal Reserve's attempts to expand or restrict the money supply
   (2) policies no longer used by the government
   (3) the right of private banks to print money
   (4) a policy of having all your money in cash
   (5) government spending for public works

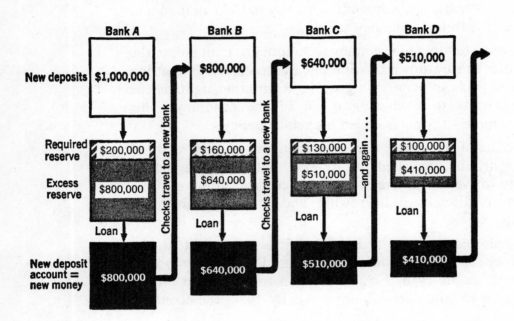

28. Based on what you read in the essay, this diagram is an   28 ① ② ③ ④ ⑤
   example of
   (1) the multiplier effect
   (2) the way economies become stagnant
   (3) internal financing by corporations
   (4) fiscal policy
   (5) the hoarding of money

For answers and explanations, see page 249.

ECONOMICS EXERCISE 4

Directions: Read the following passage and fill in the circle that corresponds to the correct answer.

The Stock Market

What is the stock market and how does it function in the economy? The stock market is a market where the stocks and bonds of corporations are bought and sold. It is economically

important because it is a form of saving and investment. Stocks
5   are shares of ownership in the corporation that entitle the owner
to dividend payments—payments made from company earnings.
The stocks may be sold at a later time for a higher or lower price
than the original purchase price. The difference between the
buying price and selling price is called a *capital gain* (or *loss*) and
10   is taxed at a lower rate than ordinary income.

How is the market seen as a barometer of the economy? When
prices move upward (bull market), it usually signals an upward
movement of the economy as a whole. When prices move
downward (bear market), it often points to economic difficulties.
15   The 1929 stock market crash, which reduced the value of stocks
by billions of dollars, signaled the beginning of the Great Depression. The market also did very poorly during the late 1960s and
1970s. The real value of stocks listed on the market fell by more
than 50 percent between 1966 and 1980. This reflected underlying
20   deterioration in the U.S. economy.

What does the stock market do for businesses? The market is
an important source of raising new capital for business expansion.
A corporation issues new stocks and sells them to raise money for
expansion. This is particularly important for new companies and
25   utilities.

What does the market do for the consumer? Expanding
markets stimulate consumer spending as the rise in prices of
stocks creates new wealth. This also provides a way for consumers
to channel their savings into productive investments. The bull
30   market of the early 1980s created several billion dollars' worth of
new wealth. This can have some impact because of the widespread
ownership of stock. In 1975, 25 million people in the United
States owned some stock (although the majority of individuals
owned only small amounts).

29. When the U.S. stock market's average prices went from   29 ① ② ③ ④ ⑤
    800 to 1,200 in 1982–83, this was a
    (1) bull market
    (2) bear market
    (3) dog market
    (4) crashing market
    (5) market that created little new wealth

30. The payments that stockholders receive from company earnings are called
(1) profits
(2) capital gains
(3) surplus value
(4) dividends
(5) investments

For answers and explanations, see page 249.

5. GOVERNMENT IN THE ECONOMY

**K
E
Y

W
O
R
D
S**

demand management—the use of a variety of forms of government measures to influence the level of demand in an economy

public goods—goods that work for the general welfare and must be provided by the government rather than by private industry

transfer payments—payments that transfer income from some people to others via the tax system

progressive tax—any tax that takes a larger portion of income as income increases

regressive tax—a tax that takes a smaller portion of a rich person's income than a poor person's income

national debt—the debt owed by the federal government on the money it has borrowed

Government Intervention

The concept of an economy regulated by the workings of a free, competitive market could be a useful starting place in understanding a capitalist economy. However, there are many things in the everyday world that alter this model. Perhaps the most important is the role of government in the economy.

At the most basic level, government provides the social peace and legal ground rules necessary for orderly economic activity. The economy could not function without laws governing contracts or the courts to enforce them.

One of the main functions of government is to provide **public goods**. These are goods that work for the general welfare and either will not or should not be produced by private business for sale on the market. For example, national defense is a public good that cannot be sold on the market for each of us to purchase whatever amount we want or can afford. Large capital construction projects such as highways, bridges, canals, and hydroelectric dams are public goods. These are part of the foundation for other economic activities. Other important public goods include education, public health, air traffic control, agricultural research, and fire protection.

Government also intervenes to help regulate the workings of the market. Antitrust laws are used to stop oligopolies from destroying market competition and to prevent the formation of monopolies. There are also numerous agencies that actively regulate some sector of the economy, such as the Food and Drug Administration (FDA) and the Federal Trade Commission (FTC).

Markets are further affected by government regulations influencing the costs and uses of some of the factors of production. Land use planning, zoning ordinances, and housing codes all affect the functioning of the real estate market. Labor laws and minimum wage laws influence the labor market. The credit market is regulated by government monetary policy through the Federal Reserve System.

All levels of government must deal with what are called the *externalities of production*. These are by-products that affect people other than those involved in making, buying, or selling a product. Over time, the problems created by technology have become complex, ranging from the disposal of simple industrial wastes to the dispersal of acid rain and the storage of nuclear wastes.

Demand management, also referred to as fiscal policy, is another key function of the federal government. **Demand management** refers to the use of a variety of forms of budget measures and taxes to influence the level of demand in an economy. Before the Great Depression, the government did little to deliberately alter the level of demand in the economy. Since the Depression, the federal government has played an active role in creating more demand for goods and services.

One of the ways that the government carries out demand management is by increasing spending when the private sector of the economy slows down and workers are unemployed. Increased government spending helps to make up for the decreased ability of people to buy goods. For example, the government might extend the length of unemployment insurance benefits in order to put some more money in the pockets of the unemployed. This keeps the level of demand from falling even further. When the economy picks up, the government can curtail such spending so as to slow the growth of inflation.

Directions: Based upon what you have just read, fill in the circle that corresponds to the correct answer.

31. Public goods are produced by the government because
    (1) the government wants to interfere in everything
    (2) a big profit can be made from them
    (3) they are goods used for the general welfare
    (4) the market produces too many of these goods
    (5) this is the way to make private industry pay for
        public welfare

    31 ① ② ③ ④ ⑤

32. *Externalities of production* refer to
    (1) by-products of production that affect people
        outside the production process
    (2) foreign competition and foreign imports
    (3) external factors that affect a corporation's labor
        problems
    (4) outside interference in production by the
        government
    (5) the influence of the environment on the production
        process

    32 ① ② ③ ④ ⑤

33. If the economy were booming and inflation looked like
    a growing problem, you would expect the government
    to
    (1) increase spending
    (2) refrain from using fiscal policy in this situation
    (3) refrain from using monetary policy
    (4) decrease spending
    (5) increase spending for public works and decrease
        taxes

    33 ① ② ③ ④ ⑤

For answers and explanations, see page 250.

Government and Finances

Welfare programs have become a rapidly growing government activity in
recent years. The provision of social welfare has been expanded from less
than 1 percent of the GNP in 1929 to 10 percent today. Social welfare
programs include Social Security, Medicare, Medicaid, and other forms of
public aid, including Aid to Dependent Children. By far, the largest
amount of the growth has been in Social Security payments.

The various types of welfare payments are called **transfer payments** because they transfer income from some people to others via the tax system. Another form of transfer payments is direct subsidies to business. For example, federal government subsidies bailed out a nearly bankrupt Lockheed in the 1970s.

Taxation is the primary source of government funding. The federal government relies on income taxes, while state and local governments use a mix of income, property, and sales taxes. The federal income tax is a **progressive tax**, which means that, as an individual makes more money, she pays a larger portion of her income on taxes. The opposite of this is a regressive tax, such as a sales tax on food. A **regressive tax** means that the rate of taxation actually increases as income decreases.

To understand the difference between a progressive tax and a regressive tax, look at the following examples. An income tax is a progressive tax. A person who makes $10,000 is taxed on a basis of 11 percent, whereas the person who makes $40,000 is taxed at the rate of 26 percent.

An example of a regressive tax is a $30 city sticker, a form of city tax. A person who makes $10,000 a year pays $30 as does the person who earns $50,000 a year. The city sticker is said to be a regressive tax because it represents a larger portion of the poor person's income.

Governments, like individuals, may finance their activities by borrowing. Savings bonds, treasury bills, and municipal bonds are examples of government borrowing. This type of borrowing has greatly added to the national debt of the government in recent years.

There has been a great amount of public debate about the growth of government expenditures. The federal budget has grown from $400 million in 1900 to $579 billion in 1980. Add to this the $300 billion spent by state and local governments, and government expenditures amount to 33 percent of the GNP. Is this too much? Is this less than adequate? These are central political questions that will be debated in the 1980s.

Directions: Based upon what you have just read, fill in the circle that corresponds to the correct answer.

34. Government spending, at all levels, amounts to how much of the GNP?
    (1) 75 percent
    (2) 50 percent
    (3) 33 percent
    (4) 22 percent
    (5) 10 percent

34 ① ② ③ ④ ⑤

35. A city government decides to add a five cents per
package tax on cigarettes. Such a tax is an example of
(1) progressive taxation
(2) regressive taxation
(3) demand management
(4) monetary policy
(5) graduated taxation

35 ① ② ③ ④ ⑤

For answers and explanations, see page 250.

ECONOMICS EXERCISE 5

Directions: Read the following passage. Answer the questions by filling in
the circle that corresponds to the correct answer.

The National Debt

In 1980, the total national debt of the United States was
$997,854,000. This comes to almost $4,300 for every man,
woman, and child in the country.

The **national debt** represents money the U.S. government has
5 borrowed to pay for government expenses above and beyond the
money it brings in from taxation. World Wars I and II have been
major causes of these deficits. The deep recessions of 1974–1975
and 1979–1982 further reduced tax revenues and greatly added to
government debt.

10 The federal government borrows money by selling financial
instruments such as Treasury certificates, notes, and U.S. Savings
Bonds. These are sold to investors, most of whom are American
citizens, or to American financial institutions. About 80 percent
of the debt is owed to American citizens.

15 The corporate world has a different way of looking at its
borrowing. Most corporations borrow for long-term development, and this shows up in their balance sheets as an investment,
not as a deficit. To the extent that government uses the money to
provide needed services and goods for the people, some degree of
20 debt could be looked upon as an investment in the future of the
country.

Today, many people are concerned about the skyrocketing
national debt. Do the long-term consequences of a large debt
outweigh the benefits to be gained through government spending?
25 Do we need a balanced (without debt) budget?

Such questions could become the center of an intense political
debate in the 1980s because, as of 1983, more than thirty states (of
a required thirty-four) have passed resolutions calling for a
Constitutional Convention to consider a balanced budget
30 amendment.

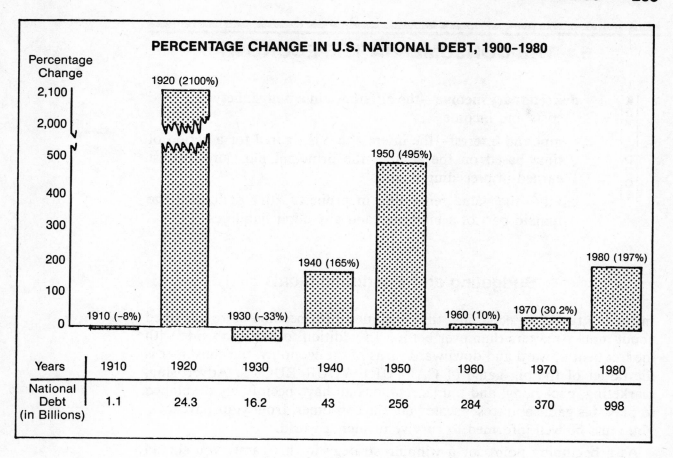

PERCENTAGE CHANGE IN U.S. NATIONAL DEBT, 1900–1980

Percentage Change

1910 (−8%)
1920 (2100%)
1930 (−33%)
1940 (165%)
1950 (495%)
1960 (10%)
1970 (30.2%)
1980 (197%)

Years	1910	1920	1930	1940	1950	1960	1970	1980
National Debt (in Billions)	1.1	24.3	16.2	43	256	284	370	998

36. This passage and the accompanying graph show that the largest increases in the national debt have been associated with

    36 ① ② ③ ④ ⑤

(1) increasing welfare
(2) financing wars
(3) increased payments to farmers
(4) increased foreign aid
(5) increased Social Security

37. Another severe recession, such as that in 1979–1982, would probably have what effect on the national debt?

    37 ① ② ③ ④ ⑤

(1) Raise the debt
(2) Lower the debt
(3) Not affect the debt
(4) Lower the interest on the debt
(5) Lower the debt ceiling

For answers and explanations, see page 250.

---

6. THE CONSUMER IN THE ECONOMY

KEY WORDS

discretionary income—the difference in a budget between fixed costs and income

compound interest—the interest that is figured for a period of time based on the sum of the principal plus any interest earned in preceding periods

equity—the value remaining in property after deducting the unpaid part of a mortgage and any other liabilities

Budgeting and Economic Goals

In today's turbulent economy, the consumer must become more informed about money matters than ever before. In addition to having to ride with the frequent upward and downward turns of the economy, the consumer is the target of the big game of CAPTURE YOUR BUCKS. Advertising, marketing, packaging, and public relations all have been finely developed to play this game and to separate you, the consumer, from your paycheck. You must be well informed to survive in such a world.

As a beginning point for a winning strategy in this game, you should decide on definite economic goals. Are you planning for a new home, a car, a vacation, or for just "making it" day to day? Without economic goals, you may wander aimlessly across the economic landscape and be blown about by any strong force that happens to come along. Once you have set your goals, you can draw up a plan to reach them.

Your budget is the most important part of such a plan. A budget is a systematic outline for using your money to achieve your goals. It involves determining the amount of money you actually have and how you will use the money. The first step, after figuring out how much money you have, is to establish your fixed costs (amounts you <u>must</u> pay) each month. These usually include food, rent or mortgage payment, utilities, car payment, insurance, etc. The difference between your fixed costs and your income is your **discretionary income**. This is the income you can devote to long-range goals.

If you are dissatisfied with the amount of your discretionary income, you have three options: (1) increase your income, (2) decrease your fixed costs, or (3) change your goals. Unless you plan what to do with discretionary income, it will probably disappear, spent on dozens of little things.

While accumulating discretionary income for your long-term goals, you can set aside this money in a savings account, where the money will earn interest. The bank will literally pay you for the use of your money. These savings accounts are very safe and are usually insured by the federal government. They pay **compound interest**, which means that the interest paid on the principal (the original amount you deposited) for a certain period (say one month) is added to the principal as a new basis for computing the next month's interest. In this way, the deposit will grow. Banks pay varying rates of interest, and the consumer can look around for the best rates.

Probably the most important economic commitment that many people will make is the purchase of a home. A home produces growing equity for the buyer, especially during periods of inflation. **Equity** represents the sales value of your property minus the unpaid amount of the mortgage.

When the value of the house rises during periods of inflation, the buyer realizes this increase in the form of greater equity. This is why real estate is considered an inflation hedge—its value goes up at least as fast as the rate of inflation; the value of other investments, like common stocks, does not rise as quickly as inflation.

Mortgages for homes have traditionally been long-term (twenty-five to thirty years) fixed-rate loans, but in recent years, a variety of different types of mortgages have been developed. Some of these new types of mortgages allow for more flexibility in payment and often have interest rates that are adjustable. The newer mortgages have made it possible for more people to plan their payments realistically, based on present and even future income.

While you are pursuing your economic goals and trying to make ends meet, you and your family need protection against serious illness and accidents. Insurance is protection for your family. Health insurance has almost become a necessity because of increased medical and hospitalization costs. If you own a home or plan to buy one, homeowners' insurance is necessary to protect the value of your home against fire and other disasters. If you rent, there is also insurance available to protect your possessions.

Directions: Based upon what you have just read, fill in the circle that corresponds to the correct answer.

38. An inflation hedge is an investment   38 ① ② ③ ④ ⑤
    (1) that goes down in value when inflation goes up
    (2) that goes up in value at least as quickly as inflation rises
    (3) that stops inflation from happening
    (4) with no reward/risk ratio
    (5) in a savings account with a high risk

39. The Jones family has the following monthly budget:

Income = $1,500 per month

Rent = $300
Food = $300
Car note = $200
Insurance = $200
Clothes = $100
Misc. = $150
$1,250

Their discretionary income is
(1) $250
(2) $1,250
(3) $1,500
(4) $500
(5) $150

40. There is an old fable about the ants who worked all
summer and stored extra food, while the grasshopper
sang and danced and fiddled away his resources. When
winter came, the ants were OK, but the grasshopper
couldn't make it The old grasshopper had
(1) forgotten to build a tax shelter
(2) failed to budget his resources
(3) no inflation hedge to hide under
(4) invested too much at low risk ratios
(5) forgotten to keep his credit rating up

41. Which of the following is <u>not</u> an example of a fixed cost?
(1) Rent
(2) Utilities
(3) Car payment
(4) Insurance
(5) Vacation

For answers and explanations, see page 250.

Credit and Consumer Fraud

It is by far the toughest opponent you will ever face in the game of
CAPTURE YOUR BUCKS, and it can be found in a variety of guises with
a variety of uses. There is nothing that has more potential power to
separate you from your money than that six-letter word—CREDIT.

When you are using credit, you are actually adding to the fixed-costs part
of your budget. This is because you must pay for credit, usually in monthly
payments. Unlike a mortgage (which is a form of using credit to make an

investment), most forms of credit are not investments. If you are not careful, credit could destroy your budget.

There are many different kinds of credit, ranging from a charge account at the department store to a loan for financing an automobile. During the past twenty years, the use of charge accounts, and especially those small plastic budget busters—credit cards—has greatly increased. Credit cards allow you to buy items that you could not afford if you had to make one cash payment.

However, credit carries a real cost. Before you arrange for any credit, you need to find out exactly what it is going to cost you. You pay for the use of credit, either through high prices or through service charges. If credit is paid off in monthly installments, interest is charged on the remaining balance. Interest on that type of account—for example, a credit card issued through a bank—is usually very high, often much higher than a loan from a bank.

In recent years, numerous federal laws have been passed to protect the consumer against excessive interest charges and other forms of consumer fraud. For instance, the Truth-in-Lending Act requires that the consumer be informed of the real rate of interest, called the *annual percent rate (APR)*. Consumers must also be informed of the total dollar cost of a loan.

Legislation on behalf of consumers has changed the relation between consumers and sellers. The old principle of *caveat emptor*, "let the buyer beware," has been partly replaced by *caveat venditor*, "let the seller beware." The consumer movement has been very important in creating safer, better made, and more honestly advertised products.

Directions: Based upon what you have just read, fill in the circle that corresponds to the correct answer.

42. Credit can be a useful means of increasing your wealth   42 ① ② ③ ④ ⑤
    (1) under no circumstances
    (2) only if a debt is very small and short-term
    (3) if the debt is due to money invested in something that is not a tax shelter
    (4) if the debt is due to money invested in real estate
    (5) only if the debt is for consumer items such as a new car or new furniture

43. The passage says that a consumer who pays off her   43 ① ② ③ ④ ⑤
    credit debt in monthly installments
    (1) pays lower interest than on a bank loan
    (2) will never be able to pay off her debts
    (3) pays higher interest than on a bank loan
    (4) will use her payments as a tax deduction
    (5) cannot qualify for a bank loan

For answers and explanations, see page 250.

ECONOMICS EXERCISE 6

Directions: Read the following passage and answer the questions that follow. Fill in the circle that corresponds to the correct answer.

Distribution of Family Income and Wealth

It has been said that the United States is a middle-class society. How does this really fit the facts of distribution of family income and wealth in America?

5   Income figures are usually compared on the basis of family income and not individual income. About 70 percent of the total U.S. family income comes from wages, salaries, and commissions. The remainder is divided into small business income (7 percent), rental income (2 percent), dividends and interest (11 percent), and government transfer payments (10 percent).

10   As the chart below shows, this income is actually distributed fairly unevenly. For instance, the top 5 percent of American families earn 15 percent of the total family income.

Family Income Rank 1970

Family Income Rank	Percentage of Income before Taxes
Lowest fifth (20%)	4.8
Second fifth (20%)	12.2
Middle fifth (20%)	17.6
Fourth fifth (20%)	23.8
Highest fifth (20%)	40.9
Top 5%	15.6

How is wealth distributed? Wealth is made up of real estate, insurance policies, stocks, bonds, savings accounts, and other

25 tangible assets with market value. American wealth is distributed even more unevenly than income. The bottom 25 percent of American families have no wealth at all, while the top 20 percent have more than 70 percent of all wealth. The very top of the population, ½ of 1 percent (0.5%), owns 25 percent of all wealth

30 in the United States.

Distribution of Wealth 1969

Percentage of Total Population	Percentage of Total Wealth
25.0	0.0
32.0	6.6
24.0	17.2
18.5	50.4
0.5	25.8

40   What has happened to the poor? Although income and wealth have remained unequally divided, the number of families under the poverty level actually declined during the 1960s and 1970s. This reduction was due to increases in government transfer payments such as Social Security, increases in the minimum
45   wage, and increases in the number of family members working. These changes occurred without a significant redistribution of wealth or income.

By the early 1980s, the declining trend of poverty began reversing itself and the number of Americans living below the
50   poverty level began to rise again. The rise in the number of poor Americans coincided with the cutbacks in the social programs under the Reagan administration and the severe recession of 1979–1982.

44. The top 0.5% of American families own approximately what percentage of all wealth?
   (1) 5 percent
   (2) 25 percent
   (3) 35 percent
   (4) 50 percent
   (5) 75 percent

44 ① ② ③ ④ ⑤

45. The idea that the increase in government transfer payments during the 1960s and 1970s had an impact on the number of families in poverty is probably
   (1) incorrect because poverty actually increased during this time
   (2) correct because the transfer programs redistributed income
   (3) correct because transfer payments did raise income levels, although they did not redistribute wealth
   (4) incorrect because so much income was taxed away from the middle class that many middle class families became poor
   (5) correct because the poverty level was raised

45 ① ② ③ ④ ⑤

46. The main idea of the passage is that
    (1) the United States is a society with different
        economic classes
    (2) the middle class runs American society and owns
        most of the wealth
    (3) the upper and middle classes receive percentages of
        total national income that are in proportion to
        their size
    (4) the number of people at the poverty level
        continued to decline during the 1980s
    (5) the United States has a classless society

For answers and explanations, see page 250.

7. THE LABOR MARKET, INDUSTRY, AND UNIONS

**K
E
Y

W
O
R
D
S**

automation—the use of machines to supplement or replace manual labor

collective bargaining—the bargaining between management and a labor union over salaries, terms of employment, working conditions, and other matters of concern

labor contract—legally binding written agreement between management and labor that sets forth salaries, terms of employment, benefits, working conditions, and the duties, responsibilities, and rights of each party

strike—the action of workers withholding their services from an employer in an attempt to force him to come to an agreement

The Labor Market and Industry in the 1980s

The term *labor market* describes that part of the economy in which workers compete for jobs. When the economy is healthy, unemployment is low and jobs are not very hard to find. When the economy is weak, unemployment is high and jobs are scarce.

During the late 1970s and into the 1980s, some parts of the labor market have been drastically affected by many changes in industry. Technological change and the decline in the traditional smokestack industries, especially in the Northeast and Midwest, have permanently eliminated many jobs. In some cases, plants have remained open with a much smaller work force. Although **automation**, the use of machines to supplement human labor, has existed throughout the industrial age, newer and more sophisticated forms of automation, such as assembly line robots, have permanently displaced many unskilled and semiskilled assembly workers.

Traditional smokestack industries, such as steel, have faced stiff foreign competition and declining profits. Their obsolete production facilities have put them in a poor competitive position, and cheaper foreign steel has taken a larger share of the U.S. market. As a result, some company owners have chosen to shut down many steel plants rather than make the long-term investments necessary to modernize the plants and to make them competitive.

There are still other factories that have been moved to foreign countries to take advantage of cheaper labor costs. Other factories have been uprooted from sites in the Frost Belt states and moved to other parts of the U.S., usually to the Sun Belt states in the South and Southwest. There, labor costs are lower and unions are traditionally weaker.

Communities in states such as Illinois, Ohio, Indiana, Michigan, and Pennsylvania have been hard hit by industrial shutdowns, and employment prospects are still bleak in many of those communities. A further decline in basic industries could cause the United States to become a deindustrialized nation with an economy based very heavily on service and technology-related industries.

At the same time that employment in traditional industry has been declining, there has been an increase in the number of jobs in the service industries, industries not involved in the production of goods. The service industries include restaurants, hotels, retail stores, health care, office jobs, government jobs, etc. Some displaced industrial workers have been absorbed by the service industries, but usually into lower-paying jobs. This has resulted in a corresponding decrease in the worker's standard of living.

There has also been a growth in the number of jobs utilizing the new microprocessor-based technology, especially in data processing. However, since the new technology is actually a labor-saving development, it is unclear whether its ultimate impact will be to expand employment opportunities or add to the problems of unemployment.

Directions: Based upon what you have just read, fill in the circle that corresponds to the correct answer.

47. If present trends continue in traditional U.S. industries, we can expect that
    (1) the steel industry will become strong and competitive again
    (2) there will be increased employment opportunities in traditional smokestack industries
    (3) employment in manufacturing will continue to decline
    (4) the Frost Belt states will continue to experience a growth in basic industries
    (5) technological change will create more jobs in traditional manufacturing

47 ① ② ③ ④ ⑤

48. Which of the following does the passage give as a
    reason for the decline in the American steel industry?
    (1) Unions are asking for too much in salary demands.
    (2) The American steel industry cannot compete
        because of outdated production facilities.
    (3) Foreign competition uses production robots.
    (4) Oil companies are buying out steel plants.
    (5) The steel industry needs more highly skilled
        workers.

48 ① ② ③ ④ ⑤

49. A large merchandise retailer announces plans to create
    new jobs by opening a department store in your
    community. Nearly all of these jobs could best be
    described by which of the following categories?
    (1) Industrial jobs
    (2) Production jobs
    (3) Shipping and receiving jobs
    (4) Blue-collar jobs
    (5) Service jobs

49 ① ② ③ ④ ⑤

For answers and explanations, see page 251.

Labor Unions

Directly related to the issue of the labor market are labor unions. Union
membership has declined in recent years to less than 20 percent of the
American work force. Much of this decrease has been a result of shrinking
work forces in the basic industries such as steel, auto, and the railroads, all
of which had traditionally been very heavily unionized. Union membership
has actually been expanding in the service sector, especially among white-
collar office workers and state and local government employees.

Unions themselves are combinations or associations of workers, usually
in a particular occupation or at a particular work site. The workers
organize because they see that they have little or no individual bargaining
power over salaries, terms of employment, and working conditions when
confronted with the power and influence of an employer—whether that
employer be a small firm, a multinational corporation, or a state or city
government.

By joining together into a union, the collective strength of the workers
provides the strength necessary to gain recognition and then to engage in
collective bargaining. **Collective bargaining** takes place between management and a union over salaries, terms of employment, working conditions,
and other matters of concern.

Management and labor normally negotiate and agree on a contract. A
labor contract is a legally binding written agreement between management
and a labor union that defines the duties and responsibilities of both
parties. It usually sets forth salaries, working conditions, terms of employ-

ment, benefits, the rights of labor, and the rights of management. It is virtually a written set of rules that both parties agree to obey and enforce.

Often, there are issues that are dealt with only partially by union contracts, since these issues are the subject of federal and state laws. Certain safety and health conditions at work sites are mandated by state and federal legislation, although a contract may go even further in raising such standards. Racial and sexual discrimination in hiring is banned by law; however, a contract may go even further to ensure that there is no discrimination in promotions, transfers, seniority, layoffs, wage increases, training, and related matters. Wages are another contract matter that are only partially affected by laws, since there are federal and state laws concerning minimum wages that an employer must observe. In recent years, there have been several unsuccessful attempts to pass subminimum wage laws that would legalize lower salary structures for workers under eighteen years of age.

Failure to agree on a contract is often a major reason for a strike. A **strike** occurs when workers withhold their services from an employer in order to force an agreement. A strike is the ultimate weapon that a union can employ. Strikes are now most often used as a last resort. When a union goes on strike, it sets up a picket line of striking union members at its work site for the purpose of explaining its side to the public as well as encouraging others to support its position by not crossing the picket line.

Directions: Based upon what you have just read, fill in the circle that corresponds to the correct answer.

50. According to the essay, union membership comprises approximately what percentage of the American work force?
    (1) 80 percent
    (2) 15 percent
    (3) 50 percent
    (4) 20 percent
    (5) 35 percent

50 ① ② ③ ④ ⑤

51. A union negotiator has been involved in around-the-clock negotiations over a new contract. The negotiations have reached a stalemate and have been broken off. The company will not budge from its position in demanding that union members take a 5-percent cut in pay. The union will not budge either and is demanding a 6-percent increase, based upon the knowledge that the company has earned money over the previous year and that the workers cannot afford any cuts.

51 ① ② ③ ④ ⑤

Since the parties have reached an impasse, what do
you believe the negotiator will recommend to the union?
(1) Take the cuts in pay
(2) Go on strike
(3) Resume negotiations
(4) Ask for smaller pay cuts
(5) Ask for a 10-percent pay increase

52. All of the following could be found in a union contract
except
(1) the setting of a federal minimum wage
(2) number of hours of work
(3) salaries of workers
(4) safety and health standards
(5) vacation leave policy

52 ① ② ③ ④ ⑤

For answers and explanations, see page 251.

ECONOMICS EXERCISE 7

Directions: Read the following passage and answer the questions that
follow. Fill in the circle that corresponds to the correct answer.

Quality Circles

For a long time, the scientific management approach emphasized
breaking down workers' tasks in production to the smallest
possible specialized task and keeping worker decision making to
a minimum. Competition from Japan has forced this method to
5   be seriously questioned. The Japanese have been able to develop
far higher levels of worker productivity than U.S. plants. Part of
this is due to the greater participation of workers in making
decisions about their work.

American corporations have begun to institute programs based
10 on the Japanese experience. In 1982, there were 6,000 U.S.
corporations involved in setting up quality circles. These circles
bring management and workers together in small groups to solve
problems of quality, efficiency, cost, and communication.

Workers have responded favorably to these programs. They
15 have long felt that they are closest to the actual process of
production, and they have many ideas about how to run industry
more efficiently and humanely. The chance to demonstrate this
knowledge has led to significant savings for many corporations.
One quality circle saved National Steel $900,000 a year because
20 of worker-designed changes in production schedules.

Although such programs have initially gained widespread acceptance, several questions remain. Many workers want some part of the company's savings to be passed on in the form of higher wages and lower consumer prices. Some unions want to
25   push ahead with worker involvement in decision making, and they believe workers should also be allowed to participate on company boards of directors. These proposals have met with resistance from many corporate leaders who fear loss of management rights and control.

30   Whatever the future of these programs, it is clear that workers have responded positively to becoming participants in decision making, and this has led to better quality and more productivity in many plants.

53. If you were managing a plant and were having a   53 ① ② ③ ④ ⑤
problem with quality control, the approach described in
the passage would suggest that you should
(1) have more supervisors in order to keep a closer eye
on the workers
(2) enlist worker cooperation in planning the
production processes
(3) break down the job tasks to smaller, more
repetitive steps
(4) tell the workers just to work and let you make the
decisions
(5) increase penalties for bad work

54. According to the passage, quality circles have been   54 ① ② ③ ④ ⑤
resisted by some corporate leaders because
(1) quality circles cost too much
(2) quality circles are too partial to unions
(3) quality circles are not efficient
(4) quality circles cause some to fear the loss of
management rights and control
(5) quality circles are un-American

55. You could infer that, if quality circles were to become a   55 ① ② ③ ④ ⑤
widespread phenomenon in the U.S.,
(1) profits would decrease
(2) unemployment would rise
(3) American products would become more
competitive in the world market
(4) unions would grow
(5) productivity would remain the same

For answers and explanations, see page 251.

ANSWERS AND EXPLANATIONS

1. INTRODUCTION TO ECONOMICS

Finding Details **1.** (5) This is the definition of the term *economy* found in the first paragraph of the essay.

Finding Details **2.** (4) This essay defines macroeconomics as the study of whole economic systems.

Application of Ideas **3.** (5) Economists are concerned with economic analysis. Choice (3) is incorrect because it involves day-to-day operations rather than analysis and forecasting.

Finding Details **4.** (5) Capitalism freed the serf from the bonds of serfdom and allowed him to sell his labor.

Drawing Conclusions **5.** (3) The essay makes the point that our economic system has evolved out of earlier forms. You could conclude that the development of economic systems will probably continue.

Drawing Conclusions **6.** (2) The essay mentions that economic changes were accompanied by political changes. For example, the growth of capitalism greatly affected the social and political structures of feudalism.

ECONOMICS EXERCISE 1

Main Idea **7.** (4) Statistics are a very important tool for understanding the economy, but they can be misused.

Evaluation of Logic **8.** (1) Remember, you should make sure that the same value is used in a comparison. The writer fails to indicate the relative value of 1880 and 1984 dollars.

2. HOW THE OVERALL ECONOMY WORKS

Application of Ideas **9.** (1) When prices are high, demand is low. Graph (1) shows demand increasing as prices decrease.

Application of Ideas **10.** (4) The events described show that demand was high but the supply was low, almost nonexistent. Under these conditions, a "seller's market" emerged, and some people were willing to pay incredible sums of money for the dolls.

Finding Details **11.** (2) The passage states that consumer spending accounts for 70 percent of the GNP.

Finding Details **12.** (2) The essay describes this situation as a recession, which may lead to a depression.

Drawing Conclusions **13.** (1) Capital goods are used to expand the productive capacity of the economy. A cutback in spending on capital goods would ultimately lead to declining production.

ECONOMICS EXERCISE 2

Finding Details **14.** (1) The title of the graph indicates that the figures given are in millions of dollars. 2,633,108 × $1,000,000 would be $2,633,108,000,000 or more than $2½ trillion. Choice (2), less than $2½ million, is much too small for the GNP.

| *Drawing Conclusions* | 15. | (3) | The NNP is less than the GNP, and the column on the left indicates that the Gross National Product **less** the Capital Consumption Allowance **equals** the Net National Product. |

3.   HOW BUSINESSES BEHAVE

Making Inferences	16.	(2)	It is possible that an owner would pass on some of the savings in costs to the consumer and to labor, as well as taking some of the increased earnings for himself or his business.
Finding Details	17.	(4)	The essay discusses some marketing techniques, and all of them are related to increasing sales.
Finding Details	18.	(1)	In the latter part of the essay, there is a discussion of monopoly—a market situation with one seller who dominates the market.
Drawing Conclusions	19.	(1)	Lower costs for factors of production combined with an increased output would certainly raise profits.
Application of Ideas	20.	(4)	The first paragraph discusses the profit motive of American industry; note the remark made by a president of General Motors. The essay also states, "The profit motive is what makes the wheels of American industry turn."

ECONOMICS EXERCISE 3

| *Making Inferences* | 21. | (2) | Since multinationals have foreign investments and production, they often move production abroad where workers are not unionized and labor costs are low. |
| *Finding Details* | 22. | (5) | The essay states that, by 1980, more than 25 percent of the assets of the largest corporations were invested abroad. |

4.   FINANCIAL INSTITUTIONS

Making Inferences	23	(3)	The essay makes it clear that credit and borrowing are a source of economic growth. They actually help to expand the money supply.
Finding Details	24.	(2)	The explanation is in the second to the last paragraph. The multiplier effect is an important factor in the expansion of the money supply.
Drawing Conclusions	25.	(5)	Our economy would be buried under paper if all economic transactions had to be based on cash. Also, the increase in the demand for cash could not keep up with the multiplier effect.
Application of Ideas	26.	(1)	The passage states that the Federal Reserve can expand the money supply to stimulate the economy and, in fact, did so to help the country come out of the 1981–82 recession.
Finding Details	27.	(1)	This term is defined in the essay.
Making Inferences	28.	(1)	The diagram shows how the chain of growth of the money supply is created by successive loans made by banks.

ECONOMICS EXERCISE 4

| *Application of Ideas* | 29. | (1) | When stock market prices move up, a bull market exists. See lines 11–13. |
| *Finding Details* | 30. | (4) | Dividend payments are explained in lines 4–6. |

5. GOVERNMENT IN THE ECONOMY

Finding Details	**31.**	(3)	The essay explains that the government provides public goods because it would be impractical for private businesses to provide goods or services for the general welfare.
Finding Details	**32.**	(1)	This is defined in the essay.
Application of Ideas	**33.**	(4)	In the section discussing demand management, the essay states that the government cuts back on spending during economic booms in order to slow down inflation.
Finding Details	**34.**	(3)	The last paragraph of the essay states that government spending accounts for 33 percent of the GNP.
Application of Ideas	**35.**	(2)	Such a tax is regressive because it applies equally to the rich, the middle class, and the poor.

ECONOMICS EXERCISE 5

Finding Details	**36.**	(2)	This is stated in the passage. Also, the graph shows the largest percentage increases in national debt during the periods of the world wars.
Application of Ideas	**37.**	(1)	The essay mentions that deep recessions in 1974–75 and 1979–82 greatly added to the national debt. You can assume that another deep recession would do the same.

6. THE CONSUMER IN THE ECONOMY

Making Inferences	**38.**	(2)	The essay says that real estate is an inflation hedge and that its value goes up at least as quickly as the rate of inflation.
Application of Ideas	**39.**	(1)	Subtract the total amount of fixed costs ($1,250) from the income ($1,500). The amount that is left ($250) is the discretionary income.
Application of Ideas	**40.**	(2)	He had eaten up his discretionary income in immediate consumption and failed to budget for the long term.
Making Inferences	**41.**	(5)	Fixed costs are expenses that you must pay on a regular basis. Money for vacations is likely to come out of discretionary income.
Finding Details	**42.**	(4)	The essay describes mortgages as a form of debt that has equity and can be a hedge against inflation.
Finding Details	**43.**	(3)	The essay notes the high cost of using credit paid off in monthly installments. This includes service charges and interest payments.

ECONOMICS EXERCISE 6

Finding Details	**44.**	(2)	The passage states that the top 0.5 percent owns 25 percent of the wealth.
Making Inferences	**45.**	(3)	This inference is based on the passage. The total number of people living in poverty in the '60s and '70s was reduced, although there was not a significant change in the overall distribution of income and wealth.
Main Idea	**46.**	(1)	The passage describes the patterns of unequal distribution of income and wealth to support the claim that social classes exist in U.S. society.

7. THE LABOR MARKET, INDUSTRY, AND UNIONS

Main Idea	47.	(3)	This is a main idea of the essay, which discusses the decline of basic industries and its impact on the labor market.
Finding Details	48.	(2)	To remain competitive, steel plants need to be modernized. The passage states that some owners are not willing to make the necessary long-term investments to modernize their factories.
Application of Ideas	49.	(5)	The essay mentions that the service industries do not involve the production of goods. Retail stores fit this category.
Finding Details	50.	(4)	This detail is mentioned in the first paragraph of the section on labor unions.
Drawing Conclusions	51.	(2)	With no prospect of an agreement in sight and both sides refusing to budge from their positions, it is quite likely that the negotiator would recommend the use of the union's "ultimate weapon."
Drawing Conclusions	52.	(1)	The legal minimum wage is not set by a union contract; instead it is set by laws passed by a state legislature or Congress. This is stated in the essay.

ECONOMICS EXERCISE 7

Main Idea	53.	(2)	This is the main idea of the passage. Worker involvement in decision making and planning has led to better quality in production.
Finding Details	54.	(4)	The passage states in lines 27–29 that there are those in management who fear the loss of management rights and control.
Making Inferences	55.	(3)	Since some corporations using quality circles have experienced savings, higher productivity, and better quality, you could infer that American goods would probably become more competitive in the world market.

Geography

---

1. INTRODUCTION TO GEOGRAPHY

KEY WORDS

latitude—the distance north or south of the equator, measured in degrees between 0 and 90

longitude—the distance east or west of the Principal Meridian, located in Greenwich, England, measured in degrees between 0 and 180

contour lines—lines on a geographic map that connect points at the same elevation

Geography is the study of the physical structure of the earth, its climate, the distribution of its resources, and the effect of these factors on people. As one of the social sciences, geography places special emphasis on man's interaction with his physical environment and the influence of this environment on human relations.

The physical aspects of man's environment include terrain, climate, natural resources, waterways, and other important features. It is always necessary, however, to keep in mind how geography and the other social sciences are related.

Geographers and other social scientists agree that there is a very important relationship between the environment in which people live and the social organization we develop. For example, it is not very likely that the people inhabiting a dry, isolated environment in the heart of the desert will become expert shipbuilders. In the same light, one can guess that, in a land divided by rivers and large lakes, the inhabitants would be more apt to learn shipbuilding and navigation skills. These are social factors that affect man's future.

On the other side of the coin is our ability to influence our physical environment. As human society becomes more and more advanced, this development will, in turn, have an effect on the physical environment. Hills will be leveled to put down new highways, rivers will be dammed to generate power, and air pollution, if unchecked, will become worse.

Approaches to the Study of Geography

There are several topics in the study of geography that you should be aware of. One aspect is purely *physical*, concentrating on such elements as climate, vegetation, and landforms. Another topic is *cultural* geography, in which one studies race, religion, and population. The study of *economic* geography shows how the people of a particular area make their living, how advanced their technology is, and how they trade with surrounding areas. *Political* geography places particular emphasis on the relationships among people and nations.

Maps

One important tool of the geographer is the map. Maps of many different varieties are used to show spatial arrangements of land and water, other natural resources, and man-made features such as political boundaries and cities. Although there is an earlier section on map reading skills, in this section, we will discuss physical and geographic maps and their usefulness to geographers.

Geographic Maps

Below is a geographic map, also called a *physical map*, of South America. As you can see, this map shows the natural features of this region, as well as the political entities (countries) created by man. With every geographic map there is a legend, or key, to explain the features found on the map. On the map below, for example, you can find a guide to the different elevations of the region, as well as the symbol used to indicate major rivers. Important cities and lakes are also labelled on the map.

SOUTH AMERICA

Latitude and Longitude Lines

Many maps make use of standard lines called *latitude* and *longitude lines*. Lines that run parallel around the Earth from east to west are called *latitude lines*. **Latitude** is measured north and south of the equator, which is midway between the North and South Poles. **Longitude** is measured by distances east and west of the Prime Meridian running through Greenwich, England. Below is a map of the Earth with some latitude and longitude lines indicated.

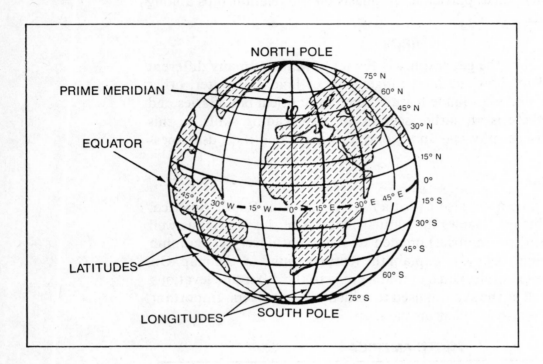

By measuring latitude and longitude, you can find the exact location of any point on the Earth. Locations north of the equator are measured in degrees between 0 (at the equator) and 90 (at the North Pole). Locations south of the equator are measured the same way—0 degrees at the equator to 90 degrees at the South Pole. Locations east and west of the Prime Meridian are measured by degrees between 0 and 180 east and west.

Latitude and longitude lines on a map are very useful in the study of geography not only because they help to cite a location, but also because they help to outline and define regions across the Earth. Terms such as *Northern* and *Southern, Eastern* and *Western Hemisphere* are used often when identifying similarities or differences between regions.

Contour Maps

Contour maps, sometimes called *topographic maps*, use connecting lines to indicate areas at the same elevation. These give you a picture of the shape of the landscape. With the **contour lines** is a number showing elevation, usually indicated in feet above sea level. The closer together the lines are, the steeper the shift in elevation.

Below is a contour map of a fictional island, accompanied by a different view of the land that the map represents.

CONTOUR MAP

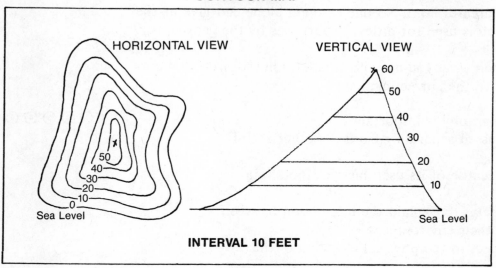

The map shows that each interval between contour lines is 10 feet. Counting from the bottom, you can see that the island rises from sea level to 60 feet at the top. A contour map, as you may have guessed, is useful to hikers and engineers as well as to geographers.

Information Maps

Some maps give the geographer some very specific information. With an information map, it is important that you take special note of the title and a key, if one is used, because it will tell you what the symbols on the map stand for. Below is an informational map.

TIME ZONES ACROSS NORTH AMERICA

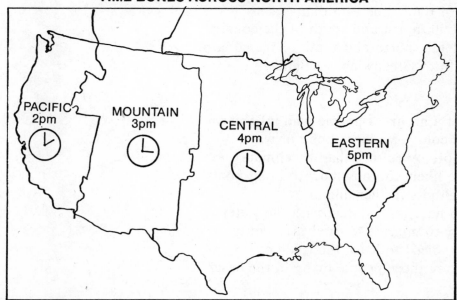

Examples of other types of information maps are the ones that show climate patterns, racial distribution, and agricultural divisions in a region.

As you can see, each of these types of maps gives us a particular piece of information about an area of land. No one of them alone can give us the "total picture," but each is used for different purposes by the geographer.

Directions: Based upon what you have just read, fill in the circle that corresponds to the correct answer.

1. The study of geography is important
   (1) only if discussed separately from the other social sciences
   (2) primarily because of its usefulness to mountain climbers
   (3) because it helps to explain the interaction between people and their environment
   (4) only in respect to the physical elements of the Earth
   (5) more for its economic implications than anything else

   1 ① ② ③ ④ ⑤

2. Geographers use contour maps
   (1) to divide one political region from another
   (2) to show physical features such as lakes and streams
   (3) more often than they use geographic maps
   (4) to emphasize the man-made features in a particular area
   (5) to show the elevation patterns of an area of land

   2 ① ② ③ ④ ⑤

3. Latitude is measured in degrees
   (1) east and west of the Prime Meridian
   (2) between 0 and 90, north and south of the equator
   (3) between 0 and 180, north and south of the equator
   (4) north and south of Greenwich, England
   (5) above sea level

   3 ① ② ③ ④ ⑤

4. You could infer that a group of people who inhabit an area of land on the coast of a large body of water
   (1) are affected more by culture than by climate
   (2) would be more likely to know how to build boats than their neighbors farther inland
   (3) are unlikely to have any contact with the water
   (4) would be likely to migrate to drier areas of land
   (5) would have less need to learn the trade of shipbuilding than those people living in the desert

   4 ① ② ③ ④ ⑤

For answers and explanations, see page 273.

GEOGRAPHY EXERCISE 1

Directions: Look at the map below and fill in the circle that corresponds to the correct answer.

EAST ASIA

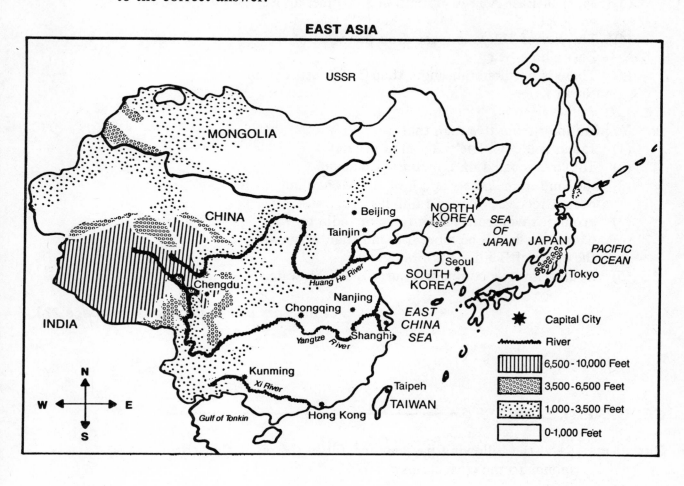

5. The majority of the land in Mongolia is what elevation above sea level?
   (1) 0 feet
   (2) 1,000 feet
   (3) Between 350 and 3,500 feet
   (4) Between 0 and 1,000 feet
   (5) More than 10,000 feet

   5 ① ② ③ ④ ⑤

6. The highest peaks in China are located
   (1) toward the western border of the country
   (2) just west of Hong Kong
   (3) to the east of Beijing
   (4) north of Mongolia
   (5) in eastern China

   6 ① ② ③ ④ ⑤

7. Which of the following statements is true?
    (1) The Sea of Japan is located west of Japan.
    (2) Taiwan is an island off the coast of Mongolia.
    (3) Most of East Asia is more than 3,000 feet above
         sea level.
    (4) The city of Tokyo is located on the coast of the
         East China Sea.
    (5) There is no mountain more than 3,200 feet high in
         North Korea.

8. You can infer from this map that
    (1) Japan is a completely flat area of land
    (2) Tokyo is located on a mountain plateau
    (3) the land immediately south of the Mongolian
         border receives a lot of rainfall
    (4) ground travel from the country of India to
         Mongolia would be more difficult than between
         the cities of Beijing and Shanghai
    (5) South Korea is completely surrounded by water

For answers and explanations, see page 273.

GEOGRAPHY EXERCISE 2

Directions: Read the following passage and fill in the circle that corresponds to the correct answer.

El Niño and the Price of Chicken in Chicago

Every eight to ten years, the waters of the Pacific off the coast of
Peru warm up. This creates a condition known as El Niño. This
warming occurs because the westerly winds that normally push
warm water west die down, and the warm water collects along the
5 Peruvian coast. This may raise the normal water temperature as
much as 10° F. What does this have to do with the price of
chicken in Chicago?

   In 1972, the warm water of El Niño kept the anchovies from
reproducing. The catch of anchovies dropped from 10.3 to 1.8
10 metric tons. At the time, anchovies provided about 40 percent of
the world's fishmeal, an important ingredient in animal food.
U.S.-grown soybeans replaced the anchovies in animal feed,
driving up the cost of soybeans. While this made soybean growers

15   happy, it, in turn, raised the price of chicken feed. This increase
was passed on to consumers, raising the price of chicken about
20¢ a pound.

El Niño affects our lives in other ways. Our weather is a
complex system based on energy exchanges between the ocean
and the atmosphere. The substantial warming of the eastern
20   Pacific during El Niño causes changes in the storm patterns that
bring rain to North America, South America, and other parts of
the world.

The unusually large and long-lasting El Niño of 1982 created
huge floods in normally dry areas of Peru, Bolivia, and southern
25   California, while creating droughts in India and Australia and
parts of the U.S. The U.S. government reported that approximately 800 people died worldwide because of weather problems
caused by El Niño. These weather conditions also caused 7 billion
dollars worth of damage.

9. The main idea of this passage is that
   (1) climate rules our lives
   (2) climatic changes have little impact on modern man
   (3) climatic changes in one area of the world can have
       profound economic effects in other areas
   (4) technology has protected modern man from
       changes created by natural disasters
   (5) water currents in the ocean affect our weather

9 ① ② ③ ④ ⑤

10. How often do the waters of the Pacific off the coast of
Peru warm up?
   (1) Every summer
   (2) Only once, in 1972
   (3) Every eight to ten months
   (4) Every eight to ten years
   (5) Every year

10 ① ② ③ ④ ⑤

11. El Niño affected the price of chicken because it
   (1) created cold weather that killed the chickens
   (2) drove up the cost of chicken feed
   (3) increased the demand for chicken
   (4) reduced the soybean crop
   (5) created hot summers that killed the chickens

11 ① ② ③ ④ ⑤

For answers and explanations, see page 273.

2. REGIONS

K
E
Y

W
O
R
D
S

region—an area of land having characteristics that distinguish it from another area of land

scale—the scope or size of a geographer's observation and investigation

topography—the physical features of a surface of land, including mountain ranges, plateaus, and lowlands

Geographers often divide land into what they call *regions*. A **region** is an area of land that has some characteristic that distinguishes it from another area of land. For example, we call a certain region in the midwestern United States the "Corn Belt." This region has no definitive boundaries and does not include a set number of states or counties. It has no distinct political or cultural barriers separating it from the Northeast region or the Southwest region of the United States. What <u>does</u> establish the Corn Belt as a region is the simple fact that a given percentage of its farmland is used for the production of corn.

Historians and geographers have developed classifications of large-scale cultural regions. It is obviously easier to break the world down into regions and to study each region separately than it would be to study "the geography of the world." Many geographers would agree that the nine basic regions of the world are North America; Central America; South America; Northwest Europe; the U.S.S.R. and Eastern Europe; the Mediterranean and the Middle East; the Far East; Africa, south of the Sahara; and the Pacific.

Regions are used by geographers in order to organize their study. In the example above, geographers chose a characteristic (50 percent of land must be corn producing) that distinguishes the Corn Belt from other areas. However, by labelling this region, they are not attempting to give us a complete description of this area of land. While its corn production may be a unifying feature, you cannot assume that the race of its inhabitants, its population, or its concentration of natural resources differs from that of other regions.

Geographers do not define regions for the purpose of dividing the world up into neat packages. This would be impossible. The division of regions depends upon what the geographer is looking for and how he wants to organize his study. For example, the region distinguished by its percentage of corn production and another region defined by its oil production may well be part of a third region defined by a similarity in economic growth.

By looking at regions, one is able to make generalizations. We can make some pretty good guesses about the states located in the Corn Belt, just by looking at its unifying characteristic. For example, we can tell that farming is one of the more important means of earning a living in those states. We have a good idea that the land is nonmountainous. By learning what temperature and rainfall are necessary to grow corn successfully, we can easily determine the climate of the Corn Belt. With these generalizations in mind, we can compare this region with others.

Generalizations are absolutely essential to the productive study and understanding of geography. The exceptions to these generalizations are also very important but should not stand in the way of defining regions. The fact that the huge majority of the inhabitants of a certain country raise wheat gives us some insight into the land and culture of this region. The fact that there are some people who grow oranges is interesting and worthy of investigation but should not detract from what we can learn about this culture through generalization.

An important aspect in defining regions is scale. **Scale** refers to the scope of our observations. Astronauts orbiting the earth are able to see and compare whole continents. Returning to Earth, they undergo a *shift in scale*. They are no longer able to see the broad scope of an entire planet, but instead see, up close, the finer distinctions of the land. The question of scale is involved in all geographic work, be it physical or cultural. Geographers must choose the scale that is appropriate to the kind of study they are undertaking. If they want to study global language patterns, they would not spend a great deal of time and effort learning about one of the seventeen dialects of Swahili spoken in tropical Africa.

Directions: Based upon what you have just read, fill in the circle that corresponds to the correct answer.

12. Why do geographers divide land into regions?   12 ① ② ③ ④ ⑤
    (1) The world is made up of nine distinct areas of land that are all completely different from one another.
    (2) One region never has anything to do with another.
    (3) This division helps the geographer to study specific physical characteristics in an organized fashion.
    (4) Geographers can, in this way, avoid generalizations.
    (5) It is not productive to study more specific areas.

13. A geographer who first studies rainfall in the entire   13 ① ② ③ ④ ⑤
    region of South America and then more closely examines the rainfall patterns in South America's tropical forests has
    (1) discovered that these regions have nothing in common
    (2) forgotten the organization of regions
    (3) little concern for rainfall patterns across South America
    (4) undergone a shift in scale in her observations
    (5) found South America to have a unique amount of rain

14. Based upon what you have read in this essay, you can conclude that

14 ① ② ③ ④ ⑤

    (1) there is little difference between one major region of the world and another

    (2) the wheat-producing region of the United States and the lumber-producing region of Canada may both be part of a third region because of common characteristics in economic development

    (3) exceptions to the rule should be more important to a geographical study than generalizations

    (4) a shift in scale is an example of poor geographic work

    (5) the nine large-scale cultural regions of the world all have the same span of area

For answers and explanations, see page 273.

GEOGRAPHY EXERCISE 3

Directions: Look at the geographic map of the region of Central America below and fill in the circle that corresponds to the correct answer.

CENTRAL AMERICA

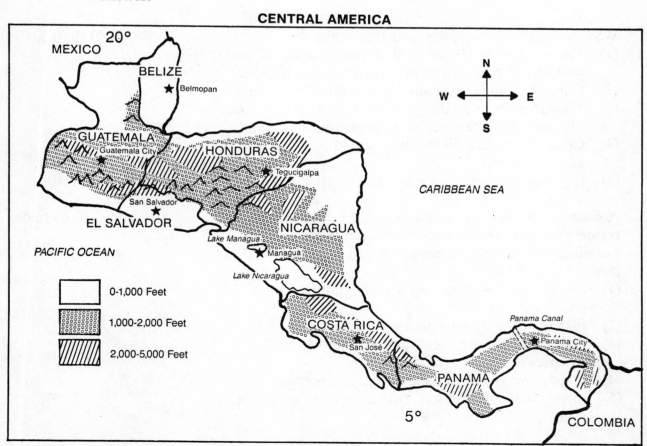

15. Which of the following most accurately describes the
topography of Central America?
    (1) Rolling hills across the majority of land
    (2) Steep mountain ranges along the coasts and flat
        farmland in the central areas
    (3) Mountainous throughout the whole region
    (4) Coastal lowlands to the east and west with
        mountain ranges toward the center region
    (5) Flatlands covered with a large number of lakes
        and rivers

15 ① ② ③ ④ ⑤

16. The body of water that cuts through a country in
Central America is
    (1) Lake Managua
    (2) Lake Nicaragua
    (3) the Panama Canal
    (4) the Caribbean Sea
    (5) the Pacific Ocean

16 ① ② ③ ④ ⑤

17. To go from Managua, Nicaragua, to San Salvador, El
Salvador, you would travel
    (1) east
    (2) south
    (3) northeast
    (4) northwest
    (5) southeast

17 ① ② ③ ④ ⑤

For answers and explanations, see page 274

3. POPULATION

KEY WORDS

demography—the study of the growth and distribution of
people

ecological system—the order of relationships between living
things and their environment

mortality rate—the rate of deaths in a particular time and place

fertility rate—the rate of births in a particular time and place

migration—the movement of people from one country or
location to another

The field of geography includes **demography**, which is the study of the
growth. distribution, and movement of people. The study of population is

important to geographers because it shows a particular aspect of our relationship with the land we inhabit. In the description of Central America's highlands and lowlands, you saw how physical realities can decide which areas of land will be heavily populated or underpopulated. Any population puts pressure on its environment, including its physical features, natural resources, and the other living organisms that happen to inhabit the same environment:

There is order in the relationships between living things and their environment. This order is called the **ecological system**. The fact that it is a system means that changes in one part of it affect changes in other parts. For example, man can change his agricultural practices to practice more intense farming. This may destroy many small animals and birds that live in the area. It may also lead to soil erosion, lowering of the water table, and the eventual end of farming in the area.

Population Growth

Man has been a very successful species. This means that he has reproduced successfully and that there is little danger of his being wiped out completely. At the end of the last Ice Age, about 12,000 years ago, there were between 5 and 10 million humans. By 1980, there were more than 4 billion humans. This growth has greatly accelerated in this century. The world population doubled between 1900 and 1960 and may double again by the year 2010. This rapid growth has often been referred to as the *population explosion*.

Population growth is a result of the relation between **mortality** rates (deaths) and **fertility** rates (births). Great increases in population growth usually come from a reduction in mortality rates (particularly for infants and children) while high fertility rates are maintained.

The decline in infant mortality has had two important consequences for population growth. One result is that more people reach adulthood, and this increases the size of a population. The second consequence comes about because more women reach childbearing age. This is the source of the population explosion. Population growth may level off because of increasing mortality rates caused by famine or war or because of lowered fertility rates maintained through family planning and birth control.

The growth or decline in population does not mean a great deal when considered on its own. To assess the influence of population on a nation or region, you must consider the pressure this population puts on its resources. For example, does a region have enough suitable land for farming to support its population? Is population growth outstripping the rate of economic development needed to support the people?

After experiencing a great burst in population growth in the last two centuries, the Western industrial countries have now gone through what is called the Demographic Transition. This is a transition from high birth rates and low mortality rates to lower birth rates and lower mortality rates. This leads to slower population growth.

The situation in nonindustrial and economically less developed countries is often quite different. The decrease in mortality rates has come about extremely rapidly, creating a true population explosion. This decrease, unlike that in the Western industrial countries, was not accompanied by a decrease in fertility, and this has created the population explosion.

Migration

Population **migration** has been a constant feature of human life since our ancient ancestors wondered what was over the next hill. People have pushed out from their origins in Africa to cover the entire globe and now have their eyes on space settlement. Migration can result when people are compelled to move because of overpopulation or bad economic conditions in their region. Migration can also result when people are attracted by better conditions in other areas.

The last century and a half have seen great migratory movements. More than 60 million people have emigrated from Europe in the last century. Thirty-seven million of them came to the U.S. The United States is currently experiencing sizeable immigration from Mexico, other Spanish-speaking countries, and Southeast Asia.

As you saw in the anthropology section of this book, migration creates what geographers and other social scientists call *cultural diffusion*, or the spread of cultural traits from one culture to another.

Directions: Based upon what you have just read, fill in the circle that corresponds to the correct answer.

18. *Demography* can best be defined as   18 ① ② ③ ④ ⑤
    (1) the study of changes in man's ecological system
    (2) the study of population and its growth and movement
    (3) the study of migration patterns
    (4) an explanation for the population explosion
    (5) the study of uninhabitable climates

19. The people of a certain region cleared all their forests of   19 ① ② ③ ④ ⑤
    trees in the 1970s to produce lumber and paper
    products. They did not follow a plan for conservation
    and in the 1980s found themselves with a great deal of
    barren land. These people
    (1) have demonstrated the danger of migration
    (2) have made no changes in their ecological system
    (3) most likely have undergone a form of cultural diffusion
    (4) have put tremendous strain on their environment and its natural resources
    (5) will be forced to migrate to new forests

20. How would an increase in birth control and an increase in the number of people killed at war affect the population of a region?

    (1)   Mortality and fertility would both increase, resulting in a growing population.

    (2)   Mortality would decrease and fertility increase; there would be no real effect on population.

    (3)   Mortality would increase and fertility decrease, resulting in a decreasing population.

    (4)   These factors would have no effect on a population's growth pattern.

    (5)   Fertility and mortality would both decrease, creating a huge growth in population.

20 ① ② ③ ④ ⑤

21. Based on the essay, you could infer that in some non-industrial and economically less developed countries

    (1)   natural resources are going to waste because of underpopulation

    (2)   Demographic Transition is occurring rapidly

    (3)   fertility rates are below the rate of replacement of the population

    (4)   there are few women reaching childbearing age

    (5)   population growth is exceeding economic development

21 ① ② ③ ④ ⑤

For answers and explanations, see page 274.

GEOGRAPHY EXERCISE 4

Directions: Read the following article and fill in the circle that corresponds to the correct answer.

> EAST AFRICA—The devastating combination of population explosion and severe drought is bringing about the worst famine in the history of this region. Hundreds of thousands of citizens from Ethiopia to South Africa have starved to death already this
>
> 5   year.
>
> Due to the pitifully small amount of rainfall this region has received during the past two years, food supplies have dwindled to nothing. Crops are burnt and dry, and livestock, without grazing land or sufficient water, are either emaciated or already
>
> 10   dead.
>
> The agony of this situation is intensified by skyrocketing birth rates. While the population of East Africa has grown by about 3 percent per year, its food production has increased by less than a third of that amount. Wars in surrounding areas are complicating

15 the population problem by driving thousands of refugees into the already overburdened countries. Nearly one-half million refugees have flooded into the Sudan from the war in Eritrea. In Somalia, as many as 1,500 refugees arrive each day.

20 Emergency measures are being taken to import food and assistance for the people of East Africa. Officials say that, as bad as the food shortage is, it will probably get worse. Millions are expected to die before the end of next year.

22. Food production in East Africa increased less than 1 percent this year. According to the article, what is the major reason for this?   22 ① ② ③ ④ ⑤
    (1) Wars in surrounding nations are cutting off supplies.
    (2) The emergency imports that these nations are accustomed to receiving have been decreased.
    (3) There are not nearly enough farmers to tend the crops.
    (4) Lack of rain has destroyed crops, and underfed cattle are dying.
    (5) Population growth has exploded.

23. You can infer from this article that   23 ① ② ③ ④ ⑤
    (1) drought is the only factor in the current famine in East Africa
    (2) man, not his environment, is to blame for this tragedy
    (3) famine occurred in East Africa because of weather problems and man's pressure on his natural resources through increased population
    (4) migration is having no effect on East Africa's widespread starvation
    (5) population growth had no effect on the famine in East Africa

24. Based on the article, which of the following is true?   24 ① ② ③ ④ ⑤
    (1) The population in East Africa has grown by about 3 percent each year.
    (2) The population in East Africa has grown by about 1 percent each year.
    (3) Food production in East Africa has grown by 3 percent.
    (4) Fifteen thousand refugees arrive in Somalia each day.
    (5) A million refugees have arrived in the Sudan from the war in Eritrea.

For answers and explanations, see page 274.

4. GEOGRAPHY AND CITIES

KEY WORDS

site—the physical qualities of a specific location

situation—the physical qualities of the area surrounding a particular site

Site and Situation

The location and growth of cities is a good illustration of the relationship between geography and the other social sciences. Some cities arose as a part of the process of economic and political development known as *industrialization.* For example, the steel-making city of Pittsburgh grew because of its proximity to the rich coal fields of Pennsylvania. Where cities are located, how big they become, and what form they take are all influenced by geographic factors.

The geographic concepts of site and situation are used to analyze city growth and location. **Site** factors refer to the physical qualities of a specific location. Historically, the most important site characteristic has been access to water routes—rivers, large lakes, and oceans. Chicago is an example of this. It originally grew up as a portage point between the Great Lakes and rivers, such as the Illinois, that drain into the upper Mississippi.

Cities have grown at these points because they are locations where travelers and cargoes must change types of transportation, either from land to water or from rivers to oceans. These changes require warehousing, laborers, merchants, financial centers, transportation company offices, repair shops, and all the other businesses associated with trade. This provides the initial nucleus for city growth. After that, additional businesses grow to support the trade activities, and the city continues to grow. Access to transportation means access to raw materials. This made some cities ideal for the growth of manufacturing and industry.

Site features are important, but the most important aspect of a location is its situation. **Situation** refers to the quality of the area surrounding a site. This surrounding area is called the city's *hinterland.* The hinterland includes the natural and human resources of the region. A river or water site is usually necessary for city growth, but growth will occur only if that water connects to a productive hinterland.

New York grew because its site at the merging of the Hudson River and the Atlantic Ocean gave it access to a productive agricultural region. In addition, the Erie Canal ties New York to the Great Lakes and expands New York's hinterland. Chicago is another example of a city with a good situation. We saw above that Chicago is located near important water routes. But the most important factor in this city's growth is its situation near the agricultural abundance of the Great Plains.

Political organization is another feature of a city's hinterland. Many county seats and state capitals, and certainly the nation's capital in Washington, DC, owe their growth to their situation in the political hinterland. These capitals have often been located in order to be central to the areas they administer. Once they become political centers, they grow to accommodate government workers and this growth creates the conditions for even more growth.

The location of competing towns is another feature of a city's situation. A size hierarchy of settlements in a region usually forms over time. There is a series of smaller settlements that are satellites around larger settlements. A settlement must be sufficiently distant from a larger settlement in order to experience any kind of growth.

Climate can also affect city growth. If the climate is so harsh that it precludes settlement of the surrounding areas, then a town is not likely to become a city. The climate can also change and affect the city's situation. This is happening in North Africa, where a long dry spell has increased the size of the Sahara Desert and destroyed local agriculture.

Technological changes can overcome some site problems and transform a town's situation. An unpromising site like hot, isolated Phoenix, Arizona, can become a boomtown because of such changes. The development of air conditioning and modern transportation helped to turn an isolated desert community into a thriving city.

Suburbanization

Nowhere is the influence of modern technology on man's geographic location more obvious than in the effects of transportation on cities and their hinterlands. As cities grew and transportation in and around these cities improved, it became easier for people to work in one place and live in another.

It was not always this way. Before the development of trains, the growth of cities was basically limited by how far people could travel on foot or on animals. Commuting distances had to be quite short. By the end of the nineteenth century, the effect of interurban trains and trolleys was very noticeable. Major cities became surrounded by growing suburbs that housed people who commuted into the city to work. For example, the area around Los Angeles became a region of sprawling communities in the early twentieth century because of the Pacific Electric interurban train system.

Industry began to move into the suburbs with the next great transportation development—the introduction of automobiles and trucks. Trucks could transport resources to and from the city, and inexpensive, mass-produced cars could transport the workers to factories in the suburbs.

Clearly, the growth of cities shows us how geography has had an effect on where we live and work. However, as technology advances and improves, we see more and more of the reverse—people influencing their environment to better suit their needs.

Directions: Based upon what you have just read, fill in the circle that corresponds to the correct answer.

25. Cities in a region usually form a hierarchy based on
    (1) size
    (2) site
    (3) climate
    (4) age
    (5) situation

    25 ① ② ③ ④ ⑤

26. From this essay, you could infer that a community located near the coast of a major body of water and blocked from its hinterland by rugged mountain peaks
    (1) has neither good site nor good situation
    (2) has good site but poor situation
    (3) has both good site and good situation
    (4) is a victim of size hierarchy
    (5) shows the effect of poor climate

    26 ① ② ③ ④ ⑤

27. Which of the following was the most important factor in the growth of Chicago?
    (1) Its proximity to the mineral-rich hinterland
    (2) Its tremendously advanced transportation systems
    (3) Its situation near the agriculturally rich Great Plains
    (4) Its situation in the midst of other prosperous cities
    (5) Its political hinterland

    27 ① ② ③ ④ ⑤

28. Suburbanization is a good example of
    (1) the effects of a poor site
    (2) the size hierarchy of central cities
    (3) the effects of the lack of sufficient water routes
    (4) the poor planning of city government
    (5) the influence of technology on man's location

    28 ① ② ③ ④ ⑤

For answers and explanations, see page 274.

GEOGRAPHY EXERCISE 5

Directions: Read the following passage and fill in the circle that corresponds to the correct answer.

When you picture Denver, Colorado, you may envision a spotlessly clean city built high in the clear mountain air of the Rocky Mountains. This, indeed, used to be the case. But today, our influence on environment is more evident than ever, as Denver
5   ranks fourth on the list of America's most polluted cities.

It is no surprise that Denver grew into a major industrial city. Its site at the convergence of important rivers and at the foot of the Rocky Mountains made it a convenient place to settle. Its situation in a region rich in agriculture and minerals is ideally
10 suited for growth. However, as Denver grew and industry and population increased, this interaction between people and environment took a turn for the worse.

The "brown cloud" that cloaks the city an average of 100 days out of the year is made up primarily of carbon monoxide, the
15 poisonous gas emitted by automobiles and industrial smokestacks. Besides its unsightly appearance, ruining some of the most spectacular views of Colorado's mountain peaks, this "cloud" poses a critical health risk for the inhabitants of this city. Although they are not conclusive, studies show that the rate of
20 lung cancer is higher in polluted urban areas and that this rate may be anywhere from 10 to 21 percent higher in cities such as Denver.

Why is Denver, in particular, so high on the list of polluted cities? As mentioned above, automobiles are a major cause of air
25 pollution. Denver has more cars per capita than any other city in America due to its poor public transportation system.

This problem is compounded by a geographic factor. Denver, located one mile above sea level, has considerably less oxygen in its atmosphere than cities at lower altitudes. This causes automo-
30 biles to work less efficiently, which in turn causes increased production of carbon monoxide. In addition, people are forced to breathe harder to get enough oxygen into their lungs, which means that they are also taking in more of the poisonous gas. Many people with respiratory diseases are being forced to move
35 out of Denver and into suburbs at lower altitudes.

29. The seriousness of the air pollution problem in Denver, Colorado,

29 ① ② ③ ④ ⑤

    (1)   is a product of man's own actions
    (2)   is a product of both man-made and natural factors
    (3)   is not necessarily affecting the citizens
    (4)   has caused innumerable deaths in the area
    (5)   is virtually unexplainable given the city's altitude

30. You can infer from the passage that   30 ① ② ③ ④ ⑤
    (1) if Denver had a better site, pollution would not be
         a problem
    (2) the state of Denver's transportation system has
         little to do with its air pollution
    (3) Denver is the worst city in America in which to
         live
    (4) industry does not affect air pollution in Denver
    (5) improvements made in Denver's public
         transportation system would help alleviate the air
         pollution problem

31. According to the passage, which of the following is   31 ① ② ③ ④ ⑤
    true?
    (1) The rate of lung cancer in Denver is at least 33
         percent higher than any other city.
    (2) There are two automobiles for every citizen of
         Denver.
    (3) The cloud of carbon monoxide cloaks the city of
         Denver an average of 100 days out of the year.
    (4) The cloud of carbon monoxide over Denver has
         existed for a total of 100 days.
    (5) Death caused by cancer in Denver is anywhere
         from 10 to 21 percent above normal.

For answers and explanations, see page 274.

ANSWERS AND EXPLANATIONS

1. INTRODUCTION TO GEOGRAPHY

Main Idea **1.** (3) The interaction between people and their environment is the most important aspect of the study of geography.

Finding Details **2.** (5) The essay describes contour lines as connecting lines on a map that indicate areas at the same elevation.

Finding Details **3.** (2) This is stated under the heading "Latitude and Longitude Lines."

Making Inferences **4.** (2) Based on the essay, you could infer that people who live near water are likely to develop skills related to water.

GEOGRAPHY EXERCISE 1

Reading Maps **5.** (4) By looking at the key, you can tell that the symbol (white) covering most of Mongolia stands for a range from 0 to 1,000 feet.

Reading Maps **6.** (1) The vertical lines indicate the highest elevation. The only place these lines appear is in the western part of China.

Reading Maps **7.** (1) According to the map, the Sea of Japan is west of Japan. None of the other statements are supported by the graph.

Making Inferences **8.** (4) Ground travel from India to Mongolia involves crossing numerous mountains, which would be considerably more difficult than traveling the short, flat distance between the Chinese cities of Beijing and Shanghai.

GEOGRAPHY EXERCISE 2

Main Idea **9.** (3) This passage describes how changes in the waters off the coast of Peru (El Niño) have had a considerable effect on the price of chicken thousands of miles away.

Finding Details **10.** (4) This is stated in the first paragraph.

Drawing Conclusions **11.** (2) When the cost of chicken feed went up, farmers passed on the cost increase to consumers.

2. REGIONS

Making Inferences **12.** (3) The essay defines a region as an area having specific distinguishing characteristics. This type of division enables geographers to study particular areas in a systematic fashion.

Application of Ideas **13.** (4) The geographer has changed the scope of her observations, creating a shift in the scale.

Drawing Conclusions **14.** (2) The essay points out that geographers use the term *region* to define areas with shared characteristics. A wheat-producing area in the U.S. and a lumber-producing area in Canada may have similar patterns of economic growth and can be looked at as an economic region.

GEOGRAPHY EXERCISE 3

Reading Maps	**15.**	(4)	Based on the map and the key that accompanies it, you can see that the coastal regions have few mountainous areas while the central area has mountains ranging from 1,000 to 5,000 feet.
Reading Maps	**16.**	(3)	The Panama Canal cuts across the country of Panama, located in the southeastern portion of Central America.
Reading Maps	**17.**	(4)	Use the directional guide at the top of the map to see that San Salvador is northwest of Managua.
Finding Details	**18.**	(2)	*Demography* is defined in the first paragraph.
Application of Ideas	**19.**	(4)	By depleting some of the natural resources in the area, the inhabitants have put a strain on their environment.
Drawing Conclusions	**20.**	(3)	Both factors, population control and war-related deaths, would result in a decrease in population.
Making Inferences	**21.**	(5)	The essay points out that, in less economically developed countries, there has been a population explosion. You could infer that this puts a further strain on the existing resources.

GEOGRAPHY EXERCISE 4

Finding Details	**22.**	(4)	According to the essay, lack of rainfall has led to poor food production.
Making Inferences	**23.**	(3)	The article describes both factors: weather problems and increased population. This combination of factors has contributed to the famine.
Finding Details	**24.**	(1)	This is stated in the third paragraph of the passage.

4.   GEOGRAPHY AND CITIES

Finding Details	**25.**	(1)	The essay states that, over time, a size hierarchy of cities develops.
Making Inferences	**26.**	(2)	The site of this community, located near a body of water, is helpful, but the connection to the hinterland is blocked by steep mountains. This means that, while the community has a good site, it has a poor situation.
Finding Details	**27.**	(3)	The essay states that the most important factor contributing to Chicago's growth was its proximity to the Great Plains.
Making Inferences	**28.**	(5)	The last two paragraphs describe how transportation-related technology has influenced the growth of suburbs.
Drawing Conclusions	**29.**	(2)	The passage describes how the altitude of Denver combines with the exhaust from cars to create pollution.
Making Inferences	**30.**	(5)	Part of the reason for Denver's excessive pollution is the abundance of automobiles. Better public transportation would decrease the number of cars and decrease the pollution as well.
Finding Details	**31.**	(3)	This is stated in the third paragraph.

SOCIAL STUDIES POST-TEST

<u>Directions</u>

This social studies post-test will give you the opportunity to evaluate your readiness for the actual GED social studies test.

This test contains 60 questions. Some of the questions are based on short reading passages, and some of them require you to interpret a chart, map, graph, or political cartoon.

You should take approximately 90 minutes to complete this test. At the end of 90 minutes, stop and mark your place. Then, go on and finish the test. This will give you an idea of whether or not you can finish the real GED test in the time allotted. Try to answer as many questions as you can. A blank will count as a wrong answer, so make a reasonable guess for questions you are not sure of.

For your convenience, we have included an answer sheet on page 297 that you can take out of the book and use along with the test.

When you are finished with the test, turn to the evaluation and scoring charts on page 296. Use the charts to evaluate whether you are ready to take the actual GED test, and, if not, what areas need more work.

1. Geographers often look at the places they study in terms of regions. Rather than having distinct boundaries or an exact population, a region is simply an area of land with a certain characteristic, differentiated for the purposes of study.

   For example, a geographer studying rainfall patterns in the Pacific Northwest might focus on a region defined by
   (1) changes in altitude moving inland from the coast to the mountains
   (2) a high annual precipitation rate
   (3) the state boundaries of Washington and Oregon
   (4) the Pacific Northwest Railroad
   (5) the greatest amount of cultivated farmland

2. Joe and Ida Wisnooski find that every month their money just seems to disappear, and they can never save for any long-term goals. The first thing they should do to correct this situation is
   (1) increase their discretionary income
   (2) draw up a family budget
   (3) buy some consumer's insurance
   (4) try a couple of get-rich-quick schemes
   (5) apply for a credit card

Questions 3 and 4 are based on the following table.

**MARRIAGES AND DIVORCES
IN THE UNITED STATES
(Per 1,000 People)**

Year	Marriages	Divorces
1930	9.2	1.6
1940	12.1	2.0
1950	11.1	2.6
1960	8.5	2.2
1970	10.6	3.5
1980	10.6	5.2

3. This chart tells you the
   (1) number of marriages that ended in divorce
   (2) percentage of the population that married or divorced
   (3) number of marriages and divorces for every 1,000 people
   (4) percentage of change in the marriage and divorce rate every ten years
   (5) statistical evidence of social deterioration in the United States

4. Based on the information in the table, you can conclude that
   (1) in general, about twice as many marriages as divorces take place
   (2) between 1950 and 1960, there was a decrease in both the number of marriages and the number of divorces
   (3) the divorce rate has been affected most by the baby boom
   (4) throughout the past fifty years, the divorce rate has been a constant percentage of the marriage rate
   (5) there are now more divorces than there are marriages

GO ON TO THE NEXT PAGE.

Questions <u>5 and 6</u> refer to the following graph.

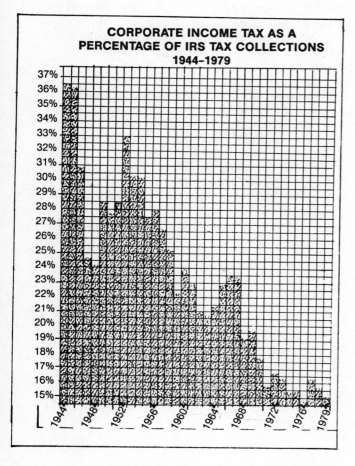

**CORPORATE INCOME TAX AS A
PERCENTAGE OF IRS TAX COLLECTIONS
1944-1979**

5. The politically and economically powerful can often avoid paying huge taxes. Based on the graph to the left, we can infer that the influence of U.S. corporations over tax legislation
   (1) has decreased since 1944
   (2) has increased since 1944
   (3) decreased to an all-time low in 1977
   (4) has not changed since 1944
   (5) will increase more than ever in the late 1980s

6. In the period from 1944 to 1979, when did corporations pay the highest percentage of income taxes to the IRS?
   (1) 1944
   (2) 1945
   (3) 1963
   (4) 1971
   (5) 1979

7. The development of mass spectator sports has replaced many of the functions of older tribal rituals. They provide occasions for ritual mass solidarity, battle between good and evil, and manipulation of tribal members by using symbols of tribal identity. What, after all, are cheerleaders but tribal shamans shaking magic pompoms and going through ritual dances to ensure the victory of good over evil?
   The main point of this passage is that
   (1) mass spectator sport has created new cultural needs
   (2) sports are important because they build character
   (3) tribal rituals have no relation to modern life
   (4) modern sport should be seen as mainly a business enterprise
   (5) mass spectator sport is a modern cultural adaptation of older tribal needs

GO ON TO THE NEXT PAGE.

Question 8 refers to the following graphs.

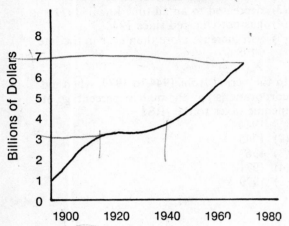

TOTAL GROSS NATIONAL PRODUCT, ADJUSTED FOR INFLATION

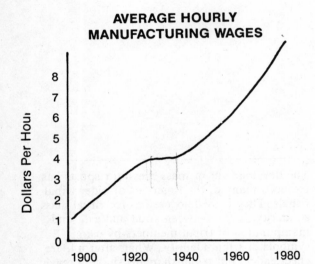

AVERAGE HOURLY MANUFACTURING WAGES

8. The story in your daily newspaper that accompanied these two graphs concluded that workers were getting more than their share of the benefits of economic growth since wages have increased 800 percent while the Gross National Product has increased only 500 percent.

   This conclusion is
   (1) correct, because wages are the only factor influencing GNP
   (2) misleading because it compares an overview of the entire economy with a small part of the economy
   (3) misleading because the two graphs use different time frames
   (4) scientific support for the idea that wages cause inflation
   (5) accurate because wages have been adjusted for inflation

9. The worldwide interest in Levi-type jeans is best described as a case of
   (1) mass hysteria
   (2) cultural conflict
   (3) role conflict
   (4) ethnocentrism
   (5) cultural diffusion

GO ON TO THE NEXT PAGE.

Questions 10 and 11 refer to the following passage.

Child care facilities first appeared in U.S. cities around 1900. They were charities, run by wealthy women who raised the money and supervised the staff. These women saw that some mothers were forced to work out of economic necessity and feared that without the day nurseries small children would be left alone. Their critics worried that these day nurseries would encourage mothers to work instead of staying home with their children.

10. Day care centers were started by
    (1) mothers who organized and hired people to take care of their children while they worked
    (2) factories who wanted to hire women workers
    (3) wealthy women who thought they would be a profitable investment
    (4) people who wanted mothers to stay home with their children
    (5) wealthy women who were worried about the safety of small children with working mothers

11. Based on the passage, you can infer that the practice of giving welfare benefits to mothers with dependent children could have developed out of some people's concern that
    (1) there were not enough jobs to keep these women working
    (2) children should have their mothers at home with them
    (3) if these women worked, there would not be enough day care centers for their children
    (4) day care is too expensive for most mothers
    (5) divorce is so common that many women have no husbands to support them

Question 12 refers to the following graph.

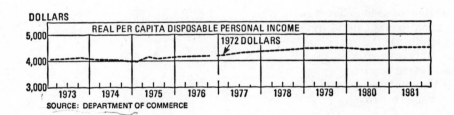

DOLLARS

REAL PER CAPITA DISPOSABLE PERSONAL INCOME

1972 DOLLARS

5,000

4,000

3,000

1973 1974 1975 1976 1977 1978 1979 1980 1981

SOURCE: DEPARTMENT OF COMMERCE

12. Real per capita disposable income is a way of showing how much buying power is left for consumers after taxes and inflation. This graph shows a period of time during which the rate of inflation in the United States was very high From this information and the data on the graph, you can conclude that
    (1) people lost buying power because of inflation
    (2) in spite of inflation, people gained buying power
    (3) real income decreased between 1976 and 1981
    (4) people were disposing of their money unwisely
    (5) the value of the dollar rose in 1972

GO ON TO THE NEXT PAGE.

Question 13 refers to the following definitions.

direct initiative—a petition process that allows citizens to draft laws and present them directly to the voters

referendum—the mechanism by which voters can repeal legislation in a general election

recall—permits citizens to vote an official out of office

13. A group of citizens who want to write tax reform legislation and present it directly to the voters should proceed with a
(1) referendum
(2) general election
(3) direct initiative
(4) recall
(5) primary vote

Questions 14 and 15 refer to the following passage.

Our schools are in crisis. They are being buried under a mountain of mediocrity. Union rule, particularly the seniority system, now runs the schools. We need a new system to establish merit pay for good teachers so that our administrators and school boards can run the schools and our students can learn.

14. The author of this passage believes there is a crisis in education that is caused by
(1) poorly disciplined students
(2) too much bureaucracy
(3) poorly motivated teachers
(4) apathetic parents
(5) uncaring school boards

15. This writer would most likely be in support of which of the following?
(1) A ban on the unionization of teachers
(2) New revenues for across-the-board teacher pay raises
(3) The right to strike for federal employees
(4) Restriction of the influence of school boards in establishing classroom policy
(5) Experimental, teacher-run schools

16. In the 1930s, England and France followed a policy of appeasement toward German territorial expansion. Germany took over all of Czechoslovakia and threatened Poland and Austria. Many experts in international relations claim that appeasing German expansionism led to World War II.
   Appeasement is
(1) refusing to allow European nations to interfere in American affairs
(2) taking in unlimited numbers of immigrants from other countries
(3) the right to use land that belongs to someone else
(4) compromising in the face of aggression
(5) German domination of international politics

GO ON TO THE NEXT PAGE.

Questions 17–19 refer to the following passage.

Consumer cooperatives are businesses that are owned and controlled by their members, the consumers who use them. Member-owners of co-ops help make decisions by voting on rules and policies and by electing officers. Co-ops can often provide their services at a lower cost since the member-owners are running the business for their own use, not to make a profit. A co-op can be any kind of business, from a grocery store to an apartment building.

17. The fundamental principle behind the decision-making process in cooperatives is control by
    (1) the government
    (2) their officers
    (3) neighborhood groups
    (4) their members
    (5) grocery-store chains

18. A cooperative townhouse complex would be owned by
    (1) the people who lived there
    (2) landlords
    (3) the people who worked there
    (4) the officers of the cooperative
    (5) city government

19. If the average cost of food is lower at your co-op store than at the regular supermarket, the reason might be that
    (1) the co-op is trying to compete with the supermarket
    (2) the co-op is receiving a subsidy from the government
    (3) the members would rather have low prices than high profits
    (4) it costs less to run a co-op than a supermarket
    (5) the supermarket sells food of higher quality

Question 20 is based on the following passage.

Since 1950, the percentage of employed black males has dropped from 75 percent to 55 percent, primarily due to the deep recessions of 1974–75 and 1979–82. This unemployment has caused many of these men to leave their families so that their wives and children could receive welfare. This situation has arisen because many states will not give welfare if there is an able-bodied man in the home.

20. From this passage, you could infer that one method of increasing the resources available to black families would be to
    (1) return to the old values of hard work
    (2) decrease welfare payments so that people would be forced to find a job
    (3) reduce the number of children people are having
    (4) increase employment opportunities for black males
    (5) arrest and imprison those men who leave their families

Question 21 refers to the following graph.

EQUILIBRIUM PRICE FOR COMPUTERS

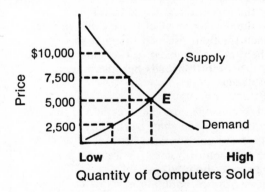

21. The equilibrium price of goods or services (E) is determined by the point at which supply is equal to demand. According to the graph above, what is the equilibrium price for computers?
    (1) $2,500
    (2) $5,000
    (3) $7,500
    (4) $10,000
    (5) $15,000

GO ON TO THE NEXT PAGE

22. Rapid population growth in developing countries is usually the result of
    (1) increased medical care for the elderly
    (2) increased migration
    (3) decreased birth rates
    (4) the demographic transition
    (5) decreased infant mortality

Questions 23 and 24 refer to the following passage.

The late nineteenth century witnessed the beginnings of a process that was to grow throughout the twentieth century. This was the process of suburbanization. Even as America was undergoing urbanization, its urban centers were decentralizing. The early suburbs, where wealthy people lived, were built on electric railroad lines. The growth of suburbs was pushed ahead by the invention of the automobile and truck. These inventions allowed factories and homeowners to locate without being dependent on the railroad lines of the cities.

23. This passage says that the growth of suburbs was advanced
    (1) by the invention of the automobile
    (2) by the development of more railroad lines
    (3) when the poor escaped the city
    (4) when industry moved to the countryside
    (5) as the use of railroads became more obsolete

24. From this passage, you could conclude that an important feature in shaping the physical growth of our environment is
    (1) the location of homes for wealthy people
    (2) the size of population
    (3) the density of population
    (4) transportation technology
    (5) the physical condition of the site

Questions 25 and 26 refer to the following passage.

Society makes a distinction between street crime and white-collar crime. Street crimes consist of car theft, burglary, robbery, homicide, rape, larceny, and assault. White-collar crimes are committed by professionals, businessmen, and corporations in the course of their business activities. The economic loss due to street crime is one-fifth of the amount lost through embezzlement, fraud, and other forms of white-collar crime. However, prison sentences for white-collar criminals are often much lighter than those for street criminals, and sometimes those convicted of white-collar crimes serve no time at all.

25. The passage says that the heaviest economic losses from crime come from
    (1) embezzlement
    (2) street crime, such as robbery
    (3) white-collar crime
    (4) home burglaries
    (5) gang activities

26. The difference in how street crime and white-collar crime are dealt with could be attributed to
    (1) the fact that street crime is much more costly
    (2) the political connections of street gangs
    (3) the courts' lenience with street criminals
    (4) the power and social status of white-collar criminals
    (5) the fact that white-collar crime is not committed by criminals

27. The idea that "our way of life" is morally better than that of other people is an example of ethnocentrism, which is
    (1) an outdated religious belief
    (2) an emotionally based psychological disorder
    (3) judgment of one culture by the values of another
    (4) typical of certain social groups
    (5) a standard for behavior in particular situations

GO ON TO THE NEXT PAGE.

Questions 28 and 29 refer to the following graph.

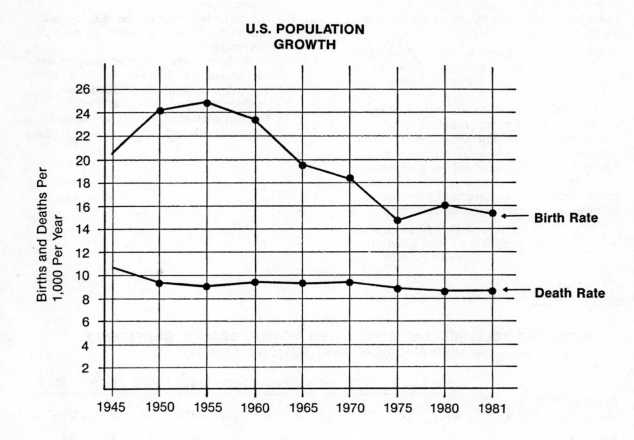

U.S. POPULATION GROWTH

28. The era known as the "baby boom" occurred in which of the following time periods?
    (1) 1945–1955
    (2) 1955–1965
    (3) 1960–1970
    (4) 1965–1975
    (5) 1975–1980

29. The graph indicates that current American population growth rates
    (1) are exploding
    (2) have remained very stable since 1945
    (3) declined during the early 1950s
    (4) have increased dramatically since 1970
    (5) have declined since 1955

30. Among the many factors affecting the long-term economic growth of a city, the most important one among the following is
    (1) weather
    (2) access to major shipping routes
    (3) size of airport facilities
    (4) population
    (5) proximity to the ocean

GO ON TO THE NEXT PAGE

Question 31 refers to the following quotations:

". . . avoid the necessity of those overgrown military establishments which, under any form of government, are inauspicious for liberty, and which are to be regarded as particularly hostile to republican liberty."

General George Washington,
1st President of the United States,
Farewell Address, 1796.

"The conjunction of an immense military establishment and a large arms industry . . . new in American experience, exercised a total influence . . . felt in every city, every state house, every office of the federal government. . . . In the councils of government, we must guard against the acquisition of unwarranted influence by the military-industrial complex."

General Dwight Eisenhower,
34th President of the United States,
Farewell Address, 1961.

Questions 32 and 33 refer to the following chart.

RESULT OF POLL: PERCENT EXPRESSING A GREAT DEAL OF CONFIDENCE IN NINE AMERICAN INSTITUTIONS, 1966–81

	1966	1971	1973	1974	1975	1976	1977	1978	1979	1981
Average of Nine Major Institutions	43%	27%	33%	28%	24%	20%	24%	25%	23%	22%
TV News	25	—	41	31	35	28	28	35	37	24
Medical Establishment	73	61	57	50	43	42	43	42	30	37
Military	62	27	40	33	24	23	27	29	29	28
Press	29	18	30	25	26	20	18	23	28	16
Organized Religion	41	27	36	32	32	24	29	34	20	22
Major Companies	55	27	29	21	19	16	20	22	18	16
Congress	42	19	29	18	13	9	17	10	18	16
Executive Branch	41	23	19	28	13	11	23	14	17	24
Organized Labor	22	14	20	18	14	10	14	15	10	12

31. Which of the following conclusions could be drawn from both of these statements?
    (1) An overgrown military establishment could pose a threat to our democratic government.
    (2) Industrial influence on the military has made our form of government more democratic.
    (3) Only the military-industrial complex can safeguard our liberties.
    (4) The military should be allowed more influence in government affairs.
    (5) Civilian control of the military should never be allowed.

32. According to this chart, the American people's confidence in major companies
    (1) has been stable and at a high level since 1966
    (2) is based on the health of the overall economy
    (3) has been increasing
    (4) has declined substantially since 1966
    (5) was higher than it was for the executive branch in 1981

33. Which of the following can you infer from the data in this chart?
    (1) Support for American institutions is very high.
    (2) From 1966 to 1981, the level of confidence in most American institutions declined.
    (3) The executive branch was always trusted more than organized labor.
    (4) In 1976, confidence in major American institutions was high.
    (5) 1966 was the year that the majority of Americans were satisfied with the condition of the country.

GO ON TO THE NEXT PAGE.

34. The rich cultural contributions of Latin Americans in the southwestern United States are not only a result of twentieth-century immigration to the region. As a matter of fact, people of Latin American origin were in the Southwest before Americans of European descent. The ownership and boundaries of the southwestern territories were a matter of dispute with Mexico for many years.

Which of the following statements is true?
(1) Cultural development in the Southwest has been held back by Latin American influence.
(2) Mexico sold Texas to the United States in an attempt to improve immigration trends.
(3) Ever since the southwestern territories became states, most Mexicans would prefer to live in the U.S.
(4) The United States had completely settled the Southwest before Mexico took an interest in the region.
(5) Latin American influence on regional culture in the southwestern U.S. is the result of a long, colorful history of interaction.

35. The New Deal, developed during the Great Depression, established which of the following governmental economic policies?
(1) The government would guarantee a high level of employment in the private sector.
(2) The government would rely on the private sector to ensure the well-being of the people.
(3) The government would completely centralize all economic decision making.
(4) The government would follow the policy of laissez-faire.
(5) The government would be responsible for a minimum level of economic security for the people.

Question 36 refers to the following table.

COSTS OF PRODUCTION & NET INCOME: ONE AUTOMOBILE

	Materials	Depreciation of plant and machinery	Total wages	Taxes	Net Income
Plant 1	$1,440	$78	$743	$176	$185
Plant 2	$1,440	$78	$650	$176	$278

36. To produce one automobile, Plant 2 paid out less in wages than Plant 1. Assuming that workers in both plants are paid the same hourly wage, what could account for the greater net income per car in Plant 2?
(1) Higher quality of materials in Plant 1
(2) Slower depreciation in Plant 2
(3) Better marketing in Plant 2
(4) Greater worker productivity in Plant 2
(5) Greater worker productivity in Plant 1

GO ON TO THE NEXT PAGE.

Question 37 is based on the following cartoon.

37. The main idea of this cartoon is that American agricultural production has evolved
    (1) away from large corporation-owned farms
    (2) as a result of farm price supports
    (3) away from small family farms
    (4) in spite of high interest rates
    (5) toward organic farming

GO ON TO THE NEXT PAGE

Question 38 is based on the following map.

LOYALIST CONCENTRATIONS DURING THE AMERICAN REVOLUTION

Loyalist Concentrations

38. The Loyalists did not want the American colonies to break off from England. According to the map, which city probably had the fewest Loyalist residents?
    (1) New York
    (2) Boston
    (3) Charleston
    (4) Baltimore
    (5) Philadelphia

GO ON TO THE NEXT PAGE.

Questions 39 and 40 are based on the following passage.

The United States Constitution guarantees American citizens protection against unreasonable search and seizure, trial by jury, the right to due process and protection against self-incrimination, the right to an attorney and a public trial, and protection against excessive bail or unusual punishment. But what about the right of innocent citizens to be protected against criminals? Our judges are too lenient with dangerous criminals who are too often let loose on the streets because of legal technicalities.

39. The author of this passage probably would like suspected criminals to be
   (1) considered innocent until proven guilty
   (2) guaranteed due process of law
   (3) kept off the streets
   (4) given lighter sentences
   (5) let out on bail

40. The Constitution guarantees Americans these rights because otherwise
   (1) innocent people might become dangerous criminals
   (2) innocent people might be treated as dangerous criminals
   (3) legal technicalities would be too time consuming
   (4) people would be considered innocent until proven guilty
   (5) the laws would be far too lenient

Questions 41 and 42 refer to the following passage.

Nitrogen and sulfur oxide pollution from factories and auto emissions in the Midwest are moved by the prevailing winds into the eastern parts of the United States and Canada. There, these pollutants become so concentrated that they give the rain a high acid content. This acid rain is killing fish and large numbers of trees in the eastern forests. The destruction of forests, if allowed to continue, will ruin watersheds, lower water tables, and cause widespread water shortages for the eastern cities.

41. This passage states that potential water shortages in the East are
   (1) inevitable
   (2) the result of negligence in the East
   (3) related to industrial activity in other regions
   (4) killing trees
   (5) killing fish

42. From this passage, you could conclude that
   (1) society can conquer nature
   (2) nature rules the development of human society
   (3) the effect of pollution is limited to the region in which it is created
   (4) just as people can affect their environment, so environmental changes can affect the lives of people
   (5) the political implications of pollution are generally overestimated

GO ON TO THE NEXT PAGE

Questions 43 and 44 refer to the following passage

A balance sheet is a financial statement that businesses use to summarize their financial position at particular points in time. A balance sheet has three sections: assets, liabilities, and net worth.

assets—everything the business has in its possession

liabilities—everything the business owes to someone else

net worth—that part of the business's assets that it owns, free and clear of debt

The balance sheet "balances" because

ASSETS − LIABILITIES = NET WORTH.

43. A balance sheet describes the financial position of a business
    (1) in terms of its debts
    (2) by counting its assets
    (3) at particular points in time
    (4) by computing profit or loss
    (5) for a fiscal year

44. If Jin Su's Chinese Restaurant has assets totaling $5,000 and liabilities totaling $3,200, its net worth is
    (1) $3,200
    (2) $1,800
    (3) $8,200
    (4) $5,000
    (5) negative

Questions 45 and 46 refer to the following passage.

The Radical Republicans were the antislavery wing of the Republican party from the mid-1850s to the mid-1870s. They persistently demanded civil rights for blacks throughout those decades. Some of their most significant successes included the passage of three constitutional amendments guaranteeing fundamental civil rights and the establishment of the Freedmen's Bureau, an agency responsible for assisting the former slaves in making the transition to citizenship.

45. The Radical Republicans advocated
    (1) slavery
    (2) the Civil War
    (3) the abolition of the Democratic Party
    (4) civil rights for the former slaves
    (5) an end to Reconstruction

46. The Freedmen's Bureau
    (1) helped former slaves learn to read and write
    (2) assisted former slaveholders in finding new servants
    (3) moved slaves North to safety
    (4) worked for the passage of constitutional amendments
    (5) established citizenship for former slaves

GO ON TO THE NEXT PAGE.

Questions 47 and 48 refer to the following passage.

Jane Benson lives in a residential working-class neighborhood in a small city. She wanted to open a small business in her area so that she could work near her home and be her own boss. She decided to do a market survey of the area. She made up a questionnaire listing the possible products and services she could provide and walked door to door every evening, asking people to answer her questions.

JANE'S RESULTS

	in favor	would spend		
		$5/wk	$10/wk.	$15/wk.
bakery	8	6	1	1
drugstore	7	2	3	2
gas station	6	3	3	0
restaurant	5	2	1	2

47. Which best describes a market survey?
    (1) A questionnaire that compares different kinds of businesses
    (2) A door-to-door poll
    (3) A measurement of how much money people will spend for something
    (4) A poll conducted in city residential neighborhoods
    (5) A way for a business to find out what people want

48. Which of the four businesses would probably attract the most customers?
    (1) The bakery
    (2) The drugstore
    (3) The gas station
    (4) The restaurant
    (5) No way to tell

Question 49 refers to the following passage.

The Constitution of the United States gives Congress the authority to make laws about certain matters. In other matters, the states are given jurisdiction. However, there is a clause in the Constitution stating that Congress may do anything "necessary and proper" to ensure the welfare of the United States and its citizens. The "implied powers" of Congress have been a subject of debate ever since the ratification of the Constitution. One view, that the "necessary and proper" clause only clarifies the power of Congress to act in matters set forth specifically as its jurisdiction, is a strict interpretation of the Constitution. The opposing view suggests a broader interpretation, allowing Congress to further the interests of the nation in any matter.

49. The nature of the "implied powers" of Congress is
    (1) not defined exactly in the Constitution
    (2) necessary and proper to ensure the welfare of the nation
    (3) the authority to act on behalf of the states
    (4) constitutional authority
    (5) a strict interpretation of the Constitution

Question 50 refers to the following dialogue.

Speaker A: I think people are less loyal to the major political parties today. This trend worries me—we need stability in our political system more than ever, and the two-party system has worked well for us for about 200 years.

Speaker B: You're right about the trend, but I think it's great. The big parties will have to work to earn the independent votes, so they'll have to find out what people really want.

50. The two speakers
    (1) think that both major political parties will soon die
    (2) disagree on the implications of the trend toward independent voting
    (3) want to have more than two political parties
    (4) disagree on whether or not voters are remaining loyal to the major parties
    (5) are not sure of their party affiliations

GO ON TO THE NEXT PAGE.

51. Which of the following statements is true?
    (1) Generally, a strict interpretation of the Constitution has been followed throughout American history.
    (2) The Constitution gives Congress the power to act in any manner it sees fit.
    (3) For the most part, the interpretation of the Constitution has reflected changing political and social trends.
    (4) The Constitution does not give the states jurisdiction over their affairs.
    (5) The Constitution only gives Congress the power to act in matters set forth specifically as Congress's jurisdiction.

Questions 52 and 53 refer to the following passage.

The term *populism* refers to a movement to organize farmers that peaked in the 1890s following two economic depressions and a worldwide decline in agricultural prices. Farmers felt that economic policy favored industry and commerce and that reforms were needed to assist agricultural producers. In particular, they asked for an increase in the amount of money in circulation in the United States, government ownership of railroads, and legislation against alien landholding.

52. Populism was
    (1) a union
    (2) an economic policy
    (3) legislation against alien landholding
    (4) a social movement
    (5) an anti-industrial sentiment

53. In the late nineteenth century, farmers were hurt by
    (1) the Populists
    (2) a worldwide decline in agricultural prices
    (3) an increase in the money supply
    (4) anti-industrial sentiment
    (5) industry and commerce

Questions 54 and 55 refer to the following passage.

The battle for women's suffrage raged for a full century. The Nineteenth Amendment, giving women the right to vote, was finally signed into law in 1920. One argument in favor of enfranchising women was that women would bring increased sensitivity, humanity, and commitment to fair dealings into the political arena. The antisuffragist response to this argument was that women's spiritual purity and moral force would be undermined by political involvement.

54. Suffrage means
    (1) suffering
    (2) civil rights
    (3) appeasement
    (4) the right to vote
    (5) emancipation

55. According to the passage, some people who opposed giving women the vote were concerned that women would
    (1) be less able to provide spiritual guidance in their communities
    (2) not want to do their housework
    (3) have fewer children
    (4) dehumanize the political arena
    (5) no longer be feminine

GO ON TO THE NEXT PAGE.

Questions 56–58 refer to the following passage.

Following World War I, many nations banded together to form the League of Nations, an alliance whose goal was to guarantee world peace. U.S. President Woodrow Wilson wanted the United States to take the lead in the League of Nations. However, Congress refused to allow the international affairs of the United States to be subject to the articles of the league. As a result, the United States did not join the League of Nations.

56. The purpose of the League of Nations was to
    (1) bring an end to World War I
    (2) allow the United States to take the lead in international politics
    (3) guarantee world peace
    (4) allow western nations a forum for communication
    (5) take over international affairs from President Wilson

57. The United States did not join the League of Nations because
    (1) President Wilson was not an effective statesman
    (2) World War I was not yet over
    (3) Congress did not want the United States to take the lead
    (4) the league could not guarantee world peace
    (5) some feared that the international affairs of the United States would have been subject to its articles

58. The League of Nations was the forerunner of the
    (1) North Atlantic Treaty Organization
    (2) Women's International League for Peace and Freedom
    (3) United Nations
    (4) European Economic Community
    (5) Iron Curtain

Questions 59 and 60 refer to the following passage.

Many westering pioneers kept diaries of their incredible journeys. Their commentary tells of their fears of hard winters, wild animals, and sickness or death and of the loneliness of leaving behind beloved families, familiar places, and personal possessions. They also wrote of the natural beauty they encountered, the camaraderie established with other travelers, and the triumph of surmounting yet another obstacle, using all the creativity and persistence they could muster.

59. Using personal diaries and journals in historical research enables us to get a sense of
    (1) the effects of natural disasters throughout history
    (2) the daily experiences and emotions of people in the past
    (3) exactly what the pioneers faced
    (4) how standard English has changed over the years
    (5) how the West has changed since it was first settled

60. What is the author's attitude toward the pioneers?
    (1) They were very courageous.
    (2) They were very afraid of bad weather.
    (3) They were foolish to leave so much behind.
    (4) They should have had more time to enjoy the natural beauty they encountered.
    (5) They made lasting friendships on their journeys.

END OF EXAMINATION

ANSWERS AND EXPLANATIONS

1. (2) Annual precipitation rate is the choice most closely related to the subject of the geographer's study: rainfall patterns.

2. (2) In order for Joe and Ida to have control over where their money goes, they need a budget that will give them some guidelines. None of the other choices would definitely help them save money.

3. (3) The title and subheading of the table give you this information.

4. (2) If you test each possible answer against the chart, you will see that only choice (2) is correct. The information does not support any of the other answers.

5. (2) In 1944, the percentage of taxes paid by corporations was just under 37% of all the taxes collected by the IRS. By 1979, it had dropped to a little more than 15%. Based on this, we can infer that corporate influence on tax legislation has resulted in tax laws favorable to corporations.

6. (1) The highest point on the graph is in 1944.

7. (5) The passage tells you that older tribal rituals served certain social functions that have been taken over by sports.

8. (2) Any conclusion drawn from these two graphs could be very misleading because so many factors affect wages, especially inflation and the value of the dollar.

9. (5) Levi-type jeans are very popular in the United States. They are not part of the traditional costume of any other culture, so their popularity throughout the world has spread, or diffused, into other places.

10. (5) The passage tells you that day nurseries were run by wealthy women who feared that small children with working mothers would be left alone.

11. (2) The passage tells you that critics of day nurseries felt that mothers should stay home with their children. From this information, you can infer that one outcome of this concern has been the granting of aid to mothers with dependent children.

12. (2) The graph shows a rise in the amount of people's disposable income. Because the data in the graph are based on the value of a dollar in 1972, you can see that, despite inflation, people actually were able to purchase more with their income.

13. (3) You can tell from the definition of *direct initiative* that it would be an appropriate tactic for these citizens since it would allow them to draft and present legislation themselves.

14. (3) The author mentions that the seniority system now runs the schools and that incentives for teachers need to be reestablished. You can infer that (3) is the best answer.

15. (1) The author says that unions now run the schools and that authority properly belongs to administrators and school boards, so she would most likely favor eliminating teachers' unions.

16. (4) You are told that Germany was able to gain territory in Europe in the 1930s. You can infer that England and France must have compromised in disputes over territory that Germany wanted to take over.

17. (4) The first sentence says that co-ops are controlled by their members.

18. (1) In a co-op, those who use certain goods and services are the owners of the enterprise.

19. (3) The passage tells you that co-ops sometimes have lower prices because they are not run in order to make a profit.

20. **(4)** The passage states that unemployed black males are being driven away from their families because welfare regulations prevent them from receiving aid. You can infer that, if these men were able to find jobs, their families would not need welfare assistance.

21. **(2)** One curve is labeled supply, and the other is labeled demand. They are equal at their point of intersection (E). The price at that point is $5,000.

22. **(5)** When fewer infants die, more people reach adulthood. Therefore, more women reach childbearing age. The result is rapid population growth, which is common in developing countries.

23. **(1)** The passage says "The growth of suburbs was pushed ahead by the invention of the automobile and truck."

24. **(4)** Because the passage describes the effects of transportation technology on the growth of a city and its surrounding areas, (4) is the best answer.

25. **(3)** The passage says that losses from street crime are only a fifth of those from embezzlement, fraud, and other forms of white-collar crime, so you can infer that (3) is the best answer.

26. **(4)** White-collar crime is committed by people with economic and political power—professionals, businessmen, and corporations.

27. **(3)** You can infer from the context of the sentence that *ethnocentrism* means "making a moral judgment about other people's way of life."

28. **(1)** The birth rate rose significantly from 1945 to 1955 and then began to fall.

29. **(5)** The graph shows a fairly stable death rate and a declining birth rate. Therefore, there is an overall decline in population.

30. **(2)** The movement of materials and products of trade and industry is critical to a city's economic growth. While all of the options will have an effect on economic growth, (2) is the broadest and best answer.

31. **(1)** Both speakers warn against allowing the military establishment to exercise too much influence on government. Washington says the military establishment is "hostile to republican liberty"; Eisenhower says that the military-industrial complex must not be allowed to acquire too much power.

32. **(4)** Confidence in major companies declined from 55% to 16% between 1966 and 1981.

33. **(2)** Looking over the chart, you can see that in each row the numbers are lower in 1981 than in 1966.

34. **(5)** You are told that Latin American influence in the Southwest is a result of more than twentieth-century immigration and are given details about a history of interaction with Mexico that goes back "many years."

35. **(5)** The New Deal was a series of programs put in place by President Franklin Roosevelt in response to widespread unemployment and other personal suffering that resulted from the Great Depression.

36. **(4)** Since you know that the workers are paid the same hourly wage in each plant, the workers in Plant 2 must produce cars more efficiently than the workers in Plant 1.

37. **(3)** The main idea of the cartoon is expressed in the last statement: small farmers are as out of date as mules in modern times.

38. **(2)** The map shows Loyalist concentrations near all of the cities except Boston. Therefore, Boston probably had the fewest Loyalist residents.

39. **(3)** The author complains that criminals are too often let back on the streets.

40. **(2)** The authors of the Constitution wanted to protect the rights of United States citizens accused of committing crimes.

41. **(3)** The passage tells you that pollution from factories in the Midwest is one of the contributions to the acid rain problem and that the killing of forests by acid rain could lead to water shortages in eastern cities.

42. (4) The passage describes a relationship in which an action of people (pollution) affects nature, creating a result that in turn, affects people (creates water shortages)

43. (3) The first sentence says, "A balance sheet is a financial statement that businesses use to summarize their financial position at particular points in time."

44. (2) The passage gives you the formula ASSETS − LIABILITIES = NET WORTH. Using the formula, $5,000 − $3,200 = $1,800.

45. (4) The passage tells you that the Radical Republicans demanded civil rights for blacks.

46. (1) You are told that the Freedmen's Bureau was an agency that assisted blacks in making the transition from slavery to citizenship. You can guess that helping them learn to read and write would serve this purpose.

47. (5) The broad purpose of Jane's survey was to find out what people wanted so she could provide her market with what was most in demand.

48. (1) The bakery has the highest score in the "in favor" column.

49. (1) The passage tells you that "The 'implied powers' have been a subject of debate ever since the ratification of the Constitution," so you can guess that they are not defined exactly.

50. (2) Speakers A and B agree that people are less loyal to the major political parties than they used to be, but they interpret the trend differently. Speaker A is worried that the result will be a lack of political stability, and Speaker B is pleased at the possibility that the major parties will become more responsive.

51. (3) The Constitution has been interpreted many different ways over the years. In fact, political scientists feel that it is this flexibility that has allowed the Constitution to endure two centuries of constant national growth and change.

52. (4) A social movement calls for fundamental social changes outside of the major political parties. You can eliminate the other answers by checking them against the information in the passage.

53. (2) The first sentence tells you that there was a worldwide decline in agricultural prices prior to the 1890s.

54. (4) This paragraph is about voting rights for women, so you can infer from the context that *suffrage* means "the right to vote."

55. (1) The last sentence tells you that some people who opposed women's suffrage thought that political activity would interfere with their spiritual purity. The other answers are not supported by the information in the passage.

56. (3) You are told in the first sentence that the goal of the alliance was to guarantee world peace.

57. (5) The passage tells you that "Congress refused to allow the international affairs of the United States to be subject to the articles of the league."

58. (3) The United Nations is an organization of nations whose purpose is to promote international cooperation. The other choices do not relate as directly to the League of Nations.

59. (2) The question asks you to explain the use of personal diaries and journals in historical research in general. Choice (2) answers the question most broadly, so it is the best answer.

60. (1) Words like "incredible," "triumph," "creativity," and "persistence" let you know of the author's respect for the bravery required on those journeys.

POST-TEST EVALUATION CHART

Below is a chart that you can use to evaluate your preparedness for the GED social studies test.

Circle the number of any questions that you missed. Then, use the headings on the chart to see which areas you need to review. Read across the chart for content areas and down the chart for the reading and interpretation skills that are discussed in the first chapter of this book. The heading *Prior Knowledge* refers to questions that require you to recall facts you may have previously learned or read.

The questions in darker type require pictorial or graphic interpretation skills. As on the GED, these questions constitute 25 percent of the test. If you missed more than 4 of these 15 questions, review the chapter that starts on page 45.

	Prior Knowledge	Main Idea	Finding Details	Inferences and Conclusions	Application of Ideas	Evaluation of Logic
History	35	59	*28*, 45, 52, 53	34, *37*, *38*, 46, 60	16	
Political Science	40, 51, 58		56, 57	31, *32*, *33*, 39, 49, 54, 55	13	39, 50
Behavioral Science	9, 27	*3*, 7, 14	10, 25	*4*, 11		15, 26
Economics	*47*	17, 43	*6*, *21*	*5*, *12*, 19, 20, 48	2, 18, *36*, 44	*8*
Geography	22, 30	*29*	23, 41	24, 42	1	

Now add the total of the numbers that you circled. Subtract this number from 60. Then use the chart below to determine what an equivalent GED score would be.

Scoring Chart	
Number Correct	**GED Standard Score**
16 or less	35 or lower
22	40
30	45
38	50
44	55
49	60
52 or more	65 or higher

SOCIAL STUDIES POST-TEST ANSWER GRID

1 ① ② ③ ④ ⑤	21 ① ② ③ ④ ⑤	41 ① ② ③ ④ ⑤
2 ① ② ③ ④ ⑤	22 ① ② ③ ④ ⑤	42 ① ② ③ ④ ⑤
3 ① ② ③ ④ ⑤	23 ① ② ③ ④ ⑤	43 ① ② ③ ④ ⑤
4 ① ② ③ ④ ⑤	24 ① ② ③ ④ ⑤	44 ① ② ③ ④ ⑤
5 ① ② ③ ④ ⑤	25 ① ② ③ ④ ⑤	45 ① ② ③ ④ ⑤
6 ① ② ③ ④ ⑤	26 ① ② ③ ④ ⑤	46 ① ② ③ ④ ⑤
7 ① ② ③ ④ ⑤	27 ① ② ③ ④ ⑤	47 ① ② ③ ④ ⑤
8 ① ② ③ ④ ⑤	28 ① ② ③ ④ ⑤	48 ① ② ③ ④ ⑤
9 ① ② ③ ④ ⑤	29 ① ② ③ ④ ⑤	49 ① ② ③ ④ ⑤
10 ① ② ③ ④ ⑤	30 ① ② ③ ④ ⑤	50 ① ② ③ ④ ⑤
11 ① ② ③ ④ ⑤	31 ① ② ③ ④ ⑤	51 ① ② ③ ④ ⑤
12 ① ② ③ ④ ⑤	32 ① ② ③ ④ ⑤	52 ① ② ③ ④ ⑤
13 ① ② ③ ④ ⑤	33 ① ② ③ ④ ⑤	53 ① ② ③ ④ ⑤
14 ① ② ③ ④ ⑤	34 ① ② ③ ④ ⑤	54 ① ② ③ ④ ⑤
15 ① ② ③ ④ ⑤	35 ① ② ③ ④ ⑤	55 ① ② ③ ④ ⑤
16 ① ② ③ ④ ⑤	36 ① ② ③ ④ ⑤	56 ① ② ③ ④ ⑤
17 ① ② ③ ④ ⑤	37 ① ② ③ ④ ⑤	57 ① ② ③ ④ ⑤
18 ① ② ③ ④ ⑤	38 ① ② ③ ④ ⑤	58 ① ② ③ ④ ⑤
19 ① ② ③ ④ ⑤	39 ① ② ③ ④ ⑤	59 ① ② ③ ④ ⑤
20 ① ② ③ ④ ⑤	40 ① ② ③ ④ ⑤	60 ① ② ③ ④ ⑤